"Greg Smith writes . . . with great knowledge of his subject. . . . [A] wonderful account."

—Jimmy Breslin

**Meet the men who made—and broke—
the DeCavalcantes**

THE BOSS

They call him **Vinny Ocean**. He's loaded. Owns a casino boat on Long Island, restaurants in Brooklyn and Jersey, and a strip joint that's driving Rudy Giuliani nuts. So who wants to snuff him?

THE SCHEMER

Fast-talking **Joey O**, wears plenty of gold, always flashing a nice roll. Big on stock-market pump-and-dumps. Unfortunately he owes everybody money and they all want it yesterday. Now he's desperate, and scheming with the wrong crowd.

THE OLD-TIMER

Good old **Joseph Tin Ear**—always does what he's told. Like whacking the brother of an underboss. At sixty-one, a real trooper. Even learning to drive a Harley so he can pull a drive-by. Still no respect. No promotion. No more Mr. Nice Guy.

THE INFORMANT

Great idea, **Ralphie**: line up three mugs to steal a World Trade Center payroll. Bad move: your Three Stooges forgot to wear masks. The FBI offers him a deal: strap on a wire and record the mob. Good job, Ralphie: *There's gotta be a book in this.*

MADE MEN

The True Rise-and-Fall Story
of a New Jersey Mob Family

Greg B. Smith

BERKLEY BOOKS, NEW YORK

MADE MEN

A Berkley Book / published by arrangement with
the author

PRINTING HISTORY
Berkley edition / February 2003

Copyright © 2003 by Greg B. Smith
Book design by Julie Rogers
Cover design by Rita Frangie
Cover photos courtesy GangLandNews.com

ISBN: 0-425-18551-6

BERKLEY®
Berkley Books are published by The Berkley Publishing Group,
a division of Penguin Putnam Inc., 375 Hudson Street,
New York, New York 10014.
BERKLEY and the "B" design
are trademarks belonging to Penguin Putnam Inc.

PRINTED IN THE UNITED STATES OF AMERICA

10 9 8 7 6 5 4 3 2 1

To Lizzy, Damon and Brendan

Acknowledgments

Much thanks is due to a number of people who supported my effort to get things right and readable. The list is long and incomplete, starting with prominent members of the New York criminal defense bar Gerald Shargel, Steve Kartagener, Francisco Celedonio, Joseph Tacopina and Gregory O'Connell. On the government side, thanks especially goes to assistant U.S. attorneys Lisa Korologos and John Hillebrecht and FBI special agent George Hanna. The story is not complete without FBI agents Eileen O'Rourke, Jay Kramer and Seamus McElearney, and, of course, New York City Police Department detective John DiCaprio. Also gratitude goes to Bob Buccino, former deputy chief of New Jersey's Criminal Justice Division for a serious history lesson and to Marvin Smilon for remembering everything. I'd also like to thank my editor, Tom Colgan, and agent, Jane Dystel, for guiding me through the forest when I lost the trail.

1

August 9, 1994

On a hot August twilight in Queens, the taxpaying citizens are up in arms and out in force. Three hundred furious people crowd onto a sidewalk in a neighborhood of mom-and-pop businesses and middle-class apartment buildings called Rego Park. They yell and holler and generally make their First Amendment rights known. Because there are so many of them, they are jammed in behind blue NYPD barricades next to Ben's Best Deli and Carpet City, a crowd of mild-mannered people wearing khaki shorts, T-shirts, and fanny packs who have gathered together to vent. A thunderstorm that rumbled through earlier is gone and the air is still thick with humidity. Occasionally inchoate shouting coalesces into a discernible chant.

"Real men don't need porn!"

"Sleaze must leave!"

They carry hand-scrawled cardboard signs such as 63RD DRIVE IS NOT 42ND ST. and XXX = NO NO NO.

There are moms and dads and babies in strollers, elementary-school teachers, a city-council woman with a microphone and a podium. Cops working overtime look on, not bothering to disguise their amusement. The crowd is jeering and cheering and jabbing their fingers in the general direction of a storefront at 96-24 Queens Boulevard from which can be vaguely heard a throbbing *dunh-dunh-dunh* of disco left over from the 1970s. Over the door of this smoked-glass storefront in lurid blue-and-red neon is one word that makes the neighbors nuts:

WIGGLES

It is a strip club, and it has landed squarely in the middle of Archie Bunker's Queens, right across the street from the old single-screen Trylon Movie Theater, around the corner from the Rego Park Jewish Center, and just up the block from Public School 139. This is the heart and soul of Queens, the borough of choice for millions of striving immigrants who come to this country of promise and McDonald's to live a better life. They expect decent schools, safe streets, and convenient parking spots. They do not expect ALL NUDE ALL THE TIME, and that is why, since Wiggles opened on July 13, 1994, there have been protests on the street outside nearly every single night.

That is saying a lot for people who have to work for a living. They are making time in their busy days to stand outside Wiggles and holler. They are writing letters to their civic representatives. They are signing petitions and cobbling together a lobby. These neighbors, to put it mildly, despise this Wiggles. They loathe this Wiggles with the enmity of property owners who fear the value of their holdings will soon decline. They also fear for their children, as they are more than happy to repeat to the one reporter who shows up with a notepad from the Queens-based newspaper *Newsday.*

"I raised my children here because of the good schools. This just isn't that kind of neighborhood." Ibn Art, a protester who's lived in Rego Park for twenty-five years, fumes without specifying exactly what "that" kind of neighborhood might be. "I'm one hundred percent against this club."

Marcia Lynn, who helped protest against another strip club down Queens Boulevard called Runway 69, puts forth a more dramatic scenario. She predicts that not only mere children but the children of dedicated religious families attending a nearby synagogue on Saturday evening will, inevitably, wander out of temple and be forced to confront Wiggles. There they will behold the photographs of headliners with interesting-sounding names like Erica Everest, Niki Knockers, and Crystal Knight.

"We need to close down all these places," she warns. "The wrong people are coming in." There is a blue wooden stage erected on the sidewalk upon which the politicians are holding forth. One of them is City Councilwoman Karen Koslowitz, who has already won votes campaigning against Runway 69 a few blocks away. Koslowitz has come to realize that standing up to strip clubs is an extremely popular stance for an ambitious politician. She has helped organize this protest, and she now stands onstage hammering away. She is a grandmotherly figure who could easily be mistaken for a Barbra Streisand fan. She has a tendency to wear tinted glasses, carry leopard-pattern handbags, and say things like "For this they have the First Amendment?"

"Children pass through here constantly!" she tells the crowd. "This is a family community!"

The crowd cheers like wrestling fans, stirred by the need to kick this trash out of the neighborhood. They are so organized, they even have their own ribbons—red, white, and blue affairs that are worn on lapels, signifying that the right to protest against the local strip joint is as American as credit cards. Suddenly the crowd notices some customers who are headed into the club. One of the activists, a middle-aged man with a receding hairline, whips out a cheap camera and begins taking photographs. One of the customers, a man wearing a black, orange, and blue Knicks warm-up suit smiles and mugs for the camera. He says the girls inside aren't worth the admission price. Another man is not so amused at having his picture taken. He pulls his turquoise windbreaker over his head like a cliché gangster. He offers up an interesting gesture involving a single finger and disappears inside the club.

The crowd spots two strippers strutting down the sidewalk on spike heels, headed for the door. Both have somehow jammed themselves into absurdly tight blue jeans that defy all the laws of physics. The blonde sneers at the amateur photographer, but the brunette, who wears a black-gauze blouse with black bra clearly visible underneath, suddenly wheels around with her own camera and begins taking pictures of the picture taker.

"Why don't you just leave us alone?" she whines as she heads into the club. "We're just trying to make a living."

Inside the club, all forms of civil protest are obliterated by the thundering disco beat. In the main room three completely naked women—they would call themselves "entertainers"—gyrate to the beat on a stage that is raised two feet off the floor. Their bodies are reflected in the mirrors on all the walls and the ceiling above. There is a "Champagne Room" in the back—a small room filled with tiny booths for "private" dances. There is a poolroom and a TV room and a number of other miscellaneous "lounges" located throughout the club's three thousand square feet of space.

Though the neighborhood protest outside cannot be heard above the din, its effects are obvious.

A sign at the entrance that wasn't there before the protests states:

WIGGLES

Don't let anyone take away your individual rights.
Celebrate your freedom of choice on us:
FREE Admission
FREE Buffet
FREE Entertainment

Wiggles has taken to mentioning—in newspaper advertisements placed in the sports sections of the local tabloids right next to the fishing column and underneath the daily football line—the presence of an ATM "available on the premises" as well as valet parking for the commuter set. On this night of grand protest, there appears to be more strippers than customers, which gives the place a lonely feel. A handful of "entertainers" do their jobs while gazing off into mirrors. A small group of men sip colas and club sodas and stare up in slack-jawed aesthetic appreciation of the dedication these girls show to their craft. Like most strip clubs, the place reeks of cigarette smoke. Unlike most strip clubs, the place does not reek of alcohol.

That's because there is none. Wiggles is booze-free, opened by people sophisticated enough to know that if you serve liquor, you have to abide by a phone-book-size list of rules and regulations that apply under New York State liquor laws. One of the laws says that if you serve booze, the strippers can't take all their clothing off—just their tops. And though Wiggles claims to be a topless club, the strippers often expand the interpretation of the term *topless* by removing their panties. Alcohol, therefore, is replaced by "juice." Wiggles is, in fact, listed in the Yellow Pages as a "topless juice bar." The club's "manager," Karen English, identifies herself as a "retired" topless dancer who has been in "the business" forever, and she is mightily offended at the slander and invective that is flying around on the sidewalk outside.

"I feel that everyone has a right to their opinion, but I have an excellent reputation in this business," she says, making the point twice that she runs a topless club, not a nude bar: "We are not a nude bar. That is a misconception. We will serve no alcohol."

She actually says, "I run a clean establishment."

But the ex-stripper named English speaks not from a position of ownership, and that is because the true owner of Wiggles is a man who prefers to stay away from the cameras and out of the headlines that have exploded around his club. In fact, his name is not on any document associated with the club. According to all forms of public documentation available to the average investigative reporter, Wiggles is actually controlled by a shell corporation with the ridiculous name of Din Din Seafood, Inc. And Din Din Seafood lists no president, treasurer, or secretary. Its "chairman of the board" is listed as Paul Ranieri, who sometimes says he is the owner of the club, and sometimes says he is the manager. But behind the scenes there is another man who calls the shots. His name is Vincent Palermo, and he is a capo known as Vinny Ocean in the littlest Mafia family in North America—the DeCavalcante crime family of New Jersey.

On this hot August night, with three hundred fuming citizens beating the drum of civil protest outside his club, Vinny Ocean is nowhere to be found.

Keeping Wiggles alive is extremely important to Vinny Ocean for a simple reason: Wiggles is a money machine. It generates hundreds of thousands of dollars in cash each week—little, crumpled-up, sweaty fives and tens and twenties that drunken patrons jam in the G-strings of the "entertainers." There are piles of dollars to be made, all handed over by leering businessmen who wind up in the Champagne Room for a personal "lap dance." They plunk down ten bucks for a can of soda and do not care because it will all reimbursed by their employers as a "business expense."

Vinny rarely stops by the club. Instead he sends his right-hand man, Joey O Masella, to pick up the weekly take. Because so many of the transactions take place in cash, Joey O often ends up carting around big fat envelopes. Much of this money is kept in a secret safe in the strip club's main office, which only a handful of employees know about. Joey O spends so much time coming and going from Wiggles, he has taken to complaining that he could hurt his back, which is not so good these days, carrying around this much cash. In short, Wiggles is good business for Vinny Ocean. The cash comes in, Vinny is happy, the DeCavalcante crime family is happy. God forbid a bunch of noisy puritans with protest signs should ruin all that.

Many of the noisy puritans, in fact, have long suspected that the club is controlled by the mob. They see these guys hanging around, and some of the protesters will swear they've been followed home after a tough night of protest.

But Vinny Ocean knows it's best to keep an extremely low profile in these matters, because he realizes that the future of Wiggles is far from certain. There is a new mayor down at City Hall named Rudy Giuliani, a former federal prosecutor who's taken on what he has deemed the pathetic "quality of life" in New York City. This Giuliani has announced a holy jihad against squeegee men and homeless people, so it is not too difficult to imagine a new campaign to shut down the strip clubs as well. In fact, just such a movement is afoot. Giuliani has put his considerable political weight behind a bill that would banish strip clubs like Wiggles from residential areas and require that they be located more than five hundred feet away from churches and schools and day-care centers. The bill has been languishing in a city council committee, but the mayor brought it back from the dead. If it passes, Wiggles could be forced to move out of the middle-class confines of Rego Park and into the kind of economic Siberia one finds in scary industrialized zones down near the waterfront or out near airports. Not the kind of places that Vinny Ocean, entrepreneur, sees as the future for exotic dancing in New York.

If anything can be said about Vinny Ocean, it is that he is a dedicated entrepreneur. "I love work," Vinny Ocean tells people. "I worked my whole life. Eleven, twelve years old. Two jobs. My whole life, I love to work. People see that you have a nice house, a nice car, they figure maybe you did something wrong. My whole life, never, *never* did I do one thing wrong. That I know of."

Vinny Ocean looks and thinks like a smart businessman. He is a short, compact man who resembles the actor Robert Wagner, with a distinguished patch of silver at the temples, a healthy head of brown hair on top, and a deep tan. He is forty-eight years old and is working on his second marriage. He has pulled himself out of debt and is now headed fast toward making his first million.

For years, he struggled financially. For years he ran a successful wholesale fish business in the Fulton Fish Market down in lower Manhattan, where he earned the nickname, Vinny Ocean, but not a whole lot else. In the mid-1980s, he owed everybody—the local hospital, local doctors, the federal government. The tax liens against his property (actually, everything was in his second wife's name) totaled $68,000. He was paying a hefty mortgage on a nice mansion on the Long Island waterfront—eight rooms, two bathrooms, one fireplace, a big pier, tucked away in an isolated section of suburban Island Park, Long Island (held under a corporate shell called Fishing Well, Inc.). He had two social security numbers and paid alimony to his first wife, with whom he had two children. He was supporting a new, second family, complete with two teenage girls and eight-year-old Vinny Jr. He was sending all three to Catholic school, with college on the horizon. He'd already put his first son, Michael, through Adelphi Academy High School in Brooklyn and then Fordham University in the Bronx. His first daughter, Renee, also attended college on his tab.

The cost of being a family guy was dear but predictable. He'd come out of a family of eight children (five girls, three boys) and was raised old-school Catholic in postwar Brooklyn. His father came to America from Italy when he was a teenager. His life was like a scene from *Once Upon a Time in America*.

"Ours is a very close-knit family," his sister Claire wrote in a letter to a judge. "We were raised in a strict Catholic household. My father who immigrated here when he was in his teens, emphasized love for one another, our fellow man, for our country and high moral standards."

Vinny was an altar boy.

When the former altar boy was just sixteen years old, his father died. He had to leave school and went to work at "two jobs to help support my mother and the younger children," his sister Claire wrote. Another sister, Nancy, remembers Vinny more or less supported the family after her father died because their mother was a bedridden asthmatic. Just about everybody who has a story to tell about Vinny Ocean would mention his devotion to family. His daughter Tara says she once saw him stop a man from beating his son. During a family barbecue, Vinny was the guy who jumped in the pool and rescued the toddler who'd accidentally fallen in.

A casual examination of Vinny's world reveals the basic résumé of the hardworking suburban dad. He and his family attended Sacred Heart Church in Island Park every Sunday. Father John Tutone knew him by his first name. Vinny Ocean watched *Annie* a thousand times with his daughter Danielle. He drove the girls to Brownies' meetings. He once took in a troubled teenager named Richie, became his godfather, and let him stay in his home every weekend for a year while Richie studied the Catholic sacraments and prepared to be baptized and to receive first Communion and confirmation.

And, of course, he was a made guy.

In the early 1960s, he met and married the niece of Simone Rizzo DeCavalcante, who would soon be known to the world as Sam the Plumber. Sam the Mafia boss took a liking to his niece's new young man and began inviting him by the social club in Kenilworth, New Jersey. Vinny was working at the fish markets in the early morning hours and hanging out with the wiseguys on Sunday afternoons at the social club or at Sam's table at Angie and Min's restaurant in Kenilworth. He was seen as an earner. In

1965, when he was just twenty years old, he became a made member of Sam the Plumber's crime family.

Never again would he be just another guy from the fish market.

Now he was *amico nos*—a friend of ours. He was part of a much larger organization that included five crime families in New York City and one in New Jersey. All six had their moments of fame over the years that became gilded and polished and placed squarely in the gauzy mythology of gangster-dom. At the time that Vinny Ocean became *amico nos,* the DeCavalcante family was a small but respected organization. It had a virtual lock on most of the unions that did construction work in northern New Jersey and a good relationship with the five New York families who ran the gangster world. Small but respected. And Vinny Ocean was a part of all that.

Nearly thirty years later, the mob wasn't what it used to be.

In Vinny's family, the FBI had successfully planted a bug in Sam the Plumber's office and captured nearly two years of conversations. Sam the Plumber was convicted and ultimately retired. The New York families were in even more of a mess. The Colombo family had lost itself in two terrible, bloody wars in the streets of Brooklyn. Its members were being prosecuted one by one. The Luchese family had gone underground ever since one of its middle managers decided it would be a good idea to violate mob "rules" and try to shoot the sister of an informant. The Bonanno clan, the smallest of the New York five, was a shell of its former self after being kicked out of the mob's famous ruling body, the Commission. The boss of the Genovese family, Vincent (the Chin) Gigante, had taken to wandering through the streets of Greenwich Village in a bathrobe, unshaven and muttering to himself about Jesus.

Subpoenas were everywhere. When he was indicted, his own lawyers said he was insane.

As of 1994, the most powerful family in America—the Gambino family—was on the ropes, brought down by its boss, John Gotti, the Dapper Don, a man whose mountainous ego was surpassed only by his inability to keep his mouth shut. The high-living Gotti dodged not one but three prosecutions (mostly by fixing juries), ate at fine Manhattan restaurants, danced till dawn, and offered a raffish Al Capone smirk to reporters who dogged his every move. By 1992, he was finished, convicted of murder and racketeering and just about every Cosa Nostra sin imaginable. He now sat in a maximum-security prison, fuming about all the rats who'd turned on him, unaware that his own words, captured by FBI bugs, were the true reason for his downfall.

Different theories emerged about the downfall of the mob. Some believed it was simply an extraordinary effort by law enforcement. Some said it was sloppy behavior by a secret society that was no longer so secret. A few saw something else—a group of criminals done in by their own mythology.

With Gotti, there was practically a cottage industry between the movies and books and talk-show discussions. His image as a boastful, well-dressed hoodlum catered to the notion that the mob was a glamorous American institution. Gotti was seen in some circles as an antihero, a guy who thumbed his nose at law enforcement while impressing the working people with old-fashioned fireworks displays every Fourth of July in his Queens neighborhood. Even Gotti believed it. He talked about "my public" as if he were George Raft or Paul Muni or Robert De Niro. Here was the myth of the crime boss as Robin Hood. Here was *The Godfather* of Mario Puzo, who had somehow managed to create the Men of Honor fiction.

In 1994, the Gambino crime family had become material for popular culture. If Jay Leno or David Letterman needed a Mafia joke, inevitably they would mention the Gambino crime family. Gotti had made the cover of *Time* as the face of organized crime in America. When people made jokes about "sleeping with the fishes" and "make him an offer he can't refuse," they thought of Gotti and the Gambino crime family, even though its power and strength had been considerably weakened by Gotti's conviction two years earlier.

When people thought of the Mafia in 1994, they most certainly did not think of the DeCavalcante crime family— New Jersey's only homegrown Mafia clan. By the time the protesters took to marching outside Vinny Palermo's strip club in Queens, the DeCavalcante crime family had fallen into a near-permanent stupor. Within seven years, the family's underboss had been murdered, the boss had been jailed, and the man who'd been appointed to replace him as acting boss on the street had been murdered by his own men. The guy left in charge, Giaciano (Jake) Amari, had cancer and was slowly dying. Most of the leadership of the family consisted of extremely old men stuck in the old ways. There was one exception in the DeCavalcante crime family in 1994—an up-and-coming capo named Vinny Ocean.

THE "FARMERS"

He was clearly headed to the top of the corporate hierarchy. Vinny Ocean's problem was that he was in the wrong corporation. If the other Mafia families of New York City were airlines, they would be Delta and USAir and American. The DeCavalcante family would be Bob and Joe's Airlines. They were openly called "farmers" by the New York goodfella crowd, and there wasn't much they could do about the name, mostly because it was true.

For years they had always been forced to glom on to other families to earn a living. For a short time when Sam the Plumber was running things, they were seen as a fairly sophisticated group, coming up with smart new ways to suck the blood out of local union pension funds. By the mid-1990s, they had reached a new low. For an aggressive, ambitious guy like Vinny Ocean, this was good news.

Vinny was an optimist. He was aware that the family's boss, John Riggi, remained in prison with no chance of walking on a sidewalk until at least 2003. There was a perception that no one was really in charge, which for Vinny could be a good thing. And while the New York families had gotten all the glamour from the mythology machine, they had also received most of the unwanted attention from law enforcement.

The way Vinny Ocean saw it, the so-called farmers of New Jersey were now ready to fill in the void. And with Vinny Ocean's help, they were doing just that. Slowly, the farmers of New Jersey were finding their way across the Hudson River and into the boroughs of Queens, Brooklyn, Staten Island, and even Manhattan. They were expanding because nobody was really paying any attention to them. The way Vinny Ocean saw it, the DeCavalcante crime family could definitely be a player in the 1990s in a way that could exceed even what the family's namesake, Sam the Plumber, had imagined. The key, as Vinny would tell his underlings, was cooperation. Like the namesake of his family, Vinny Ocean had made a career out of cultivating relationships with other families. He set up a lucrative loan-sharking deal with one Gambino capo and a book-making operation with another. He was working on a deal to partner up with a Colombo captain and kept in touch with members of the Genovese crime family he knew from the fish market. For the most part, he was well liked. He was, in the truest sense of the word, an "earner" who got the job done.

By 1994, Vinny had established himself in the usual Mafia businesses. According to the FBI, he was shaking down construction companies in the city through his control of several laborers' unions. Some of that money he put back on the street through loan-sharking and gambling operations, which allowed him to collect thousands of dollars every week in off-the-book cash. He became an off-the-book partner of one of his loan-shark victims' businesses. He opened up Wiggles in Rego Park, a tremendous source of cash.

There were only three hundred problems—all of them standing on the sidewalk outside Wiggles nearly every night, hollering about kids and morality and property rates. They were protected by the same First Amendment Vinny Ocean mentioned on the sign outside his club to justify opening an all-nude club on a mom-and-pop Queens street. They had a right to protest. And it was that very right that gave Vinny Ocean an unusual idea.

What if you use the First Amendment to fight back?

He had been talking with his lawyers about filing a free-speech lawsuit against the neighborhood activists, arguing that their aggressive behavior was scaring off his customers in violation of his rights to do business as an American. It is, he would argue, positively un-American, and certainly antientrepreneurial, to allow such a thing to continue.

On September 1, 1994, less than a month after the big protest, Wiggles officially fired back. One of Palermo's lawyers, Stanley Meyer, filed a lawsuit—one of the first of its kind—in Queens State Supreme Court arguing with a straight face that protesters were violating Wiggles's right of free expression. Meyer asks a judge for an injunction ordering the protesters to immediately cease and desist from yelling and screaming outside the door. They alleged that the protesters had repeatedly violated the privacy rights of customers by videotaping license plates. They also claimed the protesters had violated the right to be free of flying foodstuff. Wiggles employees—even those who kept their clothes on at work—had been hit by airborne tomatoes and other unspecified fruit. Granted, there was no better than a slim chance that Palermo would actually win. But Vinny Ocean knew that his quixotic effort of wrapping himself in the American flag and filing suit might, in the end, not matter a bit.

That was because the protests had actually increased business. All that publicity had been good for the club. In fact, in the city of New York in 1994, no other strip club could boast of getting so much publicity with so little effort.

All of which made Wiggles's prospects pretty good. When a reporter asked Meyer, the club's lawyer, what he thought the future would bring for Queens's only all-nude strip club, he answered swiftly and succinctly.

"We will outlast them."

SAM THE PLUMBER

February 11, 1997

Two hours past noon at Corsentino Home for Funerals in Elizabeth, New Jersey, and the cars had filled up the parking lot and jammed Second Avenue. Agents with the State of New Jersey's Organized Crime Racketeering

Bureau walked from vehicle to vehicle, jotting down license-plate numbers. Agents in a van with tinted windows videotaped the men and women entering and leaving Corsentino's. This was a big day for the funeral home. This was the day that New Jersey's one and only Mafia don, the eminent Simone Rizzo DeCavalcante, was to be waked.

This was the funeral of Sam the Plumber, the founding father of the DeCavalcante crime family, who managed to live a life as a racketeer and die of a heart attack in what the FBI deemed "semi-retirement" at the respectable age of eighty-four.

Sam the Plumber definitely fell into the category "old school." With his carefully combed silver hair and his Italian suits, DeCavalcante made a practice of claiming to be a descendant of Italian royalty. Whether or not this was true, no one knew. He was nicknamed "the Count" and was allegedly one of several real-life Mafia bosses said to have inspired Mario Puzo's entirely fictional Don Vito Corleone, the patriarchal boss of *The Godfather.* He was also the owner of Kenworth Heating and Air-conditioning in Kenilworth, New Jersey, which had earned him his nickname as a seller of sinks and pipes. Law enforcement seemed to have a certain respect for Sam the Plumber. They noted that he managed to win a spot on the Mafia's Commission, the ruling body that once governed the mob in America. They referred to him as "diplomatic" and noted that he was able to double the number of associates and made guys in his crime family between 1964, when he took over from the previous boss, and 1969, when his secret life as a mob boss became not so secret.

For a brief and strange moment during the Summer of Love, Sam the Plumber became a national sensation. On June 10, 1969, the FBI suddenly released 2,300 typed pages of transcripts gathered during a two-year wiretap of Sam the Plumber's office. On tape, Sam the Plumber was given to philosophizing about "honor." He was known to say things like "I'd give my life for our people." His most famous quote was "Honest people have no ethics." He said this because he was furious that the cops and judges he was paying off wouldn't always do what he wanted.

"Those people just don't stay fixed," he complained.

Sometimes he'd settle disputes over who was allowed to shake down whom in the manner of, say, a Roman senator. Revealing how he resolved one such affair of state, Sam the Plumber explained that he'd ordered a trusted lieutenant to administer a beating. "Then he hit him another one. He started hollering, 'Help! Help!' There were sixty guys outside, but I guess the room was soundproof."

At times Sam was a father figure. When one of his soldiers did not show sufficient respect to one of his capos, his response was quite paternalistic.

Sam: "Joe, you owe John an apology."

Joe: "Okay, I apologize."

Sam: "Joe, do you mean that? Shake hands. I won't permit it this way. Joe, I'd give my life for our people."

The tapes undermined the Count's royal legacy. They captured forever the fact that he was cheating on his wife with a secretary named Harriet, with whom he sometimes conversed in Yiddish. Sam the Plumber was momentarily famous, but also bound to spend some time in jail. On the day in 1971 when he and fifty-four of his cohorts were indicted, he was at the height of his power and the family that bore his name was as famous as it would ever be.

He pleaded guilty to running a $20-million-a-year gambling operation around the same time that a state report claimed that he and another crime family controlled 90 percent of the porno shops in the city of New York. The loquacious Sam the Plumber did two years of his five-year sentence and was released early because of good behavior and heart problems. He retired to an ocean-view high-rise condo on Collins Avenue in Miami Beach, Florida, and the crime family that bore his name was never quite the same. By the time the 1990s rolled around, law enforcement continued to believe he was advising the family on criminal matters, but in documents they listed his "hangouts" as "Miami Heart Institute."

After DeCavalcante left jail, he appointed first as acting boss and then as boss a well-spoken, extremely polite, and profoundly ruthless man named John Riggi. Riggi was business agent of Local 394 of the International Association of Laborers and Hod Carriers in Elizabeth, New Jersey, and he managed to stay out of jail until he was indicted in Newark in 1989. He was convicted the next year and began serving time, continuing to serve as boss of the family from his cell in Fort Dix federal prison.

At the time of Sam the Plumber's funeral, there was word of yet another potential void in the leadership of the DeCavalcante crime family. Riggi was still technically the boss, despite his having been in jail for seven years. Riggi had appointed an acting boss to handle matters on the street. The man's name was Jake Amari, a broken-down septuagenarian who ran AMI Construction in Elizabeth, New Jersey. Jake had always been close to Riggi, from the days when Riggi actually walked on city streets and hung around the now-defunct Café Italia in Elizabeth. Now Jake the acting boss—and by extension, his friend and real boss, Riggi—had a big problem. Jake was slowly dying of stomach cancer.

Everyone knew it, and no one talked about it. It was certain that when he passed, there would be a move to see who was in charge. As the New Jersey law enforcement agents ran their video cameras and scribbled down license plates at Sam the Plumber's funeral, they looked for clues as to where the DeCavalcante family was headed. They made some predictable findings—Jake Amari was there. So was Stefano Vitabile, the alleged consigliere who once had been Sam the Plumber's chauffeur when he traveled to New Jersey, driving a car registered to a sand and fill company. There was Charlie (Big Ears) Majuri, a captain and son of Sam the Plumber's former underboss Frank Majuri, driving a car registered in his wife's name. There was Frank Polizzi, an old-time captain who was once busted in the old Pizza Connection heroin case and then released from prison because he claimed he was dying. He was still alive.

These were all men who could end up running the family, which would make them potential targets of any investigation. The agents wrote down everything they could, and noticed that most of the license plates were from New Jersey. There were a handful of New York plates, including one from Brooklyn captains named Anthony Rotondo and Rudy Ferrone and a longtime, profoundly unsuccessful bookmaker named Joey O Masella.

But on that day, as members young and old paid their respects to the man who claimed to possess royal blood, one name did not surface on any of law enforcement's radar screens—Vincent Palermo. In fact, as of 1997, Vinny Palermo was able to attend the funeral of his mentor and did not have to worry that his name would show up on some law enforcement database listing who's who in organized crime. At the time Vinny Ocean did not exist to the FBI. For more than thirty years, Vinny Ocean had stayed off the FBI's radar.

That was about to change.

2

January 8, 1998

In the heart of a New York City winter it was actually sixty-five degrees in Central Park. People strolled giddily down sidewalks in shirtsleeves and sneakers. Stuck in traffic, they snickered when the radio said it was thirty-six degrees in Albany and trees were exploding in a Maine ice storm. By midday a thick fog settled on Manhattan from the Bronx to the Battery, turning the great architectural icons of New York into ghosts. At the bottom of the island, this meteorological oddity enshrouded the World Trade Center so that the nearly all of the massive twin towers seemed to disappear into a cloud.

From where he stood down near Battery Park, a short, chubby Brooklyn guy with a receding hairline and expanding midsection gazed up at the Trade Center towers. His name was Ralph Guarino and he was trying to see exactly where the towers ended and the fog began. It was an inspiring sight, filled with the casual majesty that is everywhere on the street corners of Manhattan. Here was one of the most impressive building complexes on earth, two 110-story citadels of power as tight as the Federal Reserve, swallowed up whole by the sky. The mighty towers seemed almost fragile this way. *Fragile* was a word Ralphie Guarino needed to explore.

He was aware that the World Trade Center was known as one of the most secure public spaces in the world. First, the huge complex of towers and office buildings was positively brimming with cops. There were all kinds of cops in there—New York City cops, Port Authority of New York and New Jersey police, Federal Police officers with their unrecognizable initials, FPO. Inside the two towers just about every federal law enforcement agency imaginable was well represented—the United States Secret Service, the U.S. Customs Service, the U.S. Bureau of Alcohol, Tobacco and Firearms—you name it. Cops were everywhere.

Added to that was an atmosphere of paranoia inspired by an incident that occurred just before noon on February 26, 1993. On that day, a group of Islamic fundamentalists drove a yellow Ryder van into the garage underneath One World Trade, parked it in a spot near a bearing wall, and quickly drove away in a beat-up sedan. A few minutes later the van, which contained canisters of liquid hydrogen and extremely volatile urea nitrate, blew into a thousand pieces. In all, six people died and thousands more were injured. A class of suburban elementary-school students was trapped in an elevator for hours. Thousands of employees had to trudge down thousands of stairs through thick black smoke, emerging from the building with their faces smeared with soot, coughing and wheezing and happy as hell to be out of there.

Ralphie knew all about this from his friend Sal Calciano, a guy from the neighborhood in Brooklyn who had worked inside the Trade Center twenty years. Calciano was a supervisor with American Building Maintenance, the company that kept the Trade Center clean, and he'd been inside one of the towers when the bomb went off. He'd carried a woman who was having problems breathing down many flights of stairs. He'd helped many others find their way out and then stayed outside watching for his coworkers, making sure they'd all escaped.

Then, in the weeks and months that followed, Sal told Ralphie, the building changed. Consultants were hired. Reports were drafted. Jersey barriers were trucked in and laid end to end around the entire building. Steel gates were erected to shut down access to certain parts of the plaza between the towers. Huge concrete flowerpots were plopped down in front of building entrances nobody had ever noticed before. And there were cameras. Lots of cameras, covering every angle—on every floor, in corners, in elevators, in dark garages. Twenty-four/seven the cameras ran, recording the face of every individual who entered or exited. And after the bomb, the building management made every employee who worked in the building wear a special plastic identification tag so they could keep track of who was doing what.

The inspiration for all these changes was simple—it's one thing when some terrorists from across the sea drive into your building and blow it up once. To allow such a thing to happen twice was simply out of the question.

Just last month Sal had told all of this to Ralphie as the two were sitting in a car in Brooklyn. Ralphie had been working on Sal for weeks. During their talk, Sal had finally agreed to hand over to Ralphie one of those special new ID badges the Port Authority gave out only to trusted employees like Sal.

Sal told Ralphie other things as well—such as the precise day and time the Brinks truck arrived each week with money to be delivered from Bank of America's many branches to the bank's foreign currency unit on the eleventh floor of One World Trade. He told Ralphie which freight elevator the guards took, how many guards stayed with the money during the eleven-story ride, how much time it took to get to the eleventh floor, approximately. He couldn't say exactly how much money the Brinks guards transported on any given day, but he knew it was a lot because the bags sure looked heavy.

Ralphie had much in common with Sal. Both had grown up near the South Brooklyn waterfront. The two men knew many of the same knock-around guys who hang out at social clubs, putting money on the street and gambling on nearly anything that moves. Ralphie always enjoyed hanging around with these guys, and he picked up a very specific type of education as a result. Stealing things, for instance, had become his career. He had been arrested many times and had cobbled together an impressive record that culminated in charges brought by the United States attorney for the Eastern District in Brooklyn in 1987 involving fraud and larceny and general felonious behavior. In fact, Ralphie had just finished paying off the fine he had incurred in that case just a few weeks ago. Over the years he stole many things from warehouses on the Brooklyn and New Jersey waterfront and sold them to a fence in a wheelchair named "Wheels." Ralphie was definitely a knock-around guy himself. He told stories about Joey Gallo and Joey Gallo's lion, although it was never sure that he ever actually met Joey Gallo or his lion. Ralphie had lots of brothers, some of whom had gone to jail at one time or another.

"In 1972," he confided to Sal, "me and my bro Tony were on a hijacking case. Four brothers in jail at one time. My mother did not know which way to run."

For all his knocking around, he didn't have much to show. He was also forty-one and worried about putting his two kids through college. He put sunscreen on his bald spot and obsessed about his weight. "I can't believe how fat I got," he said. "Fucking fat." He drank his coffee black with Sweet'N Low, liked to get a manicure once in a while, and could spend endless hours discussing the good things in life—caviar, champagne, the correct cigar. He drank Dewar's and smoked Mohegans. He was vain as hell, but very talented at getting what he wanted by convincing others that they were smarter than he was.

"If I'm rich or poor, I act the same," he said. By this he meant, in good times or bad, if there was a scam to be had, Ralphie was a willing participant.

Ralphie on Ralphie: "Everybody says if you ask anybody in the neighborhood, Sally, he's a stand-up guy. They don't tell you what he does 'cause—"

Sal: "They don't know it."

Ralph: "They don't know. Nobody knows my fucking business. Nobody knows what I'm fucking capable of. Nobody. They summize . . ."

Sal could relate to Ralphie. He lived twenty years in a three-family tenement on Twenty-third Street in south Brooklyn, a tough little no-name neighborhood that lies between the Brooklyn Piers and Greenwood Cemetery. Sal had not had it easy. His father was an alcoholic who threw Sal out of the house when he was thirteen and stepped in front of a train when Sal was thirty-eight. Sal had to identify the body. One of his brothers died in a motorcycle accident; his sister went to a party in 1984 and never came home. Another sister died from AIDS. He had a wife who was afraid to leave her house and a twenty-one-year-old son who still lived at home. Only his daughter seemed to have promise—she was an honor student at a Catholic prep school and was headed off to college, hopefully on scholarship. Sal thought "hopefully" because if not, Sal— at the age of forty-one and collecting only limited legitimate income—had no clue how he was going to pay for it. The way Sal saw it, Ralphie might just provide the answer.

He had known Ralphie for years and had come to believe that Ralphie was smart. Still, he liked him just the same because Ralphie was not the kind of guy to hold it over you that he was smarter. And Sal—who considered himself a kind of evil genius in his own right—saw Ralphie as a comrade in crime.

Now Ralpie and Sal both needed a score. Ralphie owned real estate all over Brooklyn, collecting rent from working people and people who didn't work. With his many needs, this was not enough. Sometimes he had to hire junkies as superintendents and then forget to pay them because he felt he should place his limited supply of cash elsewhere. Such as in the restaurant he was trying to run down by Hudson River near the Brooklyn anchorage of the Brooklyn Bridge. The idea of it was to grab on to the cigar craze that was sweeping New York as part of the biggest financial boon in Wall Street history. Plenty of yuppie types lived in nearby Brooklyn Heights and the neighborhood just south of the Heights that used to be called Red Hook. Some were even moving into the old factory buildings between the Brooklyn and Manhattan Bridges. People like Sal and Ralphie who had grown up in these old Brooklyn neighborhoods now felt like they no longer belonged there. Their only form of revenge was to gouge the hell out of the yuppie hordes at "upscale" restaurants like Cigargoyles. And perhaps at some point, such a thing would occur. But for now, Cigargoyles was an endless chasm into which Ralphie poured his hard-earned cash and out of which he received nothing but aggravation.

"I'm tired of fucking earning," he says to Sal. "I mean I want to fucking spend money with broads and have fun. You know, the usual bullshit. But I don't want to sit in fucking social clubs all day either."

Recently Ralphie had confided in Sal that he had a girl-friend who liked to spend time in the best of Manhattan's hotels.

Sal said, "How's your wife doing? She's nice. A very nice person, your wife. I met her a few times. Your daughter's beautiful. And you got a girlfriend, too."

Ralph: "I'm telling you, I can't fucking afford her."

"You know it and I know it."

"I've got a wife. I've got a girl," Ralphie says. "I'm telling you I'm so pressed up here. You have no idea. I'm fighting with my girl. I'm all day with her. My credit card is up to the fucking sky limit with these fucking hotels. Everybody's running out of patience. I'm running out of patience.

"You know what?" Ralphie asked. "This is sad."

Ralphie had come to the realization that he was, in fact, dead broke. Stealing maybe $3 million from the Bank of America inside the world's safest building could perhaps resolve that dilemma.

January 9, 1998

The plan was either brilliant or insane.

The idea was to gain entrance to a secure area deep inside America's most secure building on a busy weekday morning, hold up two armed Brinks guards carrying bags of cash for the Bank of America, and then wander out of the building with many bags of money in hand.

And not get caught.

The scheme was essentially Ralphie's idea, and if it went off as planned, both his wallet and his reputation would reap enormous benefits. If, on the other hand, it failed, it would be Ralphie who would lose the most.

Ralphie had done the best he could to think of every angle ahead of time.

He visited the Trade Center buildings several times, although he had never actually been able to get to the eleventh floor, where the actual robbery would take place. He had scouted out the employee entrance in the main concourse and made note of the many cameras that Sal had warned him about.

The job was set for Tuesday morning at 8:30 A.M. sharp. That was when the Brinks drivers would arrive through the underground entrance to One World Trade. Sal had explained that in the basement garage, the guards would hoist many bags of money out of the truck and onto a stainless-steel rolling cart. Sometimes there were eight bags, sometimes ten. They would roll the cart into a freight elevator—always the same freight elevator—and ride to the eleventh floor. Sal let Ralphie know that it was always just two guards, although sometimes other workers at the Trade Center got on the same elevator for the ride to whatever floor they happened to be working on. This complicated things, but only a little. They were, after all, merely employees. They did not carry guns.

The plan was that three men personally selected by Ralphie for their felonious experience and grace under pressure would arrive at the World Trade Center concourse and find their way to the employee entrance to One World Trade. They had to show up at a little before 8:30 A.M. Timing was critical. Wearing their fake employee IDs, they would have to get past security and take the elevator to the eleventh floor. They were supposed to arrive early enough to account for other stops on the way to their destination, but not so early that they'd be standing around on the eleventh floor in their ski masks looking like the Munich Olympics. They were to keep their masks and guns inside the duffel bags until the elevator reached the eleventh floor. When they stepped out, they were to keep their heads down away from the cameras and quickly put on ski masks. At the same time they were to act in a quiet and calm manner, as if they were salary-earning civil servants shuffling off to jobs they despise just like everybody else. They were to wait for the freight elevator doors to open, which should occur at precisely or just about 8:30 A.M. They were to quickly enter the elevator before anyone got out.

Two of the three robbers would pull out handguns. Each was to disarm a Brinks guard while the third man handcuffed them with plastic-covered wire. All three would then quickly remove cash from the blue Brinks bags into the duffel bags each man carried. They were to then press the button to send the elevator to a top floor, step quickly out into the hall, and walk calmly away with their newly filled bags of money.

For any of this to take place, they would first have to find their way through the concourse to the correct passenger elevator. That might not be so easy. The World Trade Center concourse was a confusing windowless mall filled with overpriced retail outlets, chain restaurants, and the entrance to the PATH trains to New Jersey. It was easy to become disoriented because everything looked the same no matter which way you turned. At 8:30 on a weekday morning, it was an incredibly busy place, with thousands of commuters streaming in from Jersey to their jobs inside the thousands of offices of the Twin Towers. It looked like the Christmas rush every morning.

That was why on this day at 8:30 A.M.—four days ahead of time—Ralphie had come to the concourse with one of the men he chose to pull off this caper of the century. The idea was to get acclimated to the morning chaos. God knew, it wouldn't do to get lost in the concourse on the big day.

Ralphie was with Richie Gillette, a guy from Windsor Terrace—another one of those Brooklyn neighborhoods that got a new name once the yuppies moved in. Richie was definitely not a yuppie. In fact, standing amid the morning rush inside the World Trade Center concourse, he looked more like a guy who might be featured on *America's Most Wanted* than a morning commuter glancing at the Charles Schwab ticker on his way to work.

Richie was thirty-nine years old, stood five feet eleven inches tall, weighed over two hundred pounds, and hadn't worked a steady job since June 1996. He smoked crack and had a seventeen-year-old son he saw only once in a while. His rap sheet was twelve pages long and dated back to the days when he was a mere sixteen-year-old lad, trucking back and forth between relatives who lived in Brooklyn and relatives who lived in Florida. His first arrest was for drug possession and bribery. Since then he'd been quite active, although never impressive. One of his most recent schemes involved stealing two bottles of EnFamil baby formula from a CVS on Third Avenue in Brooklyn. Why he stole baby formula was not clear, since he had no babies. Why he picked Bay Ridge was easier to understand. It was not the neighborhood in Brooklyn were he grew up, but it was nearby and thus convenient by subway. This was one of three men Ralphie has chosen for his caper. It was clear that Richie Gillette was not Cary Grant in *To Catch a Thief*.

Richie, in turn, picked two of his neighborhood pals to help him carry out this dangerous daylight mission. There was Melvin Folk, a forty-four-year-old alcoholic with a tenth-grade education. He had a history of drug and booze problems. That meant sometimes he was addicted to drugs, sometimes he was addicted to alcohol. Usually he was addicted to both. He had been homeless for months since his wife and five-year-old son were burned out of their home in Queens.

Then there was Mike Reed, a thirty-four-year-old long-time heroin abuser. His parents had died of heroin overdose when he was eight. He was raised by his grandmother in the Bishop Boardman Apartments in Windsor Terrace and kicked out when it was discovered that he was stealing from elderly residents—including his grandmother. Just this week he had stolen food stamps from a homeless man.

This was Team Trade Center. To the uninitiated, it might seem that Ralphie had made a huge mistake, picking three neighborhood junkies with the intellectual depth of bouncing-head dashboard dogs. But there was some reasoning behind this apparent blunder. The idea was to pick three guys who would do only what they were told to do and nothing more. Ralphie let it be known to Richie that he was a connected guy. This was to imply that if Richie, Mel, or Mike ever gave him up, they'd have to live with the knowledge that some guy in a Le Coq Sportif jogging suit might come up to them on the street someday and shoot them in the forehead.

Richie was Ralphie's go-to guy. Ralphie deliberately had little contact with Mel and Mike and kept himself behind the scenes. He never let Sal know the details and never let Richie, Mel, and Mike know about Sal. All they had to do was follow instructions, and each could expect to make $20,000. To three junkies from Windsor Terrace, that was a lot of cash.

January 13, 1998

A little bit past 8 A.M. on a chilly Tuesday morning, a heavily armored Brinks truck forced its way through the morning traffic and pulled up to the underground garage at the World Trade Center. A frigid drizzle fell from overcast skies. Security guards inside the Trade Center building waved the truck through and it proceeded to wind along the concrete labyrinth to a certain freight elevator that led to One World Trade Center. This was neither the first nor the last delivery of the day. Two Brinks employees remained in the truck, while two others unloaded seven blue Brinks bags from the bag onto a steel cart. Inside the bags was a mix of French, Italian, Japanese, and U.S. currencies totaling just over $2.6 million. Most of the American dollars were placed in bundles inside the bottom three bags. The top four bags contained mostly foreign money. Both guards carried handguns that were plainly visible. They pushed the cart over to the elevator, pressed the button, and waited. Inside they were joined by two cleaning ladies and three other building employees headed to work. The guards pressed the button for the eleventh floor and began the journey upward, headed for the Bank of America.

At about the same time three men strolled into the World Trade Center concourse in winter coats. Two of them—Michael Reed and Melvin Folk—wore nothing on their heads. The third, Richie Gillette, thoughtfully kept the hood of his Green Bay Packers jacket pulled up to hide his face. Each carried a duffel bag that appeared to contain very little, if anything. Each bag contained a ski mask; two contained handguns.

The three men pushed their way through the morning crush to the employee entrance to One World Trade. At the security desk they flashed their employee identification tags. If the guard had looked closely, he would have noticed that all three employees had the same name. The three men signed in under false names and pressed the button for the elevator bank that would take them to the eleventh floor. One of them, Richie Gillette, kept glancing at his watch.

The three men got on the passenger elevator with a number of other employees. They tried to look as bored as everyone else. At the eleventh floor they got off, and when the door closed, they found themselves in a gray-carpeted hallway with no windows that led in two directions past numerous anonymous offices. They quickly pulled on ski masks and figured out which of the elevators was marked FREIGHT. It was 8:28 A.M. In a minute, the freight door opened.

Inside, the two guards began to push out the cart full of money. They looked up to see three ski-masked men. Two were pointing guns at them.

One of the men hollered, "Don't nobody move! Everybody up against the wall!"

One of the cleaning ladies fell to her knees and began to pray loudly on the floor of the elevator. Later the guards would remember three men in ski masks in dark clothes, and that was all. A third man—it was Richie Gillette—handcuffed each of the elevator's occupants with plastic-covered wire. The men were clearly nervous. They disarmed only one of the two guards. The other guard remained handcuffed in a corner with his gun only inches away in its holster during the entire robbery. While Gillette tied up the guards and the cleaning ladies and the rest of the stunned passengers, Mel and Mike pulled out box cutters and slashed open the top four of the seven money bags. They then began jamming the contents into their duffel bags, not paying much attention to the fact that most of what they were stealing was not manufactured by the United States Treasury Department.

They moved as quickly as they could, but time was passing quickly. They had now been in the elevator for nearly eight minutes, holding the door and pointing guns at seven prone people. The cleaning lady who had been praying on her knees was now weeping. The robbers decided to call it a day, leaving behind $1.6 million in U.S. currency in carefully stacked packages inside the bottom three blue Brinks bags.

One of the men hit the button for the twenty-second floor. They stepped out of the freight elevator into the hall, still wearing their ski masks. At this moment they were confronted with confusion. They had been told again and again to hide their faces, but also to look as calm and normal as possible. Wearing ski masks in a bank unit's hallway seemed hardly a normal thing to do. Thus it was that all three men removed their ski masks at once. Only Richie Gillette, who had apparently picked up a modest amount of common sense over the years, kept his hood on. Richie and Mel carried one bag, Mike carried two. They strolled down the hallway with their bags weighted down by money, looking as relaxed as vacationers on the beach. Or perhaps they were maintenance guys headed over to check out the latest complaint about the screwy heating system that kept things too hot in the summer and freezing from December through May.

Stroll was what they did, over to a passenger elevator.

They pressed the button and waited. Soon they were on board, headed back to the concourse. In a few minutes—by 8:45 A.M.—they passed out of a set of revolving doors at One World Trade and onto a crowded New York City street.

They had to be feeling pretty fine. This was, after all, the World Trade Center, a building transformed into a fortress as a result of the acts of crazed overseas terrorists. And they had just stolen lots and lots of money from inside that very building and walked outside an actual door onto the street.

At that moment, as Richie, Mel, and Mike headed out of the revolving door, Ralphie sat across the street in a parked car, watching. He saw them leave. He saw the bags in their hands. He saw them walk down the street. He knew that they were to take different subway routes to Brooklyn and meet up that night to split up whatever they had snatched. It must have been a difficult moment for Ralphie. There he sat, knowing that his three handpicked guys had somehow managed to come out of that building without being arrested. And yet he could not know what had transpired inside, he could not know precisely how much they'd stolen, and he could not, under any circumstances, walk over at that moment and ask.

January 14, 1998

It was hard to tell from the media deluge whether the world viewed the mastermind behind the Great World Trade Center Heist of 1998 as a criminal Einstein or a comic genius.

It was full-court media bombardment, almost from the moment Richie, Mel, and Mike traipsed out of the Trade Center with their heavy loads. On TV, on the radio—hour after hour it continued. The press loved it! Three guys—in some reports "bozos"—managed to walk out of New York's most sensitive building in broad daylight (whatever that is) with more than $1 million in cash. And they did it while showing their faces to no fewer than fifty-five hidden cameras. How about that! These radio and TV people were practically laughing out loud as they read their copy to the masses.

The mastermind himself—Ralphie Guarino—remained in a state of shock. He didn't know what to think, except to know that whatever would come of this, it would surely be bad. During the previous twenty-four hours, after he watched his guys exit the towers, he headed to a rendezvous spot in Brooklyn. There he helped Richie and the other two guys count and split the cash. His first shock came when he got a look at the take. There was nary a dead U.S. president in the lot. Francs. Yen. Lire. Lots of lire.

"You know I got fucking bags of this Italian yen," Ralphie told Sal later. "I don't know, Italian lire. You know, eighty thousand of them making fucking ten dollars."

There were some good old American dollar bills, but not a whole hell of a lot, and Ralphie was forced to hand over most of the U.S. cash to his three foot soldiers in stacks of $20,000 each. Counting the rest became somewhat tricky. Ralphie—a guy from Brooklyn—had little experience with the finer details of foreign currency exchange rates. They did the best they could. He arranged to have the bulk of the overseas cash hidden away until he could figure a way to exchange it for real American bills. He made sure to tell all three of his guys to get out of town as quickly as possible, and then he went on his way. He was happy that the job itself had come off, but talking with Sal Calciano, he was not so happy about the foreign aspect of the haul.

"Maybe we can figure it out on a computer," he said. "I got to know what a pound is worth. I got to know what the Armenian dollar is worth. Excuse me. What a lire is worth. I mean, I look at the paper, but I can't understand it. You know? It's zero-zero-point-five. I'm not good at it. I have bad dreams about this."

That morning, the *New York Daily News* story headline on page 3: 1.6M LOST IN WTC HEIST.

That was bad. What was below the headline was worse. There were two photographs, taken off surveillance cameras on the eleventh floor of the World Trade Center. In one photo taken from Camera no. 4, the time was listed as 8:40:11 A.M. 1/13/98. There, for all the world to see, was Melvín Folk. His face was as clear as if he was appearing on *America's Funniest Home Videos*. He might as well have waved at the camera. Then right behind him came Michael Reed, his jacket open, carrying two bags, oblivious. Richie Gillette walked behind the three, his face obscured by a hooded jacket. The photographs were precise and clear. They offered time to the nanosecond and well-focused detail of Mel and Mike's collective mugs.

"What's the big deal about buying a hat?" Ralphie asked Sal. "No good news. Can't get no good news out of this. Sitting on a million dollars. I never lied in my whole life."

Sal: "You know what I want? We need to get somebody sharp."

Ralph: "I mean, I'm so pissed. I should be. You know what? I don't mind. You want to get caught, you get caught. These things happen, right? Can't go to fucking Mommy."

But the details. The stories alongside those horrible photos provided galling details.

"They knew the layout of the World Trade Center well,"

one law enforcement source was quoted as saying. "They seemed to know the delivery schedule."

And worst of all—the newspapers reported that the thieves left behind $1.6 million of mostly U.S. currency.

"How can you only take two bags?" Ralphie asked rhetorically. "Two bags whatever the fuck you take. He was on the elevator. He saw it. I mean, I can't believe they did this. I think they just panicked."

One question begat another, then another.

Ralph: "I mean I didn't see them. You know, they went by train. And then I saw them later on. So who knows what they fucking did. You know they're fucking junkies. All right? I mean I hate to say the fucking word *junkie,* but I mean, they're fucking thieves."

As the day wore on, more and more details of the Trade Center robbery became a matter of public entertainment. By the next morning, on the front page of the *Daily News,* it deteriorated into high comedy.

MOE, LARRY AND CURLY
Three stooges swiped $1M from WTC then went home to show off in B'klyn nabe

What did that make Ralphie? Shemp?

Now the photo of Richie, Mel, and Mike was on the front page, too, over the caption: "Oooh look, a camera!" And as a final insult, one of the suspects had already been picked up by the FBI.

Though no names were yet mentioned, it was clear everybody knew who was involved. That's because at least two of the three—Mel and Mike—had clearly ignored Ralphie's advice to get the hell out of Dodge and instead returned to their old haunts in Windsor Terrace. This indicated they either had no clue their faces were all over the newspapers and on the TV news, or they simply didn't care. Otherwise, why would Michael Reed have headed straight back to his usual barber at the Unisex Salon on Prospect Park West to drop fourteen dollars on a haircut? Barber Lou Amato got a measly three-dollar tip and was thus inspired to tell the *Daily News,* "I saw his picture in the paper and I said to myself, 'Oh my God, I cut a bank robber's hair.'"

From there, Reed walked down the street feeling mighty munificent. He walked into a local corner store where he was well-known and gave the owner a dollar he owed her. He then bought himself a carton of strawberry milk.

"All singles," she said. "He acted very normal. It was unbelievable."

Within hours after the newspapers printed a number to call the police with information about the suspects, the cops had received no fewer than fifty-six tips. It did not hurt that there was now a $26,000 reward. All over Windsor Terrace people were dropping quarters into pay phones. Mel and Mike, after all, weren't exactly well liked in the neighborhood. At Farrell's bar, for instance, the bartender— who also managed to call the tip line—made it clear that Reed was considered a bit of a skell, and was therefore unwelcome on the premises—"not even to use the bathroom."

But worse than all of the humiliation was the fact that one of the Three Stooges was now in the custody of the FBI, and Ralphie was sure he knew which one.

It had to be Mel, and Mel knew Richie's first and last name. Whether or not he knew Ralphie's name, Ralphie could not be sure. Certainly Richie had mentioned it once or twice. And even more certain was that the FBI could not in their right minds believe that Moe, Larry, and Curly had thought this thing up. As a liquor-store owner from Windsor Terrace told the *News,* "They weren't smart enough for that. Someone had to come to them and offer a deal."

Someone indeed.

Ralphie reached out to Sal to have a talk. They met for coffee.

Sal: "You want some coffee?"

Ralph: "You drink the coffee."

Sal: "I'll drink any fucking thing. I mean, I don't give a fuck."

Ralph: "I got a fucking headache."

Sal: "All right, then. What are we gonna do? Let's really start thinking."

Sal then informed Ralphie that he'd heard a kid from the neighborhood was at a local funeral home and was saying that Melvin Desmond Folk had $25,000 stashed at his house and then the federal agents came around and were asking the kid questions. Sal said the kid told them, "I was just talking out of my hat."

Ralph said, "Sally, you know, you gotta believe one thing. You gotta believe you're dealing with fucking morons, this whole neighborhood."

The FBI picked up Michael Reed on Thursday, the fifteenth of January. He was actually staying at the home of a friend right there on Twentieth Street in Brooklyn where he hung out all the time. A retired NYPD detective who'd known Reed for years from Windsor Terrace had identified him within a few hours of the robbery. That same day a photo of Richie Gillette was circulated to police stations across the nation.

Around 7:30 P.M. on Friday, January 16, a passenger on a California-bound Amtrak aroused the suspicions of railroad security because he was chain-smoking and flashing money around. The man was approached by security in his sleeper car as the train pulled into Albuquerque, New Mexico, and was asked a few questions. The man wore a Green Bay Packers jacket and produced an ID with the name George Grillo. He said he was from New York and was headed to San Bernardino. He consented to a search of the cabin and a drug-sniffing dog reacted to his red duffel bag. Inside, Amtrak agent Jonathan Salazar found lots of cash and an ID with the name Richard Gillette. The cash was confiscated because Gillette couldn't explain it. Agent Salazar did not arrest the passenger but instead headed back to his radio car to check both names. When Gillette popped up in the computer as wanted by the FBI, Salazar returned to the sleeper and discovered his man was gone.

The train had by now pulled out of Albuquerque and was headed out into the frigid desert night. Amtrak ordered it stopped and the local police in Albuquerque began searching for Gillette, street by street. A waitress pointed him out in a bar called Famous Sam's, but he ducked out the back door. An hour later they tracked him down to a nearby hotel. At 8:30 P.M., January 16, 1998, Gillette was arrested by the FBI and charged with participating in the daring January 13, 1998, robbery of Bank of America from inside the heart of the nation's safest building.

In less than four days, the Three Stooges were in the custody of the United States government. Nearly all of the stolen $1 million in lire, francs, yen, and good old American dollars was still unaccounted for.

January 19, 1998

In Brooklyn and Queens and Staten Island and the Bronx and North Jersey, the bookies prepared. Sunday, January 25, was Super Bowl XXXIII. Two weeks out, Vegas had Green Bay as thirteen-point favorites over Denver. Now it was twelve points, Green Bay. This was the week that could make or break the bank. Usually during the week leading up to Super Bowl, Ralphie was excited. This was *the* event. More money was bet on this game than on any single sports event during the year. In the New York area, millions of dollars were at stake. Fortunes were acquired; fortunes were lost. Spousal abuse was rampant. Enough beer was consumed to fill several football stadiums. In years past, Ralphie had done well on Super Bowl Sunday. This year he was betting against the spread, picking Denver over Green Bay, trying to get himself excited about earning some money as he had in years past.

But this was not years past. This was the week after the greatest failure of Ralphie's storied career. And during the last seven days, Ralphie has heard some things. For one, Sal told him the Port Authority police and the FBI now believed Moe, Larry, and Curly could not have pulled off such a well-organized heist without help from someone of more substantive intelligence. That they had names of actual individuals. That Sal and Ralphie now had their names on a list.

A few days before Super Bowl XXXIII, Ralph and Sal were driving around Brooklyn, headed for a seafood restaurant they both had known for years. Sal mentioned that the Port Authority police had been around to Sal's office asking many questions.

"They gotta be buzzin' about you inside the building because they know your fucking activity," Ralphie says.

"Everybody's thinking," Sal says.

"Yeah," Ralphie says, "they know, huh. Because, remember you said, you're gonna be all hot because of that building."

Sal: "Everybody's thinking I know about it."

Ralph: "Really."

Sal: "Hey. I'm not 'fessing up to nothing. I don't give a fuck. The only one I told, between me and you, believe it or not, is my wife." Sal stopped talking.

Ralphie says, "Say it."

Sal: "I told her my Jewish partner came over. I says, 'Steve, listen, do you know me?' And he knows me. Me and him do everything together. He's embarrassed. I says, 'Just tell me one thing. If I do get fucking nailed on this, if I gotta do twenty, will you look after my family?' He says, 'Sal, they will want for nothing.' That's all I needed to hear. So that's why I tell my wife. She's going crazy right before I'm locked up. I'm going alone."

Ralph: "Yeah, of course."

Sal: "Ain't nobody coming with me. She says, 'I know that.' She says, 'I knew it was you, you fuck.'"

They both laughed, but only for a minute.

Sal: "She says to me, 'Why?' I don't know why. Who the fuck knows why?"

Sal said the Port Authority has two detectives working on the case and they have no leads. "Everybody's protected," he says.

"Richie is protecting us, that's all I care about," Ralphie says. "All right. So what do you want to do with this money? That's the next problem. I don't want to send it away again, I don't want to keep it around me. You know what I mean?"

"My fucking head hurts when I think about it," Sal says. "I says to myself, I'm sitting here talking on the computer and I'm talking to this fucking girl in Florida. I wanna go see this girl in Florida. She's a Jewish girl. She's fifty-four years old. She is fucking twenty years older than me. She's very attractive, though. I like that in older women. She wants me to come down and spend the weekend with her and I am talking to her and I'm thinking, 'I can do this. I know I can fucking do this.' But why ain't I doing it? I don't know what we did wrong."

Ralph: "Well, you had it right the first time. I don't know what we did wrong."

Sal: "We didn't. We did everything fucking right."

They pulled up to the restaurant and walked inside. Ralph ordered a half-dozen cherrystone clams, an order of shrimp, and a Coors light for himself, and a sixteen-ounce Coke for Sal.

"Medium sauce?" asked the waitress.

"Medium sauce," Ralph says, turning back to Sal. "Feels funny without Richie here. Ah, he'll be all right. I don't know the answer anymore. You know when you don't know the answer anymore?"

Sal: "Right."

Ralph: "You get fucking razzle dazzle, dazzle razzle. I'm fucking losing my speech. I'm losing every fucking thing."

For Sal, there were certain pressures. Believing he would become a wealthy member of society once the World Trade Center score came rolling in, Sal had gone out and done a little spending in anticipation. Specifically, he'd dropped $20,000 on a new, improved bathroom, another $22,000 on an upgraded kitchen, and another $8,000 to tidy things up in the living room. All on his credit cards.

"Now all these bills that are coming, I got to take care of my credit cards. Oh my God, you got to see my cards. Oh man. I got the guy that came yesterday for the granite. I'm staying away from everybody."

Ralph had similar problems. He owed a particularly nasty member of the Gambino crime family named Joey Smash $40,000. Joey Smash was so unpleasant he had two nicknames—Joey Smash to his face, and "the Ugly Guy" behind his back. Joey Smash knew all about Ralphie's

World Trade Center caper and had decided Ralphie was sitting on a pile of money and holding back. Again and again he reached out to Ralphie to remind him of the money he is owed.

"He says, 'You know, you're gonna be all right, you know.' I says, 'Joe, what are you fucking worrying about?' I says, 'Monday, I start bringing you money.' I gotta cash this fucking money. I gotta pay him. Hgggggh. He's driving me crazy. He's like a fucking old washwoman."

And Joey Smash was not the only one who knew about Ralphie's involvement in the caper. Other wiseguys out there from Bayonne to Bensonhurst were speculating, which was something they often did when they thought somebody might have some money they could acquire. Some had even offered to help out. There was this Jimmy Gallo, a crazy guy from New Jersey who shot his partner Joe Pitts many years ago. He'd suggested to Ralphie he could find a place to exchange foreign capital for U.S. dollars. All he wanted was a mere 50 percent. Fifty percent! Ralphie was furious about it. And now Sal was telling him that somebody was bad-mouthing Ralphie as a beat artist.

Ralph: "Beat artist? How can you be a beat artist? Is that what they're trying to say? Jerk-offs. Yeah, fuck them. I don't pay attention to them. People are just buzzin' because they don't fucking know how to get around us. Don't you understand? Everybody wants to know how to get involved in this fucking thing, you understand?"

Sal: "Everybody's got an opinion."

It was a matter of not having enough information. These people out there calling him a beat artist clearly did not have enough information to know exactly what he was going through. And Ralphie himself did not have enough information to dig himself out of his hole. He could not be sure what the police knew and what they did not know. He didn't worry so much about Melvin Desmond Folk or even Michael Reed, because they didn't really know him and could say little to implicate him in the heist. Richie Gillette was an entirely different situation. There was a chance Richie Gillette might talk, and then they would come for him. That was the most likely scenario. But Ralph could not be sure. Richie's cousin was already calling Ralphie asking for money to send to Richie, who was still sitting in a New Mexico jail cell. Ralphie had to decide whether sending money was a good investment. If he did not send it, obviously Richie would talk. If, on the other hand, he did send it, Richie could decide to talk anyway, and then the money would have been wasted.

There was one other option. He could turn to Vincent Palermo, a smart, well-respected guy everybody called Vinny Ocean. Ralph was aware that Palermo was doing very well financially, and that he was known as a man who could come up with sensible resolutions to allegedly insurmountable problems. Ralphie could go to Vinny Ocean, borrow some money, pay off Joey Smash, keep paying off Richie Gillette, and slowly exchange the pile of foreign currency he was sitting on. The only problem was Vinny Ocean was out of town, headed to San Diego for Super Bowl XXXIII, and there was no way to reach out to him until January 26 at the earliest. Usually this would not have been a big problem. But each day the weight grew heavier. A quick solution was essential.

Sitting in the restaurant with Sal, Ralphie tried not to think about his many problems. He asked Sal if he'd put on weight. Sal replied, "You don't know how to eat clams, so I'm going to teach you. Look. Let me show you. Watch."

When they were finished, Ralph had to pick up his daughter and get her to a basketball game. He and Sal went their separate ways, promising to keep talking until they figured out what to do.

THE KNOCK

Sometime between the end of Sal and Ralph's seafood dinner and the next day, Ralph was at his home in Staten Island when he heard a knock on the door. His wife answered. Two men entered the living room and sat down. Ralph walked into the room and sat down, too. Even before they opened their mouths, he knew who they were. One of the men handed over a business card. In the middle was the man's name embossed in blue script over the title special agent. In the left-hand corner was a gold embossed image of a badge topped by an eagle looking to the left. Below that was the address, 26 Federal Plaza, where Ralph knew he was going to be spending quite a bit of time. In the top right-hand corner was the title in blue: FEDERAL BUREAU OF INVESTIGATION, New York Division.

They talked for a moment to be polite, and then they made it clear Ralphie needed to come with them to downtown Manhattan. When they left Ralph's house, it was dark. This was a good sign for Ralph. That meant that his neighbors probably would not notice him walking away with the two men. Ralph surmised that this might be an important point in the days and months to come.

3

January 23, 1998

The trucks arrive at dawn, pulling up to the vacant storefront on Second Avenue in a faded little New Jersey town called Elizabeth. They are miles away from the make-believe world of movies and television, but they have a job to do, and it involves pretense. They begin scrubbing off the graffiti on the storefront, sweeping off the sidewalk in front, removing debris from inside. They wipe months of grime off the windows and repaint the front door green. In the windows they hang cured hams and trussed pig carcasses, coils of pink-and-beige sausages, a denuded chicken with beak and feet still in place. All of it is plastic. Over the entrance, they mount a sign that has never hung there or anywhere before—CENTRANNI'S PORK STORE. There is no Centranni's in this world. The people of Elizabeth would fail if they tried to pick up some prosciutto or a pound of mozzarella inside this pork store. This is pure fakery, but it looks like the real thing.

This is the work of David Chase, who grew up a few miles away in nearby Caldwell, New Jersey, under the name DeCesare. He is filming a pilot for a new television show he has dreamed up about a Mafia family from New Jersey. His is a different spin on the usual Mafia shtick. He sees real people doing real-people things, such as worrying about which college their daughter will get into or complaining about the price of gasoline. In between, these real people belong to a secret society of killers who pledge total allegiance to their "thing" and promise to shoot or, if that's not possible, beat to death anyone who informs on their secret. The project does not yet have a title, but film crews have been dispatched with camcorders throughout the streets of northern New Jersey scouting locales. Authenticity is paramount. In fact, authenticity is already causing the show many problems. Chase wants to make sure the characters are not portrayed as either too good or too bad. He wants his protagonist, Anthony Soprano, a capo in a New Jersey crime family, to be sympathetic, but also to be willing to break someone's head with a baseball bat. He has built Centranni's in the heart of Elizabeth because that is where Tony will hold court. As a result of all this authenticity, the major networks have taken a pass on Chase's project. He is in talks with HBO-TV about working a deal, and in the end, it will be said that authenticity was very important to his idea.

Just a few blocks away from the pretend Mafia pork store, Centranni's, there is a real pork stork called Sacco's. Inside Sacco's there are no plastic chickens. Pigs and sausages hanging on hooks are real. In Chase's yet-to-be-named television show, Uncle Junior is a hard old nut of a man who will sit at a table near the back of the fake pork store, and the other members of his TV Mafia family will come to him for favors and advice. He gives orders. He plots murders. He is a king.

His little kingdom is also remarkably similar to the real pork store a few blocks away from the TV pork store. In Sacco's, the seasoned gangster is named Joseph Giacobbe, who is known as Uncle Joe. He is a hard old nut of a man who comes to the store every morning for coffee and a roll. The FBI sees him come and go so much they scribble in their notebook, "Giacobbe and other members of the DeCavalcante family regularly hold meetings inside Sacco's." If you call Sacco's on any given morning and ask simply for Joe, Giacobbe will come to the phone.

JOE PITTS

On the Friday afternoon of January 23, 1998, sixty-seven-year-old Joseph Conigliaro drove his four-year-old black Cadillac up Smith Street through the miserable winter rain. This was Red Hook, the neighborhood in south Brooklyn where Conigliaro grew up. Everybody knew him and everybody called him Joe Pitts. But this was no longer the same Red Hook of Joe Pitts's wild years. Everywhere there was evidence that he was a stranger in his own neighborhood. A French restaurant had opened up, followed by a store that sold precious little ceramic objects made on the premises. Next came painfully hip boutiques with retro clothes for bohemians. The yuppies were coming and there was nothing Joe Pitts could do about it.

Joe Pitts was a dinosaur.

Red Hook wasn't even called Red Hook anymore. It was now Carroll Gardens, a name dreamed up by real-estate developers intent on softening the neighborhood's longshoreman image. It was no longer just a traditional Italian neighborhood where outsiders were considered a form of infectious disease. Into this insular neighborhood in the early 1990s had come an invading army dressed all in black. They were artists, people who made a living with their hands but not in the same manner as the people of Red Hook. Most of the old shipbuilding factories down by the water were long gone, and the sons and daughters of the men who built the ships of World War II were left scrambling for a new way to get by. Now came the artists, fleeing absurd Manhattan rents for cheap space on Smith Street. They opened galleries and shops and restaurants catering to young hip people of modest means. They changed Red Hook's neighborhood for good.

Joe Pitts—who was as much a part of the neighborhood as the cracks in the sidewalks—was now beginning to stand out. His notorious social club, the One Over Golf Club, hidden behind tinted black windows and a gate that was always shuttered, had become a relic. Perhaps he knew it. Most likely he did not. He lived in Carroll Gardens, but if you asked him, he'd say he lived in Red Hook. Red Hook was where he came from. It was part of his DNA. It was a place he could understand.

Red Hook back in 1973 was to gangland what New Orleans was to jazz, a rough waterfront neighborhood where much gangster lore originated. From Red Hook came Crazy Joey Gallo, who kept a scrawny half-sized lion in the basement of a tenement on President Street. This was the Joey Gallo who spent hours watching old gangster movies of Paul Muni and Jimmy Cagney and Edward G. Robinson, and learned to imitate their body language. Years later, a Hollywood actor would come to Brooklyn and meet with Joey, who would let the clueless thespian in on how to walk and talk like a "real" gangster, without revealing that he himself was just a sucker for the silver screen. It was art imitating life imitating art.

In the Red Hook of 1973, Joe Pitts had been somebody. He was a known soldier in the crime family of Carlo Gambino. He was a made guy. You couldn't raise a hand to him without getting permission from the bosses. He made money just by walking into a business and declaring himself partner. To some, his story rivaled Crazy Joey Gallo's, mostly because no one believed half the things that were said about Gallo. The story that went along with Joe Pitts was hard to believe, but had a basis in truth. Because after it happened, Joe Pitts had to spend the rest of his days in a wheelchair.

At the time, back in 1973, Joe Pitts was forty-two years old. His partner was one of Joey Gallo's distant cousins, Jimmy Gallo, a DeCavalcante soldier. Joe Pitts and Jimmy Gallo were looking for a Brooklyn gambler named Vincent Ensulo. Ensulo had borrowed $1,200 and within a week owed $1,600, but that's not why they wanted him. Gallo and Joe Pitts had learned that Ensulo had begun secretly cooperating with law enforcement. Both men were extremely interested in finding Ensulo, and on a particular day they just happened to see him driving out of a gas station in Red Hook. They jumped into action, pulling open both doors of Ensulo's slowly moving car. Joe Pitts and Jimmy Gallo jumped inside the car, one on each side. They both drew guns and pointed them at Ensulo. Joe Pitts, who was at the wheel, began to drive away.

Within three blocks, Ensulo, who was either insane or so crazed with fear he didn't know what he was doing, suddenly jerked the wheel away from Joe Pitts. Immediately both Joe Pitts and Jimmy Gallo began firing their weapons, temporarily forgetting that there were three large men jammed inside the front seat of a moving sedan. Joe Pitts, or "Mr. Conigliaro," as the *New York Times* would later call him, shot Jimmy Gallo once in the left side. Jimmy Gallo ("Mr. Gallo") shot Joe Pitts twice in the right shoulder. The temporarily lucky Vincent Ensulo suffered only minor wounds, which allowed him to jump out of the car and flee into the Brooklyn night. Jimmy Gallo survived his wounds more or less unscathed, but Joe Pitts was partially paralyzed forever.

Both men were charged with shooting each other, and both pleaded guilty to weapons charges. Joe Pitts did his time in a wheelchair. When Gallo got out of prison, the FBI says, it took only a few days before Vincent Ensulo's body was discovered with one bullet in the head. Jimmy Gallo was later charged, but he was acquitted. He was later heard bragging about the time he "beat the system" when he "shot a rat and got away with it."

In the years that followed, Joe Pitts and Jimmy Gallo remained partners and pals, running a loan-sharking business out of John's Luncheonette in Red Hook well into the 1980s. But times changed. In 1972, Joey Gallo was gunned down at Umberto's Clam House in Little Italy. He had spent the evening at the Copacabana with the actor Jerry Orbach, who was about to play a version of Joey in the movie *The Gang That Couldn't Shoot Straight*.

The apartment building where Joey kept his lion had been demolished and replaced by subsidized senior housing with a sign, KEEP CHILDREN AND PETS OFF THE GRASS. By 1998, Crazy Joey Gallo wouldn't have recognized the neighborhood he had once ruled.

He certainly wouldn't have recognized Joe Pitts. By 1998, Joe Pitts was a bitter old man trapped in a wheelchair. He was sixty-seven years old and had been demoted from soldier to mere "associate" in the Gambino crime family by infuriating nearly everyone he came in contact with. He was now viewed by many of his peers as a washed-up, 210-pound tough old bastard who bled his victims dry. Joe Pitts the made guy wasn't what he used to be.

At this hour, as Joe drove down Smith Street toward the Gowanus Canal, few artists in black could be seen walking the rain-soaked streets. It was too early. He was alone in his Caddy. He had a nasty German shepherd that he kept in the One Over Golf Club. The dog accompanied him everywhere and barked and snapped at the invading yuppies. Joe Pitts would laugh when the dog did this. Everybody debated who was worse—Joe Pitts or his dog. On this night he intended to collect some money he decided to leave the dog behind.

It was all arranged.

He had put himself on the books of a struggling company called T&M Construction. T&M was owned by a would-be wiseguy named Mike. He was a source of regular cash for Joe Pitts. The arrangement was simple. Pitts would come by T&M and Mike would hand over a fat envelope of cash. In return, Joe Pitts would "protect" him from being shaken down by other gangsters. Mike hated Joe Pitts. Lately Joe Pitts had been stopping by more often, insisting that the fat envelopes be even fatter, and Mike was getting very tired of this.

Joe Pitts pulled up to Mike's apartment on Smith Street. Mike dashed through the rain to the Caddy. Sitting in the front seat, he told Joe Pitts there was a guy waiting with the money at Joe's social club, the One Over. They drove the few blocks to the club and Joe Pitts pulled up to the curb.

A guy called Marty Lewis came out of the club by himself. He was not the guy Mike had said would be there, but he was a guy Joe Pitts knew. Marty was a guy known to other guys. He had driven around with Joe Pitts hundreds of times and pushed him in his wheelchair when the old man needed pushing. He was wearing gloves in the rainy winter night, and he jumped in the backseat. Marty Lewis said the guy with the money was waiting just a few blocks away, but Mike said he couldn't go because he needed to get back to his apartment. Joe Pitts drove him home and dropped Mike off.

Lewis got in the front seat and told Joe Pitts the guy with the money was waiting on Lorraine Street.

Lorraine Street was down near the Gowanus highway overpass next to a bedraggled housing project. There were auto-body shops and garbage-clotted empty lots. Most New Yorkers would hear they were supposed to meet somebody on a winter night in the rainy darkness on Lorraine Street and they would drive quickly away, never to return.

Not Joe Pitts.

Joe Pitts had grown up in this neighborhood and feared no one, even from his wheelchair.

Joe Pitts drove through the quiet residential brownstone neighborhood with its pizza shops and Italian pork stores and yuppie boutiques south on Court. The farther south he drove, the more uncivilized his neighborhood became.

By the time he passed under the Gowanus Expressway, Joe Pitts had crossed over into another world. Gone were the orderly brownstones with flower boxes and kids on bikes. Now there was razor-wire fences and pocked streets and dangerous alleyways. Here, packs of dogs ran leashless through empty lots. Marty Lewis told Pitts to pull up to the curb on Lorraine Street past the highway overpass. This was where the guy with the money was supposed to be. Joe Pitts could not see the guy with the money anywhere in the rain and the dark, but he pulled over anyway.

Marty Lewis took off one glove as he opened the passenger door and stepped out of the car. Rain thrummed on the windshield.

Marty stood up outside the car, turned around, and leaned back in the Caddy. He had a revolver in his hand pointed at Joe's head and he squeezed off six shots. Five entered Joe Pitts. Bullets entered Joe Pitts's face, his right arm, his torso, and his right lung.

"I can't believe it was you," Joe Pitts grunted. "Motherfucker."

Lewis stepped back, perhaps surprised by the fact that Joe Pitts was still talking. But Joe Pitts wasn't just talking—he was driving. He put the car in drive and drove slowly away from the curb. The door shut as he accelerated, and when he got to the corner, Joe Pitts, nearly seventy years old, with five bullets in his body, clicked on his turn signal.

Marty Lewis stood on the corner with the rain pounding down, watching the red light of that turn signal click on and off in the darkness. On and off, on and off. Marty Lewis almost had a heart attack on the spot as Joe Pitts drove away.

Carrying five bullets, Joe Pitts not only managed to obey all traffic laws, but he somehow was able to navigate his huge automobile back to his social club on Court Street, bleeding all over the upholstery. Somehow he managed to get one of his cohorts, a big three-hundred-pound DeCavalcante associate, who lived in an apartment above the club, to come down to the car.

The three-hundred-pound associate drove Pitts the seven blocks under the IND subway el tracks, over the foul waters of the Gowanus Canal, and right up to the emergency entrance of Methodist Hospital in Park Slope. They arrived at 6:17 P.M., and Pitts was placed on a gurney, where he remained for the next four hours, waiting for surgery.

Because he had been shot, the police from the Seventy-eighth Precinct were summoned. A detective asked Joe Pitts what happened. He said a black man from the Red Hook housing projects shot him. Clearly it was his intention to distract law enforcement while he took care of business himself. Clearly he believed he would survive to take care of business.

At 10:22 P.M., Joe Pitts was still waiting when he had a heart attack and died.

VINNY OCEAN

At the hour of Joe Pitts's death, Vinny Ocean was just arriving in San Diego in anticipation of Sunday's big Super Bowl extravaganza. His mind was most likely on having a good time, on whether Green Bay would be as dominant as everyone was saying, on how much money he'd make if he guessed right on the spread. This was the good life—he was far away from the cold January streets of New York in sunny California with his first son, a stockbroker named Michael, and several of his closest friends. He could afford Super Bowl tickets. He could afford to be in San Diego. He was doing well, and was about to do even better.

Vinny knew all about Joe Pitts. Mike of T&M had come to him and asked him for help after another DeCavalcante captain named Rudy Ferrone had died. Rudy had been put in charge of Joe Pitts and had essentially let him do whatever he wanted. Now that Rudy was dead, Mike went to Vinny Ocean and asked if it was okay to kill Joe Pitts. Joe Pitts was no longer a made guy, but he did have friends, and Mike didn't want any trouble. Vinny Ocean had looked Mike in the eye and said, "What's the matter with you? I don't want to hear anything about this."

Mike, the FBI came to believe, had interpreted this as approval.

After Joe Pitts was gone, Vinny Ocean could rightfully say that he had nothing to do with the chain of events. He could not say he had nothing to do with Joe Pitts. As a result of Joe Pitts's death, Vinny Ocean wound up making a lot more money. When a wiseguy dies, somebody has to figure out what to do with all the money he's taking in through various schemes. In this case, it was decided that Vinny would get Joe Pitts's payments. He did this by putting his driver, Joey O, on the payroll of the victims' companies in no-show jobs. Each week Joey O would get paid and kick his share up to Vinny Ocean.

Immediately.

Besides the weekly paycheck Joe Pitts had been extorting from Mike at T&M Construction, Joe Pitts had also been shaking down a man named Al Manti for $1,000 a week. Al Manti owned a bus company on Long Island called Manti Transportation. He was not a very good businessman, and as a result, his company was about to sink under a sea of debt. Still, a business is a business, and some business owners in New York City have been known to turn to subsidiaries of La Cosa Nostra for a little fast cash. Manti Transportation was such a company, and Joe Pitts had sunk his hooks into Al Manti for months. Now that Joe was gone, Vinny Ocean took over the task of collecting $1,000 a week from Al Manti to protect him from being exploited by some other unfeeling, unscrupulous Mafia family.

Thus, on one rainy January night, Vinny Ocean got himself an extra $52,000 a year for doing exactly nothing.

Each week Joey O would show up at T&M Construction and Manti Transportation and pick up his "paycheck." He would keep half and send the other half up to Vinny. Of course, this arrangement was never called "protection." It would be called something else.

Salary.

At one point Al Manti was not happy about this and actually complained in person to Vinny Ocean. "Why," he asked Vinny, "do I have to pay protection to Joey?"

Vinny Ocean frowned and shook his head sadly. "Let me tell you something," he said. "You don't ever mention that word in front of me. You're not paying for no protection. I'm your partner. That's my salary every week. Like your salary. Don't ever ask that again."

Manti immediately backed down. "I was just kidding," he said, handing over yet another envelope stuffed with ten $100 bills toward Vinny Ocean's "salary."

In January 1998, that was how it was going for Vinny Ocean. The money was rolling in. Life was good. He was an experienced capo with a crew of both old-timers and newcomers. The strip club he secretly owned, Wiggles, was still up and running, having so far survived attacks from all sides by the politicians of Queens County and beyond. The city had passed a law shutting down all businesses that traffic in "adult entertainment" in residential neighborhoods or within five hundred feet of schools, churches, or day-care centers.

"Wiggles" was within five hundred feet of just about everything. But the strip clubs of New York had hired a lawyer and banded together under the American flag, waving around the First Amendment and taking their case all the way through the New York courts. So far, they'd been losers. The courts weren't buying the sex industry's claim that the city was denying exotic dancers the right to ex-press themselves through the medium of lap dancing. City officials, in fact, could legitimately state that they were not shutting strip clubs down. Instead, they were simply packing them off to urban Siberia, allowing them to relocate to industrial waterfront neighborhoods and other out-of-the-way locales hard by the Fresh Kills Landfill and the Coney Island Cyclone. But the state's top court had yet to issue a final decision on the question, and as a result, all the clubs were allowed to remain open for business three years after the strip-club law first passed in 1995. During that time, "Wiggles" had built up a loyal customer base of leering drunken men with fistfuls of sweaty dollar bills. And many of those sweaty dollar bills were secretly finding their way into Vinny Ocean's pocket.

Plus there were many other deals. There was the $1,300 a week Vinny pocketed from his take of a gambling operation that took bets from across metro New York. There was the untold thousands in loan-shark interest Vinny picked up by buying his money at a point and a half weekly interest from a Gambino capo and putting it on the street at two points. Then there were the secret partnerships. He had designated himself a "partner" of T&M Construction, which then went and won a big contract to renovate the New Yorker hotel in midtown Manhattan. He was looking into becoming a secret partner in a new gambling boat operating out of Freeport, Long Island. None of this money showed up on his tax forms. All of it was collected in bundles of cash.

Still, Vinny Ocean wanted more. Much of his income in 1998 came from the usual Mafia sources—preying on degenerate gamblers, lightening the wallets of loan-sharking victims, shaking down local unions. Thirty years after Joe Valachi first went on national television and revealed the inner secrets of the Mafia, these three activities remained the mainstays of the mob. In business terms, this refusal to evolve was not a good thing. This was like the automobile industry failing to predict the ascendancy during the 1970s of small, affordable Japanese cars that didn't consume massive quantities of gasoline. Except in this case, Toyota was the FBI, and the FBI had long ago figured out how to investigate the mob when it was involved in gambling, loan sharking, and extortion. What the mob needed in the late 1990s was to figure out new ways to make money. And by 1998, some of the more clued in were doing their all-American best. Vinny Ocean was definitely one of the more clued in.

Like most Americans who did not live in dark spaces beneath the ground, he was vaguely aware of the unusually strong boom in the stock market that was making some amateur investors a lot of money. Therefore, Vinny invested. He talked about puts and buys. He consulted with a DeCavalcante captain named Phil Abramo who thought of himself as the Michael Milken of La Cosa Nostra. He discussed "this new thing, this Viagra."

"Somebody's going to make a lot of money on that one," he said.

But the stock market was still a risky place, and some of what Abramo was doing—secretly paying off brokers to pump up the worth of worthless stock and then dumping the stock when it peaked—was not exactly legal. Vinny Ocean was clearly looking for ways to go legit.

Consistently he sought out business deals that might be considered forward-thinking. In January 1998, for instance, he was talking about investing in a cell-phone distributorship through the German communications giant Siemens. He had a partner. To the Germans they did business with, the partner's name was William Cutolo, a businessman in a suit. Cutolo was like Vinny Ocean—a good-looking, fifty-something New York guy with silver sideburns that implied distinguished banker at work. Prudence was the message. Of course, on the streets of Brooklyn, Cutolo was known as Wild Bill. This was because Wild Bill had once beaten a man bloody with a baseball bat in front of a group of stunned Teamsters. This was the Wild Bill who was heavily involved in the Colombo crime family wars of the early 1990s, when ten gangsters and two innocent bystanders were shot down in the streets of Brooklyn because of a dispute over who would run the family. At that time one side of the family had decided it was better than the other side. In one episode of this two-year saga, Cutolo lured to a suburban home in Staten Island a rival from the other side who many felt held too high an opinion of himself. When the rival showed up, he was pointed toward the stairs leading to the second floor and told to walk up. The rival began walking and looked up to see two men—a Colombo soldier named Carmine Sessa and Cutolo—standing there with weapons drawn. Cutolo, according to Sessa, suddenly thought he was in a movie.

"Fucking godfather," Cutolo muttered, emptying his revolver into the rival gangster at the foot of the stairs. Later, the rival was rolled up inside a rug and dumped in a landfill.

Cutolo was a man who spent much time massaging his public image. He was, for instance, a fund-raising chairman for a local charity that raised hundreds of thousands of dollars each year for research into multiple sclerosis. He posed for photographs and offered toasts at annual dinners. Many of those who paid for tables at these dinners were members of unions the FBI believed were secretly kicking back thousands to Cutolo. But as of January 1998, Cutolo was not in jail, and was not anticipating spending any time in jail. He'd been acquitted of all charges for his alleged role in the Colombo crime family war and now he was out on the streets, behaving like a businessman just trying to make a little here and there. The Siemens partnership on the Russian cell-phone deal with Vinny Ocean, of course, was not exactly public knowledge. They worked behind other investors. Their names appeared on no documents. If Cutolo's involvement in the deal became known, the Siemens deal would surely evaporate.

For that reason, Vinny Ocean was looking to do business with a big-name entrepreneur. He yearned for the imprimatur of legitimacy. One of those risk takers with a big name was, according to the FBI, Bob Guccione, the founder and president of one of America's favorite girlie-magazine empires—*Penthouse*.

Guccione was, of course, really a guy from Brooklyn with gold chains, the son of a Sicilian accountant. He grew up in a place where gangsters thrived but chose a legitimate way to make a living. He founded his General Media in 1967 and built it up to a $21 million company by out-*Playboy*ing *Playboy*. He was willing to do what hundreds of successful businessmen had done before to make a killing—take another step down. Of late, however, circulation of his slick porno magazines had taken a beating. He'd nearly defaulted on bond payments, had to cut forty jobs and shut two magazines. The extraordinary growth of the Internet and the new availability of product far raunchier than anything Guccione could dream up was killing him. Diversification, as they say in business school, was the only option. Thus Bob Guccione was talking about branching out into several new areas. One idea involved a vague plan to build a noncasino hotel with "masculine" amenities in Atlantic City. Guccione was in the process of finding investors.

Another idea was strip clubs. He was thinking about using the *Penthouse* name to open a string of upscale topless clubs in New York and New Jersey. A lawyer his daughter knew had put him in touch with a very charming businessman who looked a bit like the actor Robert Wagner with silver sideburns. The man's name was Vincent Palermo and he had much experience with a club in Queens called Wiggles. Palermo said he and Guccione were talking about getting together for a club in Manhattan, or if the mayor of the city didn't like that, in the Five Towns on Long Island. Vincent Palermo believed that Guccione was impressed with Vincent Palermo. And it was clear from Palermo's talks with one of the DeCavalcante family's new associates, Ralphie Guarino, that Vinny Ocean was very much taken by Guccione and his millions.

Ralphie, of course, was trying out the new secret-agent equipment given to him by the FBI, a fact he did not mention to Vinny. Ralphie pretended to be fascinated with Bob Guccione.

"Does he go out much?" Ralphie asked.

"No, not at all," Palermo said as if he had known Guccione his whole life. "He goes to the summer house for the weekend."

Vinny made it clear he was on a first-name basis with "Bob." He dropped in conversation numerous times that he had Bob's home number, that he had visited Bob's enormous town house on the Upper East Side with its built-in swimming pool and Icelandic goat pelts covering marble floors. Vinny claimed he was hoping to put together a club with Bob that would attract Wall Street guys, with door-to-door limousine service for convenience.

"He said, 'Vinny, you feel it is good,' he says, 'you got it.' Swear on my kids. Forget about it. 'You got it,' he says."

Ralphie asked, "I wonder how much this guy makes a year."

"Ah, forget about it," Vinny said. "Fucking unbelievable . . . He even says he is so far ahead of *Playboy*. Forget about it. *Playboy* ain't even in the same fucking class."

Ralphie: "I think *Penthouse* is a nice magazine, actually."

"There is no comparison," Vinny said, claiming the *Penthouse* Web site got more hits on the Internet "than anybody in the world. Right now."

"Does he really work anymore?"

"No, he doesn't go into the office, no. He was telling me a story, that he went to his office and the girl in the front there says, 'Can I help you?' Didn't even know who the fuck he was."

Vinny mentioned that Guccione's "right-hand man" was a lawyer named Gene, which made Ralphie light up like a game-show contestant with the right answer.

"I know him," Ralphie says. "I was in the can with him."

"You're kidding me," Vinny says.

"Old man Gene," Ralphie says. "You know what he does? He loves to knit. Swear to God."

Vinny: "He does what?"

Ralphie: "To knit. He used to knit."

Vinny—who apparently knew nothing about knitting—got uncomfortable and tried to change the subject. "Oh, I don't know about that."

"I'm serious. In the can, that's what he did. He was a lawyer, he got caught up in a swindle."

"Yeah."

"A stock swindle. Gene Bo. I can't believe that."

Vinny was beginning to like this Ralphie. Here was a street guy who was known as an earner. Vinny had heard that Ralphie was in a bit of a jam with the World Trade Center heist, but he was still impressed. It was true that the three guys Ralphie had picked to actually go inside and do the job turned out to be Moe, Larry, and Curly, but it appeared as if Ralphie had successfully insulated himself from their foolishness.

Ralph had told Vinny he was confident the three were not competent enough to link him to the scheme. And it had been a bold scheme. It had taken place in the middle of a weekday morning in a building that had more security than a nuclear weapons factory. This was, after all, *the* World Trade Center, the place that a mere five years before had been attacked by a band of dedicated and none-too-stable Islamic terrorists in a rented Ryder truck. Here were three of Ralphie's guys actually getting in and out of the building without getting caught, and walking away with who knows how much cash. How much of it was still missing nobody knew for sure. This was the kind of bold plan that Vinny admired, and hoped it would inspire his second-rate crime family, the DeCavalcantes. This kind of thinking would, perhaps, result in added respect. Perhaps, if Vinny was lucky, the term *farmer* would go out of fashion.

Vinny made a managerial decision that he would one day regret: he decided to put Ralphie with his driver and longtime friend, Joey O. That way he could keep an eye on this up-and-coming kid Ralphie.

And Ralphie could keep an eye on him.

4

By the time the FBI knocked on Ralphie Guarino's front door, much had changed in La Cosa Nostra regarding the ramifications of becoming a dreaded *rattus norvegicus*.

In the autumn of 1963, the ramifications were simple. You talk, you die. When sixty-year-old Joseph Michael Valachi sat in a roomful of United States senators and television cameras and became the first made member of the American Mafia to publicly reveal the corrupt inner machinery of his claustrophobic world, everyone knew he was a human target from then on. At the time, Valachi portrayed his decision to turn informant as a kind of business maneuver, a matter of pure pragmatism. His boss, Vito Genovese, had given him a theatrical "kiss of death" inside the federal prison in Atlanta, labeling him to the rest of gangland as an informant. This, of course, meant he should be killed as soon as possible. At the moment this occurred, Valachi was actually not an informant. A few months later, after pondering the fact that his own boss had publicly turned on him, he decided, "If the shoe fits . . ." As a result, he rejected his oath of *omerta,* knowing there was a $100,000 contract out on him, and talked. And talked and talked and talked.

In his talks, Valachi portrayed some members of his Mafia (the ones he still admired) as "men of honor." He never talked about his own family, and he was acutely aware that what he was doing ran contrary to everything he'd believed for most of six decades. He seemed almost to find acceptable the fact that anyone even loosely affiliated with any family from Bayonne to Berkeley would try to kill him if they could. In those days, the vow of *omerta* was serious business.

Nevertheless, Valachi did something that was a little ahead of its time. Despite the constant threat of sudden death, he decided to write a book, or more specifically have Peter Maas write it for him. The result was *The Valachi Papers* in 1969. It was a huge success and even became a Charles Bronson movie. It was the first of its kind, but far from the last.

Who could have known what this thug from East Harlem would inspire?

Thirty-one years after Valachi made his TV debut and wrote all about it, becoming an informant in La Cosa Nostra was old news. It started off slow. A low-level associate turned informant here, a slightly higher-up soldier decided to blab there. Then capos—midlevel bureaucrats in the mob hierarchy—jumped on the government bandwagon and agreed to tell all. There was Joe (Fish) Cafaro and Joe Cantalupo and Jimmy (the Weasel) Fratianno. The stakes grew. Phil Leonetti, the underboss of a Philadelphia crime family, flipped in 1986. Five years later, on September 21, 1991, Little Al D'Arco, acting boss of the Luchese crime family in New York, called up the FBI even before he was arrested and offered to help out. Forty-eight days later, on November 16, 1991, Salvatore (Sammy the Bull) Gravano, the underboss of what was then the nation's most powerful crime family, the Gambino clan, decided that he, too, had had enough of "the life" and agreed to cooperate. Gravano boasted openly during his court testimony that when he got out of prison, he would go back into the construction business and live a normal life. That pretty much made it official—the notion of a feared code of silence in which talk meant death had pretty much become a national joke. The secret society was no longer such a secret.

In fact, it was now a commodity. There was money to be made in all this chatter.

Some of the informants—including Gravano and Leonetti—showed up as the central characters of books. Criminals who hadn't even informed decided to get in on the action. The brother and godson of Sam Giancana wrote a book about the infamous Chicago crime boss. The boss of New York's Bonanno crime family, Joseph Bonanno, wrote his own self-serving book, making sure to declare that "Informers don't deserve to be called omu (men)." Sammy the Bull read both Giancana's and Bonanno's book.

The negative image of the "rat" was altered forever. Thirty-three years after Joe Valachi, you now had one Lawrence Mazza, known to his friends as Legitimate Larry.

Here was a young associate rising through the ranks of the Brooklyn-based Colombo crime family, jailed in a murder-racketeering indictment that could keep him in prison for twenty years. Not surprisingly, he decided to become a witness for the prosecution. Sitting in the Metropolitan Correctional Center in lower Manhattan, Legitimate Larry had a series of conversations with his father and mother in which he outlined the rationale and benefits of becoming what he, for years, derisively referred to as a rat.

In his many talks, all of which were recorded (with his knowledge), he outlined a complex rationale for informing on friends and associates that started with the premise that the Mafia wasn't what he thought it was. This "men of honor" stuff somehow seemed overblown.

"We're thinking we just have to be, you know, loyal and honorable," he tells his father. "But it's bullshit. Like that's why I don't feel anything derogatory toward myself for this. Nothing at all. I really don't. Put it this way: If I had something to stand up for, I think you'd know I would stand up. This life isn't what I thought it was, so I'm not turning on it. I'm not turning on a loyal bunch of friends, real close guys, family guys. You know, they break every other rule, and I'm not supposed to break this rule?"

Legitimate Larry then let a tiny bit of momentary fame get to him. According to a March 1994 *Daily News* article in which his exploits as the protégé of a particularly deranged Colombo gangster named Greg Scarpa had been dutifully recorded, his relationship with Scarpa was somewhat unusual, even by mob standards. Legitimate Larry was actually conducting a regular sexual relationship with Scarpa's common-law wife of twenty years, and Scarpa—who was dying of AIDS—heartily approved. Now, as he sat in the Metropolitan Correctional Center in lower Manhattan chatting with his father, Legitimate Larry got an idea.

"I've been writing a lot," he revealed. "First I did just like notes. Now I'm trying to make it in a, you know, story form."

"Well," offered his father, "if you get one of the big guys interested, all these big book publishers. . . ."

Larry's idea was to sell his story to the newspaper reporter who had written the *News* feature, who would then turn it into a bestseller that could possibly make Legitimate Larry . . . well, legitimate.

Over the weeks he refined his idea. Talking with his mother, he scoffed at the idea that any one would actually try to kill him for revealing the inner secrets of this reputedly secret society.

"I'm not afraid of them at all," he said. "Don't worry about that." He then brought up, again, the newspaper article that he hoped would lead him to Hollywood. By now he was working on theme development. "The article that came out was good," he says. "It showed how I started out one way and, you know, wound up with the devil."

Mother: "Yeah."

Larry: "Like I says, hopefully I could write somethin' good."

Mother: "Yeah, that would be good, too."

Larry: "That would be nice. Others have done it. And I've got a very good story there, so . . . from here to the war."

Mother: "Yeah, yeah."

Larry: "You know?"

January 20, 1998

For hours and then days Ralphie Guarino sat with FBI agents in a windowless room inside 26 Federal Plaza in lower Manhattan learning things. He first learned that the FBI had collected not a little bit of evidence indicating that he was the criminal mastermind behind the World Trade Center heist. He learned that he could go to jail for twenty years and watch his two children grow up only from the confines of a prison visiting room. He would lose everything he had—his real estate, his wife, his family. There was an option. He could reject all he had been told about the evils of the informant, the rat, the squealer, the canary, and agree to cooperate with the Manhattan United States Attorney's Office.

"Where do I sign?" Ralphie asked.

It was true that his friends in the DeCavalcante crime family still referred to informants as rats and would kill him on the spot if they knew. It was true that several members of the DeCavalcante crime family who were believed to be rats had, in fact, been killed. In fact, over the years the DeCavalcante family had earned a particularly nasty reputation when it came to disposing of informants, both suspected and real. In 1989, members of the family murdered a guy named Fred Weiss in August and a guy named Joseph Garofano a month later. Both were suspected informants. The boss of the family, John Riggi, ordered the deaths of Danny Annunziata and Gaetano (Corky) Vastols— also suspected rats. Both men escaped death. These were facts Ralphie Guarino had to face.

Still, it wasn't like the old days. Guys who flipped and became government witnesses survived and even thrived. Look at Sammy the Bull. As of early 1998, he'd killed nineteen people, including his brother-in-law, testified against his boss, John Gotti, and lots of other wiseguys, and received just over five years in jail for his behavior. Now he was living large somewhere in America, having earned nearly $1 million from his book, and had even gotten the opportunity to smile knowingly at Diane Sawyer during a carefully arranged TV interview at an undisclosed but sunny location.

There were many good reasons for making the leap to Team America. Facing the possibility of becoming an informant was, perhaps, a bit like being the captain of a sub-

marine in one of those old clichéd World War II movies.
The American captain takes his aging sub down deeper
than perhaps it should go to avoid being detected by the
German destroyer patrolling the gray Atlantic above. The
hull makes funny groaning noises, sweat collects on the brow
of the captain and every member of his crew, and gauges
and rivets sprout ominous leaks. The pressure is enormous.
Thousands of tons of water threaten to crush the hull and
the crew. The captain brings the sub up far enough to keep
it from being crushed by a million pounds of water pressure but not so far that it's detected by the enemy.

Becoming an informant was just like that. You brought
the sub up just enough but not too much. It was a middle
ground of reason. Ralphie Guarino faced the facts. He had
a wife, a daughter, a son, a *goomad*, a house on Staten Island, a failing cigar restaurant in yuppie Brooklyn, and
real-estate holdings all over New York that had to be maintained. He'd been busted by the federal government just
eleven years ago and served his time, and that would become part of the equation the federal judges would use
when deciding how long a guy from Brooklyn should
spend in a federal facility. It was called "prior criminal history" and it could mean an extra five years in jail. That, of
course, would be on top of whatever one got for a Hobbs
Act Robbery conviction, which carried an exposure level
of up to twenty years.

For a guy in his mid-forties, twenty-five years in jail
was serious business. He had much to lose by keeping
his mouth shut. *Omerta schmomerta.* Silence no longer
equaled death. Silence now equaled many sad years in a
lonely prison cell away from everyone you loved and
everything you knew.

A day after the FBI showed up at his house in Staten Island, Ralphie was back on the street. That was the idea—

make it seem as if nothing had happened. Meanwhile, his life was forever changed. He was now meeting with his "handlers," working out the arrangements of his deal. Maria Barton, the assistant United States attorney assigned to Ralphie's case, said he could plead guilty to three charges related to the World Trade Center robbery: one count of conspiracy to commit robbery, one count of committing a violent felony that involved a firearm, and one count of interstate receipt of stolen property. Under the guidelines federal judges must abide by in meting out sentences, Guarino would still face twenty years in prison, but with a very important caveat: If the prosecutors wrote him a nice letter saying what a great job he had done informing on his friends and neighbors, the number of years he would have to spend in jail would drop precipitously. That would allow him to walk out of prison while he was still a relatively young man and spend the rest of his life with his family living under an assumed name somewhere out there in America.

The only problem was that he had to deliver the goods. He had to go out on the street and collect incriminating statements from members of the criminal class. He had to make the FBI's case.

He had one advantage. At the time he was escorted to a windowless room in a high-security section of the FBI's headquarters at 26 Federal Plaza, the bureau's New York office had become very interested in doing something about that pesky little DeCavalcante crime family over in New Jersey.

For years, the DeCavalcante family had simply been ignored. New York–based federal prosecutors in Manhattan and Brooklyn spent twenty years east of the Hudson, systematically attacking the five New York crime families. In the fall of 1998, the boss of each family was sitting in prison cells doing serious time: John Gotti of the Gambino family, Carmine Persico of the Colombo family, Vincent Gigante of the Genovese family, Vittorio Amuso of the Luchese family, and Joseph Massino of the Bonanno family. Accomplishing this feat had not been inexpensive. The Department of Justice had expended much time and money on New York.

New Jersey was a different matter. The FBI's Newark office and New Jersey attorney general's Organized Crime Task Force did the best they could, making arrests here and there. But without the major resources of the New York office, it could not stop these farmers from Jersey from growing into a seventy-member outfit and expanding their criminal organization across the river and into New York. They remained much smaller than the most powerful New York family, the Genovese clan, with its three hundred members. But sometimes size is not an advantage.

"There's a different trend now," said Prosecutor Barton. "The five [New York] families are somewhat crippled in their leadership. The DeCavalcante family is still very active . . . The DeCavalcante family is a strong organized crime family that has been very active for years. The only lucky thing that has happened for them is that they have been off the [New York] law enforcement radar for quite some time."

Until Ralphie Guarino came along.

As is true in comedy and cooking, timing is everything, and Ralphie had got it just right. Here was a trusted DeCavalcante associate, a good earner, a known schemer, a knock-around guy from the neighborhood. A perfect guy to take up a new career—acting. The actual role of the informant was relatively simple. The informant gathered information and handed it to his "handler," an FBI special agent assigned to supervise the case. In this instance, it was

Special Agent George Hanna. Hanna was known for his work with informants. He had worked with Sammy the Bull and knew how to win the confidence of career gangsters by following a simple rule—tell them the truth. He told Ralphie the truth: If you wear a wire and collect enough incriminating evidence to convict most of the De-Cavalcante crime family, you will spend not a day in jail. If you don't, prepare for a life at Fort Dix.

Hanna made clear to Ralphie the informant's role. The informant gathered as much information as possible without crossing that delicate legal line and creating crime. Creating crime was not allowed. The informant had to convince people to talk openly about criminal acts without setting off their rat radar. And to make matters more difficult, the informant had to do all this while wearing a small but incredibly easy-to-detect recording device under his Gap-wear. The FBI usually taped the device to the informant's body and prayed that the informant's violence-prone cohorts didn't check too closely. If they did, it was all over. Wearing a wire, they called it. It was, to put it mildly, a very tricky job.

Others had tried and failed.

The legendary FBI agent Joseph Pistone, who posed as mob wannabe Donnie Brasco and gained the confidence of a Bonanno crime family crew (as well as a book and a movie), wore a wire only rarely. Most of his testimony was based on his memory. Pistone's position was that wearing a wire was much too dangerous.

For Ralphie, however, there was no choice. He was a low-level mob associate, not even a made member of a real crime family. He had almost nothing of evidentiary significance to offer about the DeCavalcante hierarchy. He had to go out there and get the facts, and get it all on tape. He would have to wear the recording device on his person, and agree to have the FBI install a bug in his car.

And the FBI had a new idea they'd been toying with for quite a while. They would give Ralphie cell phones to hand out to his buddies (specially wired up by the FBI). He had no choice. It was wear the wire or serve the time.

He started out small.

January 21, 1998

Around 11:40 on the morning of January 21, 1998, Ralphie placed a call from a pay phone in Brooklyn that the FBI had bugged. At a prearranged time, with his handlers listening in, Ralph punched in the number of Sal Calciano, his coconspirator in the World Trade Center heist. This was a mere eight days after the crime of the century, which was beginning to look more like an episode of *I Love Lucy*. Since the heist, Sal had no clue that Ralphie had been arrested and was now working with the FBI. Ralphie's job was to pretend that everything was normal. This would not be such a problem for Ralph. He was the kind of guy who pretended every day. He could make you feel like you were the driver even as he himself steered the car. He reached Sal on his cell phone. Sal was in Bay Ridge at the time, getting his weekly manicure.

"Hey, smiley," said the unsuspecting Sal.

Within seconds of his very first FBI-recorded call, Sal noticed some kind of sound on the phone. "Hello . . . Are you okay on the phone you're at?"

"I'm on a pay phone," Ralphie explained. Sal did not hang up.

During their chat, Sal discussed an unnamed wiseguy who wanted his share of the robbery "now" and mentioned that the wiseguy "doesn't want it in foreign, he wants it in

U.S." They made arrangements to meet for lunch at a pizzeria, as soon as the manicure was over. Ralphie did not mention the name of the pizzeria. He simply referred to it as "our pizzeria."

Already he was in character, talking evasive. The idea was if you talk evasive, you must be hiding the same kind of something everybody else was hiding, therefore you couldn't possibly be a rat. Everyone talked evasive. "I gotta see a guy about a thing"—that kind of talk. Ralphie was comfortable doing this, though he had not yet gotten comfortable in his new role. Whatever conversation took place at "our pizzeria" that day was not recorded.

Throughout January and February 1998 Sal Calciano was the star of Ralphie's show. The two men met or talked on the phone nearly every day, and Ralphie encouraged Sal to believe that the danger of arrest in the Twin Towers robbery had passed. The more the two conspirators talked, the more Ralph tried to convince Sal that this was so.

"I'm burned out," Ralphie says. "I can't think anymore."

"You're burned out?" Sal answers. "I'm confused like a motherfucker."

"I mean the only thing I'm glad about is the angel of death passed over us. That I know this is over. You know what I'm trying to say?"

Naturally he and Sal cast blame elsewhere. They blamed the three robbers—Melvin, Mike, and Richie—for picking up the wrong bags. They suspected one or two or all three stuffed cash in their coats on the way out. They generally made themselves feel better about the fact that Melvin, Mike, and Richie were in jail and they were not. Ralphie apologized a lot.

"I had this thing down to a science," he said. "I'm sorry."

"That's just not you," Sal said. "They're the fuckups."

"No, but you know what? What I would say, Sally, is we're okay. You know what? Money don't mean a fucking thing. I'll say it to all of them. 'Cause with all the money in the world, you can't spend it."

Sal: "I know that."

"All right," Ralphie concluded, "so consider ourselves lucky. Does that make sense?"

"Of course," Sal said, happy to believe he was free and clear. Sal, who still had to go to work at the Trade Center every day as if nothing had happened, said the Port Authority police were concentrating on a Brinks employee they believed was in on the robbery, which was wrong and that made Sal happy. He was even more delighted that after the robbery, the Port Authority was forced to change its security. Now all employees had to get new IDs that were checked under an ultraviolet light. Sal called it "an ultra light."

"There's things, there's ribbons in there," he said.

"No shit," Ralph said.

"It's wild to see how you fucked up everything and made them change their whole system," Sal said.

Ralphie: "It's supposed to be the most secure building in the whole world."

Sal: "Well, how do you say it? After the cow got out of the kennel? Some shit like that."

The resurgence of self-confidence inspired Ralphie and Sal to get back in their old scheming mode, to come up with a list of scams to commit now that they weren't going to jail for stealing piles of foreign currency they couldn't spend. This was normal. People like Ralphie—who wouldn't be caught dead working an honest day in his life—spent hours dreaming up scams. Anything could inspire them. A conversation in the subway. A conductor talking about picking up his paycheck at the Bergen Street stop would send Ralphie into a tailspin of speculation: Where is the money kept? When does it come in? Is there somebody inside who could be bought off? Chatting with Sal, Ralphie knew it was all right to suggest schemes, but it was not all right to create crime. He tried not to forget this FBI warning as he began recording his talks with Sal. It would turn out that with Sal, creating crime was not a problem. Sal was a willing participant. In fact, at times Sal seemed to be trying to outdo Ralphie. He bragged about all the crimes he knew about. He especially liked to brag about crimes involving celebrities. He talked of a friend of his hitting the celebrity jackpot.

"He already took Madonna's dress that time that was worth a fortune. Remember that place?"

Ralphie: "Who?"

Sal: "There was a place around here that had it."

Ralphie: "Madonna's?"

Sal: "She had a storage room in Manhattan and they stole it."

Ralphie: "Madonna?"

Sal: "Yeah, Madonna. Madonna the babe."

"Yeah?" said Ralphie, always willing to listen. "Go ahead."

Sal: "You know the dress she wore in 'Like a Virgin'? It was worth fucking money."

Ralphie: "No shit."

The two knock-around guys began to perform a Mafia version of the dozens, seeing who could come up with the best scam. Ralphie suggested selling fake oil paintings as "masterpieces" over the Internet. Sal did him three better.

First, he suggested selling an original *Wizard of Oz* screenplay stolen from some kid's grandfather. Then he suggested a blackmail scheme that involved photographs of a married Staten Island college professor engaged in sexual acts with a married sanitation worker. Then he suggested renting a drug-sniffing dog from a corrupt cop and checking out warehouses on the Brooklyn and New Jersey waterfront.

"It's got to be a good dog," Sal said. "A smart one that knows."

Ralphie said, "Well, a fucking dog's a dog, no?"

Sal said, "Well, he's got to be one that's going to walk up to the fucking gate and smell it and start scratching on the door. I know that's it. I tag it. Bingo. That's one. There's fucking four thousand rooms. I walk him through the whole fucking building in the middle of the night. I'll get him in. Getting him in, believe me, I'll have no fucking trouble."

"Can we rent a fucking dog?" Ralphie asked.

"No," Sal admitted. "I mean, I tried. Believe me. I had a guy fucking train one for me. He wanted like twenty grand."

Finally Sal came up with his version of *Ocean's Eleven,* a brilliant plan in its own right: selling swag on the Internet.

"The fucking thing really works, huh?" Ralphie asked.

"Sell it in no time . . . I don't give a fuck what it is, you can sell anything. Any fucking thing."

Ralphie said, "Anything and it doesn't come back to you."

"How can it come back?" Sal asked. "They don't even know who I am and shit. I bought it in a flea market. Who's to say I didn't buy it in a flea market? You should've seen some of the shit I sold on there. Forget about it."

Ralphie said, "Are you serious?"

"Ridiculous shit," said Sal. "Comic books are one of the hottest items on there."

The idea was simple: Sal had a friend who was an expert in rare comic books. Pay somebody to draw a fake version of the first Superman comic or the first Batman comic, have Sal's pal check it to make sure it looks real, print up a thousand copies, and sell them on the 'net. Simple.

"That would kill the comic industry," Sal said.

"Will it?" Ralphie asked. "Nobody ever did that, huh?"

Sal said, "Nobody every fucking thought of it before. I got such an evil mind, only because I know the big shots in the business. I've talked to him. He says if you can make me a book where I can't tell the difference between mine and yours, it's going to make millions. We'll make fucking millions. Duplicating it, it's cheap fucking rag paper . . . We made fucking two hundred Superman Ones, for the next ten years, fifteen years, we're sitting pretty. We buy property all over the place."

Ralph said, "No shit."

Sal said, "Superman One is worth a hundred fifty thousand dollars, tops . . . Then, after, we make copies of Batman One at eighty thousand. Now we push one of each out of every fucking—"

Ralphie said, "And you think we could sell them?"

Sal said, "I don't *think*. I know. Yeah. There's always something. As long as you keep your fucking eyes open, and you got an evil mind like me. You can always see something. I got an evil fucking mind."

The more Ralphie performed, the better he got. Within days he was testing his limits, seeing what he could get away with. He openly discussed his ability to listen in on other people's cell-phone conversations. It was a kind of test, this talk.

"I listen in on everybody's phone calls," said Ralphie, who at that moment was secretly recording his friend's words. "I can sit five blocks from your house and listen to every conversation."

Sal: "You're a fucking electronic whiz."

Ralph: "Everything you're talking about."

Sal: "On the portable?"

Ralph: "On the portable."

Sal: "But on the regular phone, no."

Ralph: "No, just on the cordless."

Sal: "I never knew that."

Ralph: "Everything you're talking about I can hear and record."

Sal: "That's terrific."

Ralph: "Sure. I love to know what's going on. One day I was sitting on the fucking thing listening. I'm sitting on my desk playing on my computer. I hear two niggers talking on the cellular phone on my scanner. One says 'All right, bro, we gonna take these motherfucking white boys. We're gonna take this fucking hundred thirty thousand cash. We're just gonna meet them on the corner and we're gonna take this fucking hundred thirty grand and go two different ways.' I'm sitting there going, 'What fucking corner, you motherfuckers? Say what corner!' I'm getting dressed, my wife says, 'What are you doing?' I says, 'Nothing.' I was waiting to say what corner they were going to rip these guys and I was gonna rip them off." He pauses.

"I'm already fucking dressed, ready to run out of my fucking house," he confides to Sal.

"But they never said."

Unfortunately for Ralph, capturing Sal and his "evil fucking mind" was not what the FBI had in mind when it signed up its new informant. Ralph was spending much of his time talking with a low-level street nobody about one caper that was already solved and numerous new capers that would probably go exactly nowhere. The FBI had something else in mind. Three days after strapping on his secret device, Ralph was talking with a DeCavalcante associate named Tommy DiTorra about this and that when DiTorra mentioned a Vinny. No last name, just Vinny.

DiTorra was explaining how the DeCavalcante crime family had decided to take over a financially unstable school-bus company, Manti Transportation, which was run by one of their loan-shark victims. The guy owed everybody—the banks, the taxman, his landlord, and, most important, the DeCavalcante crime family. Therefore this Vinny with no last name had decided that he was going to make himself partner of the company and put one of his people on the payroll at Manti Transportation. That way Vinny with no last name could keep the company afloat and make some money. This Vinny put his driver, Joey O, on the payroll as employee of the month at Manti, and the bus-company owner was complaining to the mystery Vinny. DiTorra recounted the conversation for Ralphie in fairly obvious terminology anyone familiar with the average Mafia movie would know and understand completely.

"He didn't want Joey O to shake him down," DiTorra said. "He said, 'Who is he to threaten me?' and everything. 'They're gonna block my buses in and bah, bah, bah.' It's all bullshit, now he can't even pay. Now he don't even have enough money to pay. Then he told Vinny at the table, 'You know, I gotta pay protection.' Vinny said, 'Let me tell you something. You don't ever mention that word in front of me.' " DiTorra laughed. "He's such a fucking jerk when he talks, this guy Manti."

This Vinny had come up before in Ralphie's talks with Sal. The FBI wasn't sure who he was. Ralphie had mentioned Vinny as someone powerful enough to help him out. He implied that Vinny, who was, at the time, at the Super Bowl, might be able to get him cash when he returned while Ralphie figured out how to exchange foreign currency stolen from the Trade Center.

"You know he knew about this," Ralphie said. "Maybe he's got somebody who's reasonable, maybe ten, fifteen percent. But I don't mind giving him a kick. You know, give him fifty thousand."

Then Ralphie mentioned Vinny as someone powerful enough to be obeyed. Ralphie mentioned that Vinny had sent down an order to stop trying to get rid of the foreign money all at once. "Let me explain to you what's going on," he said. "Vinny Ocean sends this message to stop peddling. The whole neighborhood is talking about it. So I just stopped."

And there it was—Vinny Ocean. Vincent Palermo. At the time when Ralphie signed up as a government informant and the New York FBI decided it wanted to cross the Hudson River, Vincent Palermo was a name the bureau wanted to hear about on tape. They knew very little about him. His name emerged hardly at all in organized-crime intelligence files. He was the future for the DeCavalcante crime family: a made guy who really looked like a legitimate guy. He was a smart businessman, had been married to a niece of Sam the Plumber, and had only one arrest in his background—a misdemeanor charge for stealing frozen shrimp down at the Fulton Fish Market in lower Manhattan. The brief mention of him by Ralphie and DiTorra was hardly enough to get a grand jury to indict, but it implied things. If Ralphie was able to work his way closer to Vinny Ocean, there could be developments.

It would not be easy. There was a reason Vinny had no significant arrests during his more than thirty years in the

Mafia. He said very little, spoke only to a very few close associates, and stayed the hell out of social clubs. He was known as a wiseguy who would much rather attend the Italian Day parade in Little Italy with his family than hang out at the Ravenite Social Club on Mulberry Street to exchange inflated tales of self-worth with John Gotti and Sammy the Bull. He was, in short, extremely difficult to get. He was also Ralphie's Get-Out-of-Jail-Free card, and Ralphie knew it.

5

March 24, 1998

Late in the morning Joey O Masella sat in traffic in lower Manhattan with his old friend Ralphie Guarino. Ralphie was driving, Joey O was talking. The traffic down by the World Trade Center was miserable. The exit ramp from the Battery Tunnel had dumped its morning load of Brooklyn commuters into the claustrophobic streets near Battery Park City, and Ralphie was having a tough time negotiating through them. He was trying to get near enough to 17 Battery Place to see what he had to see. The two men were discussing the mayor of New York, Rudy Giuliani, a former federal prosecutor who was now forcing the police to enforce every little law ever enacted in the city's history. For the first time ever, jaywalking in New York City was illegal.

"I want to go a hundred miles an hour," Ralphie muttered, his speedometer hovering around the three-miles-per-hour mark.

"Fucking Giuliani with his new laws," Joey O fumed. "Speeders, kissing, cursing—it's all fucking illegal."

The two men were stuck in lower Manhattan in order to watch a man walk out of 17 Battery Place and get into his car. For more than an hour they parked in different spots near where they believed the man would come out of the building, hoping to catch a glimpse of his face. The man was involved with a jewelry business, and on this day his job was to deliver a bag filled with jewels to a spot in midtown Manhattan. Joey O and Ralphie were following him because they planned on ripping him off.

Just like Ralphie, Joey O was a knock-around guy. He talked about criminal acts the way normal people discussed buying a minivan. He was always trying to get over on some unsuspecting dupe. The life of getting up in the morning, putting on a white shirt, taking the subway to work with a little bag of lunch—this was a life Joey O could not imagine. He was saying to Ralphie how he was thinking about opening up a car wash on Staten Island with his brother-in-law from New Jersey, the big vice president of some paper company over there. But maybe not. Maybe he would just stay in the knock-around life. Even if it had turned out to be not quite what he had originally thought it would be.

Joey O's Mafia was most definitely not the Mafia portrayed in the movies.

Joey O did not have a guy to get out of the car first to open the door and hold Joey O's coat for him. He did not eat lunch gratis in the back rooms of the best Little Italy restaurants. He did not own a diamond pinkie ring or drive a new black Lincoln with tinted windows. He did, however, own a beat-up late-model BMW with mechanical troubles. He had diabetes. He had two wives—an ex who'd run off with a plastic surgeon and left their daughter with him, and a new wife whom the daughter ignored in front of him just to make him crazy. His mother-in-law lived at home with him. He had a girlfriend, but she smoked too much weed and Joey O had got it into his head that her breasts needed to be bigger. He was going to fund the necessary surgically implanted enlargements. This would mean yet another expense for a guy whose liabilities overwhelmed his assets. He owed everybody—the Gambinos, the Colombos, the Lucheses, and, naturally, the DeCavalcante crime family that gave him his status. Everybody said he owed these people $100,000 or more, but nobody knew for sure.

As they drove around lower Manhattan looking for the jewelry guy's blue Pontiac, Joey O and Ralphie began to talk about something they often talked about—getting and keeping money. Joey O's new boss, Vinny Ocean, had lots of it, while neither Ralphie nor Joey O seemed to have any at all. Joey O had just been "put with" Vinny Ocean, a capo, after his former boss, a capo named Rudy Ferrone, had died of natural causes.

As they crawled through city traffic, Ralphie had quietly triggered the FBI recording device hidden inside his car. He was aware that he had to get Joey O to stop talking about Joey O and start talking about all the illegal activity Joey O was performing for his boss, Vincent Palermo. His FBI handlers had made it clear to him that doing undercover work involved knowledge of "biology." By beginning with the species of mafioso at the bottom of the food chain, you can work your way to the top of the food chain. Ralphie has been trying for some time now to get Joey O to talk about Vinny, so he brought up one of Vinny's many business ventures, a Chinese restaurant in Flushing, Queens.

The owner owed Vinny a lot of money, so Vinny decided to make himself a secret partner in the restaurant. The owner's name was Frankie and he was Korean. Ralphie was asking Joey questions designed to illicit the exact nature of Vinny's ownership, but Joey was having none of it. Instead, Joey decided to let Ralphie know his opinions regarding Koreans in general.

"They are very funny people. You can't say 'fuck' in front of them," Joey O explained. "One day he wanted to be needled. I told him, 'All you want to do is fuck.' He said, 'Joey, please don't be offended, but we don't talk like that.' I said, 'What do you mean? What do you do?' He said, 'You can say anything you want but "fuck."'"

"He told me the same thing," Ralphie said.

Joey O had clearly been perplexed by this behavior. He recounted for Ralphie the time he casually threw money onto a table for Frankie, and Frankie offered up what Joey perceived as a "Korean" response. "I had to give him back fifty dollars. I took the fifty dollars out of my pocket and I threw it on the desk. He picked it up and handed it back to me. He said, 'Did I throw the money at you?' I said no. So he says, 'Please, we are very easily offended people, hand it to me.' So I handed it to him."

"He's right," Ralphie said.

This was a typical conversation with Joey O. Days would pass, Ralphie would find himself again and again trying to get Joey O to provide the government handlers probable cause to keep the tapes rolling. Then he hit on an idea—Joey O's former boss, Rudy the capo, had always cut Joey some slack, forgiving his debts, getting Joey out of scrapes with other gangsters. Vinny Ocean did not have the same bottomless reserve of patience for Joey O's many problems. This was a source of much concern to Joey O, and Ralphie decided he could exploit it to learn more about

Vinny Ocean. He asked Joey about the good old days with Rudy.

"When that guy—Rudy—died," Joey O said, "my life went with him."

Ralphie asked, "Why?"

"They ain't gonna make them like that anymore," Joey O said. "I would trust him with a hundred million dollars of my money."

Ralphie was curious about Joey O's relationship with Vinny as opposed to Rudy. "You don't have that trust with your goombatta, huh?"

Joey said, "Nope.

"Is he that bad with money?"

"It's fucking greed."

"Really?" said Ralphie. "I mean, how could he be where he is if he's greedy? He can't be greedy. You got to be able to give and take."

"He's got a lot of people bullshitted. I know the real him. I've seen him rich, I've seen him broke. And I've seen him rich again."

To Joey O, Vinny Ocean was changing from a knock-around guy to a guy who didn't want anything to do with his roots. He told Ralphie about the days when Vinny acted like a real wiseguy.

"He'd spend money like a wiseguy. We walked in elevators; the kid was in there with the papers and we would give the kid a hundred dollars. Like a paper route. Here, this is for you. I would see him blow fucking money unbelievable."

But Joey O also saw Vinny Ocean when Vinny ran out of money and had to scramble to support his growing families. "He would fucking run bad and he got like a crazy man," Joey recalled.

As soon as Vinny Ocean started making money again,

Joey O claimed he forgot all the people who helped him get where he was. "He started making it again and fucking greed took over. Maybe he was afraid that he would go broke again, I don't know. You know what I mean? He fucking changed unbelievable. I know him all my life. I mean, I know things about him that fucking wiseguys don't know."

They spotted the blue Pontiac in a parking lot with only one exit, so they double-parked on the street nearby and waited for a spot to open up. From where they sat, they thought they might be able to make out the jewelry man's face, but they weren't sure. Ralphie decided to push a little harder to keep Vinny in the talk.

"Thank God that you're very close to Vinny, you know what I mean? 'Cause you're going to go right to the top, you know that."

"He's a maneuverer."

"You see Vinnie's young. He's alive. You know, I mean, there's still a lot of earning power in him."

"I was with him yesterday," Joey O said. "I met him eleven-thirty. I left him at a quarter to four. I went home, showered, shaved. He was going to the city. He called me eight o'clock. I was in the city. He was in Queens. 'Do you want to go for dinner?' I says, 'Nope. I'm going the fuck home.'"

Ralphie pushed a little harder. "I guess he'll come and hang out."

"Yeah, he'll come. He'll hang out. He'll pass by!" Joey O said. "He never hangs out nowhere. You don't see him by the club. Never."

Ralphie: "What, he drives around all day?"

"He drives around all fucking day," Joey O said. "He don't stay nowhere. You'll never catch him in a club."

Ralphie went all the way, asking questions not usually

asked. "Not in a club? I was talking about the office, the apartment, the back room, right?"

"Very rare," Joey said. "Very rare."

Now Joey—who was born without any evidence of a gift for patience in his DNA—began to get distracted sitting in the car all morning with nothing to do but talk to the always-patient Ralphie.

"You want to sit here all fuckin' day?"

"I don't care," Ralphie said. "We just see him get in the car. I just want to see. You know what I mean? You're right, I don't want to sit all day, but I mean, things don't come easy, Joey."

"Yeah, I know that. But I got fucking things to do."

"Oh, you got things to do."

Joey said, "Well sure."

Ralphie pointed out the window at the World Trade Center across the street, scene of much embarrassment and humility for Ralphie. "Do you know how long I sat in those buildings down the block? Six fucking months. You know what? I see this, this is nothing for me."

"You want coffee? I'll get a cup there."

Joey O got out of the sedan and went into a deli on the corner. The minute he walked inside, the jewelry guy they were waiting for and a woman companion walked out of 17 Battery Place and got into a blue Pontiac. Joey came out of the deli with the coffee just in time for Ralphie to pull away from the curb and begin to follow their mark.

"I didn't see what he was carrying," Ralphie said. "Did he open the trunk? Did you see anything?"

"He drives like a fucking Hebe," Joey replied.

"You go out for coffee, the fucking guy gets in his car," Ralphie said.

"All right, fuck him," Joey said. "If he gets out for

coffee, goes into a restaurant, whatever the fuck he does, we hit the car."

"What's the name of that wine you wanted?"

"It's not an Italian wine," Joey said. "I don't know what the fuck it is. Old Mary she drinks."

"Old? Are you sure?"

"Yeah, it's Old Mary, some shit. Peno agretio is good."

"Peno," Ralphie said. "You want a case of peno agretio."

"Yeah, Santa whatever-the-fuck-it-is."

The men inched through the traffic, trying to keep far enough away but not too far. Their plan was to wait until the man parked the car and went into a restaurant or any-place, then walk over, pop the trunk, and walk away with the bag of jewels. The hope was that the woman who was with him would go inside as well, so they would not have to do anything that would attract attention. That was the plan.

The man with the jewels drove across town, uptown, downtown in no apparent direction. Soon he pulled over and dropped the woman at curbside. That was one less problem for Ralphie and Joey O. He pulled back into traf-fic, still unaware he was being followed. Soon he pulled over again and walked inside a restaurant.

Ralphie parked a few cars back, walked over to the blue Pontiac, and returned to his car with a bag from the Pon-tiac in his hands. He headed for the Battery Tunnel leading out of lower Manhattan back to Brooklyn.

Paying the toll at the Battery Tunnel plaza, Ralphie steered the sedan into the streets of Red Hook driving to-ward a building he owned on Sixth Avenue and Eighteenth Street in Brooklyn's Windsor Terrace. It was a typical three-story walk-up with a commercially zoned first floor just a few feet away from the perpetual thrum of traffic on the Prospect Expressway. A junior high school was across the street. When they arrived, Joey O used the phone inside to beep Vinny Ocean. He wanted Vinny there when they got the jewels appraised. They dumped the contents of the bag on a table. Inside there were twenty-five diamond set pieces, eighteen emeralds, thirteen sapphires, and six rubies. They figured they had $200,000 in their hands but would take $65,000 if they could unload the whole thing at once.

Soon enough Vinny Ocean showed up and all three of them piled back in Ralphie's car. Ralphie suggested having some guy named John the Gypsy give them an estimate on the stones, but Vinny had his own guy. They headed toward Third Avenue and deeper into Brooklyn.

In the car, Vinny was clearly in a good mood. Lately all he talked about was the problems he was having with this Giuliani and the mayor's insistence that all strip clubs should be driven out of New York City. That would include Vinny's club, Wiggles, which at the time was making Vinny rich. It was depressing to be around Vinny when he started talking about Wiggles. But now Vinny was talking giddily about opening up a new strip club where Mayor Puritan could not touch him because it would be located across the Hudson River in New Jersey.

"My brother said he found a beautiful fucking disco that's doing really bad," Vinny said. "I'll turn it into topless. Beautiful. Forget about it. Five million, ten million . . . What a fucking place, Joey." Vinny directed his conversation to Joey, whom he knew better. He was just getting used to Ralphie.

"It's ten thousand square feet, commercial area," Vinny said. "Parking for fucking one thousand, fifteen hundred cars, three big rooms, two big bars, plus it's a regular disco. Just walking around, I spent a half hour in there. The fucking ideas what I could do with that." He said he has reached out to the DeCavalcante crime family members in New Jersey to see who the landlord of the disco "[was] with." Vinny was going on and on about the strip club when Ralphie felt it was time to talk about Vinny's guy, the guy who was going to look at the stones. Ask some questions, but not too many.

"These guys, are they stonecutters?" he asked. "They still cut stones?"

Vinny said, "Yeah, he cuts stones."

"Like he does it himself?"

"Yeah, they got their own cutter, oh sure. He would chop them, you know, the big ones, take it off a little bit, two points, two percent, just to change it. It's amazing."

Ralphie acted like a babe in the woods for a day, making everybody else sound smarter than him. "Oh, that's what he meant by taking off two points," he said. "I didn't know what he meant."

"Yeah," Vinny said. "This way nobody knows. These fucking things are like taking a car. They all look the same. These motherfuckers, I don't understand it. They know. They'll cut them all down a little bit, you know? So you ain't getting no headache."

Ralphie said, "Change the look?"

"Yeah, but he buys lots of this and that, sells them. He does very, very well. I mean, I was setting up a deal with him to buy, ah, stuff. A guy wanted two million dollars, he said no fucking problem."

It was not much of a conversation, but to the FBI agents who were listening in as they drove around Brooklyn several car lengths behind Ralphie and Vinny and Joey O, it was music to their ears.

It was the first time that their new informant, Ralphie, had managed to capture on tape the words of a ranking member of the crime family they were targeting. The first time the previous week, Vinny told Ralphie he was trying to open a gambling boat with the help of a retired county judge in Nassau County who had the "hook" to obtain a license for the boat. Not a word was recorded on tape. This time, every syllable came through and a ranking member of the crime family was recorded saying something incriminating. Granted it was just a little cryptic chat about fencing stolen swag. It was not operatic conversation about severing the head of an enemy or *Godfather* dialogue about ordering somebody dead because they'd refused to "come in" when called by a boss. But it was enough to give the FBI the magic words they needed to keep their informant on the street with a Sony strapped to his undershorts. Those words were *probable cause,* and without them, the investigation would have been dead in the water.

PROBABLE CAUSE

The FBI, working with prosecutors in the Southern District of New York, hoped that Ralphie would lead them all the way to the top of the DeCavalcante crime family. They knew that to reach this goal, they would have to listen to a lot of talk about a lot of things. To be allowed to do that, they needed to go back to a federal judge every three months and show him what they'd found. If they overheard discussions of crimes past or future, they would have "probable cause" to continue listening. If they went for months and no crimes were discussed, the judge would turn off their tape recorders and that would be that.

With that in mind, the case agents in charge of the investigation—George Hanna and Andre Cicero—had to listen to every word, figure out who was talking, and write down their interpretation of what was being discussed. This was not always easy. Often the gangsters and wannabe gangsters talked eliptically or in code. They often made references to people by first names only, which could get confusing when you had more than one Vinny or a half-dozen Joey's dropping into the dialogue.

Each day the agents would summarize the meaning of conversations. They were supposed to make a distinction between what they deemed "pertinent" (talk of crimes past, present, and future) and nonpertinent (talk of girlfriends, wives, and diabetes). But making that distinction was not always simple. Gangsters, for instance, never put anything in their own name. Everything went under the names of their wives and children. To avoid missing a pertinent conversation buried deep within a nonpertinent conversation, the agents simply listened to everything. This put them in an unusual position—here they were chasing bad guys but listening in on conversations that were extremely personal. It was true that perhaps half the time these guys opened their mouths they were discussing some new scheme to make money illegally. But it was also true that the other half of the time they were discussing what most people discuss—life. In FBI summaries, life looked like this:

Discussion about sex; a stripper sucking air out of a can and getting high (called whipping it).

Discuss movies, red wine, and steak.

Discuss speeding tickets.

Discuss eating and local restaurants.

Discuss how, due to safe sex, kids today don't get
   laid as much as they [themselves] did when they
   were kids.

In one tape, Ralphie picked up two low-level associates
identified only as "SS" and "RD" for a wired-up drive to
Atlantic City. The agent who was forced to listen to this
voyage summarized the drama and excitement of the trip:

SS says wife pissed because he bought himself shoes
for Xmas. SS rambles on on how generous he is to
others during the holiday and how he deserves to
purchase a gift for himself. Bought his son a Rolex,
gave him cash. SS angry at wife's attitude toward
him. [Ralphie] and SS discuss fine dining, caviar,
champagne, wines, Dewar's, and alcohol. SS dis-
cusses eating, relaxing, and watching TV. He enjoys
sitting on the couch and having a cigarette. RD falls
asleep in backseat.

In their summary notes the day Vinny Ocean and
Ralphie and Joey O drove around Brooklyn looking to
fence stolen gems, the agents wrote down everything they
could hear and tried to make sense of it. When Vinny
talked about boats the FBI agent wrote down, "Vinny talks
about the boat show, and buying a 26-foot boat." Then the
boat grew. "Vinny says that Paul is going to get a boat, a
63-foot Manhattan Sunseeker, and that he is going to keep
it at Pier 66." The agents made no distinction between the
felonious and the mundane. They scribbled down their interpretation of what the three men were talking about.
Sometimes it was clear, sometimes it was not.

Listening in on Joey O was a particular challenge. He
had an unfortunate tendency to say things that were meant

to impress people. He was always talking about some huge scheme that was going to put him over the top so he would no longer have to hustle sports books. He talked about delivering beatings. One guy owed a DeCavalcante associate named Joey Cars $10,000. Joey Cars said he firebombed the guy's van, so the guy went out and bought another van. Joey Cars put sugar in the gas tank and slashed all four tires. Joey O said that wasn't enough.

"Every time you see him, give him a fucking beating until he comes up with the money. He only works across the street from you . . . Give him another four fucking flats."

"I'm going to burn it this time," Joey Cars replied. "It's a Volvo. I want to burn it."

Who knew if any of this was true?

In the piles of paper the bureau created to track Ralphie's progress, Ralphie was always referred to as CW for "Confidential Witness." This was done to protect his true identity. In these summaries, it was clear the FBI agents made note of everything CW and his talkative friends said, even if the agents had no clue what was being discussed. They did this because they were never sure what could potentially become relevant down the line. Thus, Vinny Ocean's chat about buying a failed disco in New Jersey—hardly a crime, though perhaps not a wise business move—could become important later if, for example, somebody found either a body or piles of cash in the disco's basement.

The FBI summaries also made it clear that gangsters liked to brag. On one FBI tape, Vinny Palermo boasted of his involvement in a half-dozen big-money business deals. He talked about stolen Ming dynasty paintings he owned, about a twenty-three-karat diamond he stole, about how he was going to get a huge maintenance contract to clean buildings owned by Leona Helmsley. All of these guys, in fact, were premiere name-droppers. They dropped more names than a gossip columnist, and the FBI was there to write them all down.

At the end of the FBI summary of the March 24, 1998, conversation, the agent wrote that Vinny, Joey O, and CW (Ralphie) got out of the car and went to see Vinny's jeweler. Everything that happened outside of the car remained a mystery because the bug stayed in the car. When the three men returned to Ralphie's car, where the bug was still running, the FBI summarized their disappointment regarding their meeting with Vinny's jewelry appraiser: "They get back in the car and discuss the fact that the stones are not worth what they thought."

At no time during the entire day did Joey O or Vinny Ocean figure out that Ralphie was not what he seemed. They confided in him, they drove all over New York with him trying to fence stolen property. They never noticed the FBI van tailing far behind. They had no way to know that the jewels Ralphie boosted from the jeweler's car were actually put there by the FBI. It was all a big setup designed to keep Ralphie credible with his criminal peers. Anyone who talked about crime but did not actually commit it was sure to attract attention. The idea was to give Ralphie a "crime" to commit to make him fit in.

The pursuit of probable cause was no simple matter.

6

July 31, 1998

The civil servants arrived on a warm Friday evening, traditionally a busy night at Wiggles. They slapped big Day-Glo–orange stickers on the smoked-glass front door. The signs warned that "use and occupancy" of Vinny Ocean's prized all-nude strip club was against the law. The city inspectors who did the slapping explained that the club was being shut down temporarily because undercover police officers had made several visits in the previous months and witnessed dancers "engage in acts simulating sex." This was vague, but the city promised to explain in court in six days, at which time it would ask a Queens judge to shut down Wiggles for good.

For four years a legion of city officials had tried unsuccessfully to shut down Wiggles. Now they had the law on their side.

The law prohibited "adult establishments" from operating either in a residential neighborhood or within five hundred feet of schools, churches, synagogues, and day-care centers. Wiggles had all four as neighbors. Vinny Ocean tried to find a way to get around this law, but it was not easy. Chatting on the free cell phone Ralphie had given him with Gus, one of the workers at Wiggles, he was getting one wave of bad news after another.

"A lot of the girls are worried about the new law," Gus was saying. "They worry you don't come around anymore because you're afraid of getting into trouble."

"They're morons," Vinny replied. "They're a bunch of fucking morons."

With one of his best soldiers, Anthony Capo, Vinny indulged in whining. "I might be out of a fucking job," he said. "Can you believe that? What the fuck am I going to do?"

He had hired plenty of lawyers, and they had found what they'd thought was a loophole big enough to drive a bus through. The sex-club law the mayor had championed defined "adult establishments" as businesses in which 40 percent or more of the square footage was devoted to selling some form of sex—videotapes and strippers being the two most common. An "establishment" like Wiggles could get around the law by simply keeping the "adult" square footage to less than 40 percent. There were many ways to do this. The strippers, for example, could start wearing bikinis. Vinny Ocean was having none of that. Or Wiggles could confine the strippers to one location in the middle of the room, onstage, and keep them from taking off their clothes in other parts of the club. That became the plan. The only problem was that the strippers had a habit of wandering out of the "adult" area into the "nonadult" area to perform lap dances, sometimes on undercover cops. This expanded substantially what the city considered "adult square footage." The crew at Wiggles brainstormed to make the 40 percent rule work. One of them, Frankie Stellini, suggested reducing the adult square footage by putting flower beds on stage with the strippers.

"I don't think so," said Vinny.

Instead, Vinny came up with an idea. Shortly after the big orange stickers went up, he called up the real owner of the construction company he secretly controlled, T&M Construction, and put him to work building walls inside the huge, cavernous space. The idea was to wall off more sections of the club and keep the strippers in the main room only. He hired an architect to keep the "adult space" to 38 percent. The architect had to get out a calculator and compute the maximum amount of space allowed in which adult men could sit and watch adult women wearing nothing but jewelry gyrate to electronic music. The precision was almost comical—997 square feet of "viewing area," 2,289 of "nonviewing area." The viewing area consisted of the main room. In the middle sat a 43-by-30-foot stage set four feet off the ground and two brass poles around which the artists created their art. The rest of the club would be chopped up into several individual "lounges" and rooms—the poolroom, the TV room, the cigar room. The club looked more or less like what it had always looked like, except now the dancers had to make sure to put on bikini tops and bottoms when wandering into the newly sectioned-off rooms. And there were plenty more rules. Each night each dancer had to sign a form that explained twelve rules. The forms were written in extremely simple English. They included:

I will not engage myself in prostitution inside or
    outside the premises.

Customers cannot touch me on stage. I cannot
touch myself on stage—specifically my breasts,
buttocks or groin area. I cannot accept a tip
between my breasts or in any other way except
in my hand.

I cannot do a lap dance!

If the dancer violated the rules, she was fired. If the customer violated the rules, he was asked to leave by one of
the bouncers Vinny employed to act as sex police. The
bouncers—who called all the customers "degenerates"—
had to keep action inside the main room from becoming a
violation of the 40 percent rule. They were, in a sense, like
cowboys keeping the horses in the corral. If a horse
strayed, their job was to rope it and quickly move it back
into the corral. This was especially tricky in the cigar
room, which consisted of eighteen small couches with mirrors on the walls and ceiling. There a customer could buy
a cheap cigar and watch a dancer who was allowed to
dance a few inches away, clad only in a full bikini. This
was called "bikini entertainment." Or, as bouncer Michael
Peranio put it, it was a "simulated lap dance."

"No contact. Meaning the guy cannot put his hands on
the girl, the girl cannot put her hands on the guy. No lap
dancing. No grinding. Just a dance. A simulated lap dance.
About two or three inches away from the customer. A customer would sit down, a girl works under, over, around,
but still three, four inches away. Very far away from the
customer. A simulated lap dance. That's all it is. If anything happens, it's by accident. The girl taking off her
dress slips, falls, what can you do? It's an accident."

"It's not a whorehouse, it's a club," said Evelyn Coffin,
a barmaid and floor manager of Wiggles. "There is no

spreading onstage, no touching the genital area onstage. No smoking, no drinking, no drugs, okay? My God, the list is long. We will be here all night." If a customer did not like the rules, Coffin would tell them, "We don't make the rules. We just follow them. Write to Giuliani."

To keep the errors to a minimum, Vinny Ocean was willing to spend money. He installed video cameras everywhere and set up a bank of monitors in a back office. He hired a retired Queens vice-squad cop to watch over everything—the dancers, the bouncers, the barmaids, the customers. If a bouncer saw a dancer handing a customer her business card, the customer was asked to leave and the dancer was to be fired. If a dancer saw another dancer performing a dreaded lap dance, she was to inform on her sister artist. This was the new Giuliani strip club—sex with a thousand rules.

For two days in August hearings were held in the Supreme Court of Queens. During this hearing Vinny Ocean learned there were some problems with Wiggles' adherence to the 40 percent rule. The Queens vice squad had made several undercover visits in the previous few months and discovered many incidents involving alleged or perceived nonsimulated lap dances in the so-called cigar room. The undercover officers alleged the dancers were exposing all parts of their anatomy and rubbing themselves against the customers. These undercover officers had had to endure this illegal behavior several times. Some of the officers had gone back on more than one occasion just to make sure that all this exposing and rubbing was, in fact, illegal. One, a Sergeant Vincent LaRocca of the Queens vice squad, asked a Wiggles dancer, "What about taking care of me with a blow job?"

She had replied, "That's two hundred dollars in a room where we're alone."

This was the wrong answer for Vinny Ocean. This gave the city the ammunition it needed to shut Vinny Ocean down. On August 12, 1998, Judge Stephen Fisher of the Supreme Court of Queens ordered Wiggles closed permanently because of math problems—specifically, the inability to stay within the 40 percent rule.

"I tell you, I'm sick," he told one of his top lieutenants, an old-time gangster named Joseph Giacobbe. Uncle Joe they called him, an aging DeCavalcante soldier who hung out in Sacco's pork store in Linden, a few blocks away from the fake pork store those people in Hollywood used for their TV show *The Sopranos*. He rarely left New Jersey.

"He just wants to see every place closed," Giacobbe said, referring to Giuliani. "That's what all this bullshit is about."

"Either that or move into the designated areas."

"Yeah, but that's down in no-man's-land, you know what I'm saying? Who the heck wants to go there?"

"Yup," Vinny said.

"Only the real tough degenerates."

"My customers would be scared to go," Vinny said.

As far as timing went, the closing of Wiggles was the worst.

BIG EARS MAJURI

The house on Ercama Street looked like *Leave It to Beaver*. It was small, a one-story brick ranch on a corner lot with a magnolia tree in the middle of the tiny front lawn. A plastic deer stood guard next to rows of salmon and pink impatiens and a red Japanese maple. The lawn looked like it was mowed every day. In the front bay window, a foot-tall blue plastic Madonna perched on the sill, her arms outstretched, her head slightly tilted, impassive. Next to the front door was a big sign made of ersatz wood: MAJURI. It was hard to make out the letters in the dark, but the three men sitting in a stolen car across the street from the plastic deer knew it was the right house.

There they sat, three grown men in a parked car on an empty suburban Linden, New Jersey, street in the middle of the night. It was Joey O Masella and two of the nastiest soldiers of the DeCavalcante crime family—Jimmy Gallo and Anthony Capo. Both men were made guys who had committed multiple murders. Both were willing to do so again. They were parked across from a sign that read NO PARKING 7 A.M.–11 A.M. TUESDAY. They had made sure that it wasn't a Tuesday. This was their second visit and they had learned.

Inside the house, Big Ears Charlie Majuri slept unaware. He was, according to the FBI, a member of the ruling panel of the DeCavalcante crime family. He was the son of the family's longtime underboss, Frank Majuri, and he had been involved in "the life" since he was a teenager. His résumé included gambling, larceny, stolen property, and bookmaking. He was once involved in shaking down a record company. He was a hulking, 210-pound, extremely ugly fifty-eight-year-old man with sticking-out ears whose parents—including the former underboss—were still alive. In fact, they both lived with him in this tiny ranch house. His underboss father was now ninety-one years old.

Big Ears Charlie was in a situation. In the last few months, John Riggi, the boss of the DeCavalcante crime family, had implemented some corporate restructuring. His acting street boss, Jake Amari, had finally died of stomach cancer. He himself was not scheduled to leave his federal prison cell until the year 2003. The way the FBI saw it, Riggi decided to create a ruling panel to run the family business that would include two men named Palermo who were not related—Vinny Ocean Palermo and Girolamo (Jimmy) Palermo. Vinny and Jimmy were to make decisions that would benefit the DeCavalcante family and result in more money being sent up to John Riggi. The plan had not worked out as intended. Big Ears Charlie—who had been around forever and whose father had been one of the group's founding members—threw a fit. He insisted that he be made part of the panel. When no one listened, he decided to eliminate the two unrelated Palermos, Vincent and Jimmy. That would leave Big Ears in charge. He asked Jimmy Gallo to take care of Vinny Ocean Palermo. Jimmy Gallo, who had been around, immediately went to Vinny Ocean with this information.

Vinny Ocean made a plan of his own. He was aware that Charlie Majuri controlled a union local in New Jersey and had lately been kicking wiseguys of other families off the payroll. This was making Big Ears extremely unpopular, which would mean there would be many suspects should anything happen to him. Vinny Ocean told Jimmy Gallo that he would appreciate it if he and Joey O and Anthony Capo would investigate the possibility of killing Big Ears Charlie. Vinny then made plans to visit Florida so he could be far away when the event in question took place.

This was night two of staking out Big Ears' tidy little ranch house. It didn't look like the home of a Mafia boss. It was tiny, especially compared with the home of the other two panel leaders, Vinny and Jimmy Palermo. Vinny had a huge waterfront mansion on Long Island with a hundred-foot pier. Jimmy Palermo had a sweeping estate in Island Heights, New Jersey. Big Ears Charlie had a plastic deer.

Jimmy Gallo had to be thinking he'd made the right choice. He dreamed up a way to get the job done.

His plan was to check out the house, wait until there were no cars around or people on the street. They would sleep in shifts. When the moment presented itself, Jimmy would walk up to the front door in the middle of suburbia and ring the doorbell next to the Madonna. If Big Ears' mother or father came to the door, Jimmy would ask for their son. The mother and father knew him. If Charlie himself opened the door, *boom!*

"This is stupid," Joey O said inside the car. "There's a cop three houses down."

This was true. Several houses away was a lieutenant from the local police, whose cruiser sat in the driveway. That's where most of the cars in the neighborhood sat—in driveways. The car with Joey and Jimmy and Anthony was the only one parked by the curb.

"It's a deserted area," Joey O said. "You sit there for three hours . . ."

The other two men ignored him. They watched Big Ears' house in the dark.

"Sit there for three hours, they're gonna see you," Joey O said out loud but to himself.

"Anthony, you want me to go shoot the guy now, I'll shoot the guy now. But not here. I pass on the way youse wanna do this."

"No," said Anthony Capo. "We got everything figured out."

The night passed and Big Ears Charlie was still alive to read his morning paper.

In a few days, Joey O flew down to Florida to give Vinny Ocean the bad news. Vinny would listen and consider the circumstances. He would decide that Big Ears was not a threat, and that he was infuriating so many other wiseguys that somebody else might just take care of the job for him. In the end, Vinny decided to call off the hit.

WALKER, TEXAS RANGER

As the summer of 1998 ended, Vinny Palermo—just a few months from his fifty-third birthday—sat nearly at the top of the crime family to which he had sworn his allegiance thirty-five years before. He has had to make executive decisions. Once he became a boss, he had to step down as captain of his crews in New Jersey, New York, and Florida and give each of them new assignments. He named as his replacement the old soldier Uncle Joe Giacobbe, promoting him to capo. Now he got calls from people asking for help with their everyday problems. An old family friend named Karen called to say her son and two friends had gotten into a fight with an off-duty cop. What could he do to help? He was now a boss, and everybody knew it.

At the same time he surrounded himself with legitimacy. He could, on any given day, spend an afternoon chatting about a plan to shoot Charlie Majuri in the head in front of his parents, and in the evening sit down with a vice president of Smith Barney to discuss a multimillion-dollar deal. In July of 1998, for instance, the FBI carefully chronicled many Vinny Ocean business deals in the making. On July 2, 1998, Vinny met for two hours at the Upper East Side home of *Penthouse* magazine founder Bob Guccione, who had no idea Vinny Ocean was anything more than a guy with big ideas. There they discussed convincing deep-pocket investors to sink millions into a hotel in Atlantic City that would be modeled after the old Sands Bugsy Siegel created in Las Vegas in the 1950s. During the meeting at Guccione's extravagant house, a vice president for Smith Barney showed up.

"These people were very interested in the Atlantic City project," Vinny was overheard saying. "Either way, they could do all the financing. Their eyes lit up when he [Guccione] mentioned the Sands."

A few hours later the same day, the FBI recorded a talk in which Vinny Palermo claimed he'd just signed a contract with the German telecommunications giant Siemens to distribute cell phones in Russia. The deal went through, Palermo said, because his connection had promised the Germans that Chuck Norris, the TV tough guy known as *Walker, Texas Ranger,* would be the company's spokesman. One of Vinny's lawyers, John Daniels, was saying, "Now that's got to be worth some money if a guy like Chuck Norris is willing to lend his name to a product."

"Yeah," said Vinny, "but he's gonna want to get paid from Siemens. Where do we come in?"

"We'll get a piece of it," Daniels said.

"In other words, if we can get him on there."

"If we can get him on there," Daniels replied, "I mean his show in Russia is the number-one show. *Walker, Texas Ranger.* Norris's show."

"Oh."

"And the number-one show in Germany."

"Wow."

"So Siemens can relate to that."

"Yeah definitely," Vinny said. "Not only that, maybe we can get close to him that way."

Nothing was too small. One day he was discussing the possibility of opening up McDonalds' franchises in Russia. The deal would probably take years to consummate, but there was a possibility the Russian government would help finance it. A few days later he was talking about doing business with the Reverend Sun Yung Moon. Palermo's thoughts on working with the good reverend were simple: "He's a good connection," he said. "Total cash."

He was no longer just another guy from the Fulton Fish Market, working all night in the middle of the winter schlepping pallets of frozen mackerel for middle-class wages. Now he was near the top. He claimed to have Bob Guccione's unlisted phone number. He was doing deals with big guys. He had a hundred-foot dock at his waterfront mansion in Island Park. He had a twenty-by-forty-foot heated pool. He was taking his second family—his wife, Debbie, his daughters, Danielle and Tara, and his son, Vincent Jr.—to Disney World.

Here was the big crime boss and hard-charging business man cruising along, buoyed by luck and talent. Who would have imagined the personal problems a man like this could face?

For instance, there was the Jet Ski incident.

His daughter Tara and one of her girlfriends, Vinny couldn't remember which one, were at the house on a Saturday while his wife was out. He was Mister Mom. The two of them wanted to use the Jet Skis, but Vinny was busy eating his lunch. He wasn't paying attention. Tara said, "Come on, Daddy" again and again, and he said, "Okay, go outside and get ready, I'll be right out." But he didn't come right out, and the girls got on the Jet Skis and went for a spin. Unfortunately they were both only thirteen years old, which meant they weren't even supposed to be on the things. There was an accident. The friend was thrown off her Jet Ski and cut her leg good enough to pick up five stitches and be hospitalized. When his girl went to visit her friend, she brought flowers but the girl's father started asking questions about what happened.

"The father's questioning her," Vinny was telling a

friend named Frank. "Like, 'Did you have life jackets on?' You know what I'm saying."

"Like he was pumping her for information," Frank said.

"Yeah, but she was smart. She says, you know, 'Sure we had life jackets on'."

"Maybc it'll appease him."

"I don't think so," Vinny said. "He looks like a miserable bastard."

"Really? It's shitty, eh. Is the kid all right?"

"Yeah, she's got five stitches on her leg. But you know what happens when you go to a lawyer. She was gonna model her legs. She wanted to be a model. And she's saying she can't sleep and—"

"Yeah, I know, it's upsetting," Frank said. "I understand."

"It's upsetting because I'm mad at myself. 'Cause I never let them go out without me. And I was eating and I says, 'Ten more minutes, we'll go out.' 'No, come on, come on.' 'Ten minutes, let me finish eating.' 'Okay, we'll stay behind the house.'" He paused. "Well, that's kids. What are you gonna do?"

Meanwhile he's got his older daughter Danielle being stalked by the son of one of his more promising crew members. Ralphie Guarino's boy, a high-schooler, was repeatedly calling Danielle, claiming he was madly in love with her and insisting that she see him. She wanted nothing to do with him. She told him again and again, but he kept calling and even showing up outside the family home. He even swore he would take the train out from Brooklyn and stay in the Long Beach hotel every night until she agreed to see him. Vinny was forced to call Ralphie, and Ralphie promised to take care of things. It was embarrassing.

But perhaps his biggest problem at the time was his old

friend and driver, Joseph Masella. Good old Joey O. The man seemed positively insistent on crashing and burning. No one could say for sure how much and how many he owed, but it was definitely six figures and more than one crime family. He owed this guy and that guy and he was making many headaches for Vinny. It was not right to have a guy like Joey O refusing to pay and then going out and gambling and dropping big bucks on his dope-smoking girlfriend. The Joey O problem had become a very public problem. Vinny was now watching a guy he had known most of his life fall apart in front of his eyes.

For years, Joey O had been there for him, picking up his blood pressure medicine, getting him coffee and breakfast, listening to his plans. Joey O was the one he trusted to pick up the little envelopes of cash that fueled the Palermo fortune. When he took him on as a crew member after Joey's old mentor, Rudy, passed away, Vinny knew he was picking up some baggage. He did not know how much. Now Joey's baggage had become Vinny's baggage, and that was not good for a man in his position.

His frustration emerged during a talk with Joseph Abruzzo, a DeCavalcante associate who also happened to be Joey O's brother-in-law. Vinny Ocean had put Abruzzo in to run a gambling boat he controlled that operated on Long Island. The boat shuttled hundreds of gamblers just far enough off the coast of Long Island to enter international waters and be free of New York's gaming laws. The Long Island officials who'd given a license to the company that ran the boat, had no clue that it was just another money-maker for the DeCavalcante crime family. Joseph Abruzzo was listed as chief executive officer. Vincent Palermo's name was nowhere in sight. When Abruzzo brought up his brother-in-law, Joey O, with Vinny, he clearly had no idea how infuriated his boss was on the subject.

"You hear from Joey?" Abruzzo asked innocently.

"I told him just don't fucking call me no more," Vinny fumed. "I don't even want to fucking talk to him. He's such a fucking asshole. I wish I never see him again."

The two men then presented a clear case of gangster logic: It's all right to have a *goomad* and spend all your money on her, as long as you take care of your wife and kids first.

"When you neglect your family, you're a fucking asshole," Vinny said. "You wanna have somebody on the side, you fucked 'em, you chased 'em, whatever you gotta do. You know what I'm saying?"

"Yeah," Abruzzo said.

"He's a fucking moron is what he is. He's a lowlife. I told him, you got a lot of money and you take care of your wife and your kids."

"And then you wanna do something else, fine," said the brother-in-law Abruzzo. "Now he's being nice nice."

"Yeah, nice nice. Because the girl don't want no part of him no more. It's the same fucking story all the time. He's with a nice broad, he's feeding her all kinds of money and jewelry and champagne and everything, and that's why she's with him. She figures, 'Look, what a score.' And then all of a sudden on the one or two days you don't do it, that's it. They leave."

"That's right."

"But in the meantime, when it's happening, he thinks she's in love with him and he don't need nobody else. And you know this is it."

Vinny Ocean now presented an imaginative litany of epithets to describe his old and close friend Joey O, then railed against gambling while failing to note that he was personally pocketing hundreds of thousands of dollars a year from it. "It's just like drugs," he said. "It's no different."

"It's like my son," Abruzzo said. "You know my son did the same thing. I had to bail him out—fifteen hundred bucks."

"You got to stop him quick," Vinny said.

"I said, 'That's it.' I said, 'Now you learned.' I said, 'You won once and now you thought it was an easy score.' I said, 'No more. I'm not bailing you out anymore.' And he stopped."

"The one time you win, you lose ten," Palermo said. "Stupid."

And then Vinny began to refer to Joey O in the past tense. "He had the world by the balls," Vinny declared, "and he blew it."

September 16, 1998

Back from Disney World, Vinny Ocean has turned around his problems with Wiggles. The city inspectors had returned after he had the new walls installed and tightened up enforcement of the sex-police rules. It had not been easy. After the city first shut him down in July, Wiggles showed up on the cover of *Newsday*. His lawyers had gone back and forth to the courthouse in Jamaica several times in an all-out effort to convince the judge to reopen the club. They filed legal briefs; they brought in witnesses during a three-day hearing. The night before Vinny called his stockbroker son, Michael, and said, "Say a prayer for me." During the hearing, his lawyers showed off a new, improved Wiggles, and on September 16, 1998, a Wednesday, Administrative Judge Fisher of the Supreme Court in Queens declared that Wiggles was no longer a "public nuisance."

Within hours, the doors were open and the dancers were back onstage.

Within two days, Palermo was on the phone talking with his lawyer, John Daniels, as if Wiggles had never shut its doors. In fact, it was clear he had embraced the saying that no publicity is bad publicity because he was now talking about how high profile the Wiggles name was. He talked with Daniels about how he had been negotiating with Bob Guccione to open up a strip club under the *Penthouse* name in New Jersey, but now that Wiggles had picked up so much publicity, he didn't seem to care if the *Penthouse* strip-club deal went through.

"Put a Wiggles up in Jersey," Palermo suggested. "It's a tremendous name. It's got the best name in the business now."

"It certainly made the papers," Daniels replied, and both men had a good laugh.

7

BOOBIE AND DONNIE

In the world of what is now called "traditional" organized crime, where rules allegedly exist to keep criminal activity organized, nicknames can get a little disorganized. Some have an old-world charm to them. Vincent (Chin) Gigante got his either because his Italian name is Vincenzo, or because he was a not-very-successful boxer who led with his chin. Some are easy to understand. Vinny Ocean once worked in the Fulton Fish Market, where the most felonious thing he ever did was to get caught with boxes of allegedly stolen shrimp. Tin Ear Sclafani has a bad ear. Big Ears Charlie Majuri's nickname is easy to understand if you see him in person. Some nicknames are complex. Anthony Casso, a truly scary guy who confessed to killing thirty people, got his nickname—Gaspipe—because his father worked for the gas company. Some nicknames imply a man's place in the food chain. John A. Gotti is called Junior because he will always be first and foremost the son of John J. Gotti, who got his nickname—the Dapper Don—strictly for sartorial reasons. Then there is Boobie Cerasani.

John Cerasani, whose nickname was Boobie, was a square man with a face like a closed fist. He wore black turtlenecks and black suit coats to court, even if his lawyer told him not to. He was also a made guy in the Bonanno crime family.

It is hard to know this Boobie. He had been a soldier with the Bonannos for nearly twenty years, according to the FBI. In 1985, he pleaded guilty to a racketeering conspiracy that included conspiring to rob a bank and possessing marijuana, cocaine, and heroin. In 1994, he pleaded guilty to criminal possession of narcotics in the fifth degree. At the time he was under investigation by the FBI, which believed he was an enforcer for the Bonanno family in a scheme to take control of a corrupt stockbrokerage house. Most important, Boobie had been involved in numerous crimes in the 1970s and early 1980s when an FBI agent named Joseph Pistone succeeded in infiltrating the Bonanno family using the name Donnie Brasco.

Donnie Brasco, it should be noted, had no nickname.

During the time Donnie the FBI agent was hanging around with Boobie and his boss, Dominick (Sonny Black) Napolitano, who has black hair, Donnie described Sonny as "quiet and smart, a chess lover." He also described Boobie as "one mean fucker." Donnie the FBI agent recalled another gangster, Lefty Guns Ruggiero, describing how Boobie and three other gangsters were involved in shotgunning to death an enormous Mafia capo named Dominick "Big Trin" Trinchera (the origin of whose nickname is self-evident). Ruggiero did not actually say that Boobie pulled the trigger, but he did say that after the deed was done, the assassins had difficulty disposing of Big Trin's body because it was so, well, big. Boobie, Ruggiero claimed, somehow managed to pick the guy up.

"I was amazed," Donnie quotes Ruggiero as saying, "Boobie could move him. They cut him up and put him in green plastic garbage bags."

In 1982, Donnie the FBI agent left his life as an undercover associate of the Bonanno crime family and began testifying in court. Boobie and numerous others with whom Donnie had spent many loquacious hours were indicted, but Boobie was acquitted of all charges. He was never charged with murdering Big Trin, never mind moving him or cutting him up and placing him in green plastic garbage bags.

In 1987, Donnie the FBI agent wrote a book about his experiences. Presumably Boobie read it, being that he was mentioned in it fifty-five times, including the description of Big Trin's demise. The book, *Donnie Brasco: My Undercover Life in the Mafia,* made the *New York Times* bestseller list, and Boobie made not a peep.

Ten years later times had changed in La Cosa Nostra. Gone were the days when a wiseguy said with a straight face that the Mafia did not even exist. No longer did a goodfella describe any allegation against him as mere fabrication. Gone were the days when silence was the universal response to newspaper stories, TV exposés, and even movie spectaculars portraying life in the mob. By 1997, if you were a gangster and you didn't like what people were saying about you in a book, you didn't whack the author. You sued.

Sometime in 1996, years after the book debuted, somebody managed to sneak a video camera into a prerelease screening of *Donnie Brasco,* starring Johnny Depp and Al

Pacino. The unnamed somebody managed to get a pirated copy of this soon-to-be-released movie to Boobie Cerasani. This time he was not amused.

In the movie, the actor who portrays Boobie and several other gangsters portrayed by actors are seen kicking the owner of a Japanese restaurant in the face and smashing him in the head with a garbage can. Worse, the actor playing Boobie is seen blasting three gangsters with a shotgun, blowing off pieces of one head and a chunk out of the leg of another. The Boobie character is then seen helping other gangsters saw the bodies into pieces for disposal in garbage bags, which, unlike the description in the book, are black, not green. When Boobie saw this, he reached for the phone.

A series of letters ensued.

Boobie's lawyer, Barry Slotnick, threatened to sue for libel and defamation of character, even though the picture had not yet been released. He argued that because enough people had seen the pirated version, the damage was already done to Boobie's reputation. This worked, somewhat. Sony Pictures Entertainment shortened the murder scene and deep-sixed a scene in which the Boobie character reloads during the shotgun murder. They also changed the Boobie character's name to Paulie. They did this by having actors dub the name Paulie every time they had previously said Boobie. They missed one reference, so when the picture was released in early 1997, there was still one Boobie involved. In addition, the Boobie character, now named Paulie, still helps dismember a victim with what is described by all involved as a "sawlike knife."

On April 3, 1997, Boobie Cerasani—who was not satisfied with the Paulie version of the film—took the position of the new gangster and filed suit in Manhattan Federal Court. He sued Sony, he sued the distributor, the executive producers, the producers, the director, even the screen-writer. He alleged many things. There was "damage to his reputation in an amount exceeding $50,000." He alleged that the film had caused him "extreme emotional distress, including fear of retaliation by organized crime seeking revenge." This onetime "mean fucker" was now asking a federal judge to protect him from the Mafia. He did not even bother to deny the existence of the Mafia. In fact, he acknowledged its existence to collect damages. He demanded compensatory damages, punitive damages, and, of course, financial reimbursement for the cost of bringing suit.

United States District Court Judge Denny Chin got Boobie's case. A few months later he got another case involving Boobie. This time it was a new criminal indictment that came out of the stock-fraud investigation. Boobie was charged with being an enforcer and threatening stockbrokers and promoters to do what they were told so the mob could capitalize on the booming stock market through illegal "pump and dump" schemes. These were, of course, mere allegations. Judge Chin allowed Sony Pictures to file a motion demanding that Boobie's suit over *Donnie* be tossed out. He then took a full six months to make up his mind.

On January 15, 1998, Judge Chin issued his opinion. In thirty-four typewritten pages, double-spaced, the judge did the only responsible thing a distinguished member of the court could do. He laughed Boobie out of court.

First, Judge Chin wondered why Boobie hadn't sued when the Donnie Brasco book came out eleven years earlier. Then Judge Chin declared that Boobie was "generally reputed to be an associate of organized crime," and, even worse, "not a model citizen." Finally Judge Chin declared Boobie "libel proof." This is an extremely rare declaration that essentially says you are such a bad person no one can possibly defame you. "I hold that Cerasani's reputation is so 'badly tarnished,' that, even assuming the pre-release version of the film is defamatory, he can suffer no further harm and hence no reasonable jury could award him anything more than nominal damages," Chin wrote.

Boobie declined to appeal, and a few months later pleaded guilty before Judge Chin in the stock-fraud case. One defense lawyer pointed out privately that Judge Chin was relatively new to the bench and probably had little grounding in the history of "traditional" organized crime. This defense lawyer wondered if Judge Chin would have even been aware of Boobie's involvement in the Donnie Brasco case if Boobie hadn't told him.

June 5, 1998

The movie in question was *Carlito's Way*. It was the somewhat predictable story of New York heroin dealer Carlito Brigante, who is released from prison and is determined to go straight. The prisoner, of course, finds himself slipping back into his old and larcenous ways. It stars Al Pacino, who presents a toned-down version of the psychotic Tony Montana character he played in his *Scarface* remake a decade earlier. It was the kind of performance and the kind of movie that would impress guys like Joey O Masella and Ralphie Guarino. As they cruised down Flatbush Avenue in Brooklyn looking for an electronics store called the Wiz, Ralphie was driving and Joey was explaining about *Carlito's Way*. It was a typical Joey explanation—elliptical, filled with digressions. It started with Joey telling Ralphie about his trip the previous day to Seaside Heights on the New Jersey shore. Joey drove Vinny Ocean down to the shore to visit with Giuseppe Schifilliti, a capo in the DeCavalcante crime family. Nobody called him Giuseppe. Everybody called him Pino. Pino was a veteran gangster with a little white Vandyke beard who owned a restaurant, By The Sea Too, right on the boardwalk, next to a cigar store owned by a guy who shows up as an actor in movies a lot. This fact had impressed Joey O mightily.

Joey O told Ralphie that during the Seaside visit he stopped by Pino's restaurant and sampled some of his homemade wine. Then Pino went next door and picked up some Mohegan cigars for everybody from the movie guy. Vinny Ocean smoked his and was not happy.

"He got sick as a fucking dog," Joey O told Ralphie as they drove. "He said, 'I'll never smoke a cigar again.' "

"It goes right to your brains," Ralphie said.

"I can't smoke that cigar," Joey O said.

"If you inhale it too much, it goes right to your fucking brains."

Joey O the name-dropper mentioned that the guy who owned the cigar store that nearly did in Vinny Ocean was an actor in movies that guys like Joey O liked to watch.

"This guy was in the movie *Carlito's Way.* You ever see that movie with Al Pacino? Where he sold the drugs? A Spanish guy. It was a good movie. Well, this guy"—the one with the cigar store—"was a big fat fuck. He was Colombian. He ended up shot at the end of the movie."

Joey O was obviously very impressed. "He was in a lot of parts. He's an actor; he opened up a cigar place right next to Pino's down in Seaside. He's got pictures all over the place of him and Al Pacino, Robert De Niro. He says whenever you wanna come down, you come down."

By now Ralphie had gotten used to listening to Joey O and his stories. Mostly Joey O's stories consisted of the many problems of Joey O. Ralphie noticed Joey was looking more slumped over than usual. Joey had once been a strong, wiry guy, deeply tanned, with a certain kind of rough charm. Now his belly protruded under his black silk shirt and he had to make do with a cheesy comb-over to hide his thinning hair. He smoked too much, his diabetes was killing him. Driving down Flatbush, he had trouble managing Ralph's cell phone. "How do you use this fucking thing?" He called his doctor about something called Protac that Ralphie thought was Prozac.

"Let me ask you a question," Ralphie said. "What's the matter with you?"

"What do you mean?"

"What you got to do with this fucking Pro—"

"Diabetic."

"Oh," Ralphie said. "I thought . . ."

Joey O was forty-nine, headed rapidly toward fifty. "I'm driving a car with no muffler," Joey O said. "The fucking thing is shimmying."

Ralphie knew Joey O's problems by heart. He also knew they were becoming legendary among the nylon-jogging-suit set. He'd been talking with Joey Cars, another DeCavalcante associate, who let him know that Joey O was now stealing from his own friend and boss, Vinny Ocean. Joey O was going around telling people that Vinny Ocean was putting money out on the street at two points per week interest, which was not true. Vinny was actually putting the money out at a point and a half, and Joey O was pocketing the difference. This he was doing in violation of just about every rule of La Cosa Nostra. Joey Cars said he borrowed $4,000 from Vinny and paid back the money to Joey O. Joey O, however, neglected to give the money to Vinny, which put Joey Cars in a bad spot.

"He's a friend of mine," Joey Cars said, "I don't wanna embarrass him."

"Like my father used to say," Ralphie offered. "When you feel sorry for sorry people, they make you sorry. And guess what? He is making everybody sorry."

Ralphie was now in the middle. If Vinny Ocean found out that Joey O was stealing from him, that could be the end of Joey O, and Ralphie needed Joey O to get close to Vinny. The FBI was clearly interested in Vinny Ocean quite a bit and interested in Joey O Masella not at all. Therefore, it was important that Ralphie get more information on Vinny. The problem was that six months into his role as a secret informant for the FBI, Ralphie had not done so well getting Vinny Palermo to say things that could get him in trouble. He'd given him free cell phones and the FBI had plenty of hours of Vinny Palermo on tape, but Vinny was smart. He rarely talked about illegal business on the phone, and when he did, the conversation was usually too cryptic to understand.

Ralphie took another approach. He had noticed that when Vinny discussed Joey O, he had a tendency to fly into a rage. Rage implied lack of self-control. The FBI figured that during one of his tirades about Joey O, Vinny Ocean might slip up. Ralphie was instructed to take advantage of this weakness by keeping the two men in constant contact.

The two men found the Wiz, did their business, then got back in Ralphie's FBI-wired car and cruised into Manhattan toward Canal Street and Chinatown. They needed to fence some stolen watches.

Canal Street used to mark the northern border between Chinatown and the old Mafia neighborhood of Little Italy. This was the Little Italy where John Gotti strutted down Mulberry Street, where Crazy Joey Gallo was shot inside Umberto's Clam House, and where the Genovese crime family controlled the Feast of San Gennaro every

September by charging mob tax on everything from the scungilli stands to the water guns. Now Canal Street marked the center of Chinatown, and Little Italy was a shadow of its former self. Chinese immigrants had continued pouring into this country. Italians did not. The Chinese drifted north into Little Italy. The Chinese who flooded the city year after year took over the Italian neighborhood, and most of the Italians fled to Staten Island and New Jersey. Gotti's social club, the Ravenite, had been sold off to somebody who was planning on putting in a trendy shoe store. The old Umberto's Clam House where Joey Gallo got shot in the head over his scungilli had shut down and moved. Most of the Italian restaurants that were left had become tourist traps. Most of Little Italy was now owned by the Chinese. Only one fact remained constant over all the years—Canal Street was still the best place in New York to buy and sell stolen goods.

As Ralphie and Joey O drove over the Manhattan Bridge and into the mess of traffic that was Chinatown, Ralphie (and the FBI) began to get a clearer picture of Vinny Ocean's illegal behavior.

Joey was happy that Vinny picked him to shake down the owner of a Long Island bus company called Manti Transportation. The setup was good. The capo put in charge of collecting, Joe Pitts, was gone. Vinny Ocean took over and put Joey O into the company in a no-show job. This was not a legal thing to do. This was more "probable cause." Joey O put the company in the name of Joey's daughter. He talked like a big businessman about borrowing money from his wife so he could get a $3 million line of credit from a bank to buy more buses to drive customers to Great Adventure theme park in New Jersey. He told Ralphie that every Wednesday Joey would show up at

Manti Transportation and pick up a paycheck. He would cash it and kick a percentage up to Vinny as tribute. He needed the money desperately.

"The more you want, the more you need," Joey O said.

"The more you got, the more you want," Ralphie said.

But Ralphie could see that the more Joey talked, the more Joey wanted to talk about himself. All of a sudden, with Joey trying to keep himself upbeat about making money scheming, he dropped the F-word into the conversation.

"The FBI," Joey said.

This could have given Ralphie a heart attack. He could have suddenly felt extremely self-conscious about the casual mention of the people he was really working for who had planted a bug in his car. Then again Ralphie could have felt Joey O would never have mentioned the FBI so casually if he ever suspected Ralphie. And it would seem that the latter was true, because Joey just prattled on and on about some agents in a boat taking photographs of him hanging out at Vinny Ocean's hundred-foot dock on Long Island Sound.

"There was a degenerate taking pictures of us while I had my bathing suit on," Joey O said. "They were agents. The guy on the left would make a call, the guy on the right would pick it up. They were talking to each other, these fucking agents. Taking pictures of me while I'm taking my clothes off. Cocksuckers."

Ralphie said nothing, and Joey went on. Other FBI agents had come to Joey's home in Staten Island, where he lived with his ancient grandmother. "My grandmother answers. She says in Italian, 'Who's this?' I say, 'The cops.' She says in English, 'Get the hell outta here!' So the cop is saying, 'I have a subpoena for you.' He says, 'Here,' and he gives me a subpoena."

Ralphie cautiously ventured back in: "For the grand jury."

"My lawyer told us just give your address and phone number. They ask, 'Do you know a Vincent Palermo? How long do you associate with Vincent Palermo?' They ask you four or five questions."

"Then they let you go?" Ralphie asked, but Joey ignored him.

"So the Justice Department came down and they put on about seventy-eight people. They got neighbors."

"Neighbors?"

"Everybody," Joey O said. "You want to write a book? I can write a book."

June 17, 1998

The Marriott Harbor Beach of Fort Lauderdale sat on a street called Holiday Drive in a state named after sunshine. It sat on the edge of the Atlantic on a huge private beach of powder-white sand and palm trees that clicked and rustled in the warm ocean breeze. It was one of two dozen hotels that dotted the very strip where Concetta Franconero sang "Where the Boys Are" using the name Connie Francis. This was also the very beach upon which thousands of college students descended during spring break to frolic and drink alcoholic beverages and enjoy such American pastimes as the "wet T-shirt contest."

The Harbor Beach was set away from all that, a fifteen-story concrete high-rise with a huge outdoor swimming pool that lit up at night. On this day, two of its 637 rooms were booked by a group of men from New York City who were down for the weekend on business.

The most expensive rooms faced the ocean, the cheaper ones faced the pool, the cheapest ones faced the

Intercostal Waterway behind the hotel. Joey O Masella and Ralphie Guarino—two guys who spent most of their time lamenting how broke they were—booked two of the most expensive rooms in the hotel: Rooms 1411 and 1417, two suites on the fourteenth floor looking out on the white sand beach. They were typical Florida hotel suites, with seashell-pink sofas and black lacquer furniture and balconies looking out on the Atlantic. The TV had all the cable channels and there was a huge vase filled with fake flowers. There was also a video camera secretly installed in the wall by specially trained FBI agents.

It was set up to capture most of the room with a wide-angle lens but specifically anybody who happened to sit on the sofa in the main room. It faced the sofa directly, slightly tilted toward the ceiling so anyone caught in its focus would be presented in the slightly menacing camera angles of *Citizen Kane*. Its microphones were not terribly sophisticated, so that if the TV set was on, it was sometimes easy to hear *Oprah* but difficult to hear what people in the room were talking about. The FBI agents listening in a few rooms away did the best they could.

On this day in the middle of a working week, Joey O and Ralphie were supposed to be meeting with Vinny Ocean and a lawyer named Kenny Weinstein. Later Anthony Capo was supposed to show up. On this first day, Joey and Ralphie and Vinny sat around in the middle of the afternoon when most taxpaying citizens were out working for a living, making fun of Anthony. They made fun of the fact that he liked golf. They made fun of the fact that he stole nearly everything not nailed down from hotel rooms. Meanwhile, Vinny was on the phone with his daughter Danielle, asking her about school. Then he was on the phone with somebody else, talking about stocks.

Outside, the Florida sun blazed down; inside, the air-conditioning was cranked all the way up.

They ordered coffee and dessert. There was some discussion about whether anybody wanted cookies, and everybody did. Ralphie was flipping through the TV channels, checking it out. He found a movie with Alec Baldwin and Kim Basinger.

"He thinks he's so good-looking," Vinny Ocean said while still on the phone.

"Who is she?" Joey O said.

"This is ah . . . Alec Baldwin's wife," Ralphie said.

"It all depends on what she's wearing," Joey said.

"I'm telling you," Vinny said, off the phone but still on stocks, "that Viagra stock is gonna go big."

The movie was *The Getaway*. It was a new version of an old movie starring Steve McQueen as Doc McCoy. Alec Baldwin portrayed a prison inmate with some redeeming qualities. The men in the hotel room seemed familiar with the entire plotline, but were mostly concerned about why a woman who looked like Kim Basinger would be married to a guy who behaved like Alec Baldwin.

"I mean with the cigarettes, with the dirty underwear on the fuckin' chair," Joey said. "No wonder his fuckin' wife wants to throw him out."

The cookies and pot of coffee arrived. They switched the TV to football and began discussing a strip club called Rachel's in West Palm. They discussed Michael Jackson and Dan Quayle. Joey O said, "He can't spell *potato,*" and Ralphie replied, "And he wants to run for president." Inside the room a few doors away, the FBI agents were getting frustrated.

This was not the stuff of probable cause. This kind of talk about Kim Basinger and cookies and *potato* would surely make the federal judge they needed to keep the bugs up and running shake his head in dismay. The agents also were now sure someone else had entered the room and they couldn't tell who. In their notes, they scrawled the acronym *UM* for *unidentified male*.

UM suggested going to the Gap to buy clothes. They fought over who would have to drive to the airport to pick up Anthony Capo. Still no probable cause on the menu. Somebody mentioned doing something that might be illegal, although it was hard to tell—smuggling bootleg Absolut vodka into Europe.

"Sixty dollars for a bottle of Absolut in Norway," said UM.

"Yeah," Joey O said, "but who the fuck wants to go to Norway?"

Somebody paged through the cable listings and found yet another movie.

"Kiss the Girls," Ralphie said. "Channel Forty-two."

This was a new movie with Morgan Freeman as a Washington, D.C., detective with a doctorate in psychology. He believes his niece has been kidnapped by a psychotic killer who commits atrocities but is portrayed as intelligent. Morgan Freeman the detective must travel to North Carolina to rescue the niece. He brings with him one of the psychotic killer's intended victims, played by Ashley Judd, the one who got away. The members and associates of the DeCavalcantc crime family who are supposed to be conducting a "business meeting" in Room 1417 at the Marriott cannot seem to get away from the silver screen.

"Kiss the Girls Good-bye," Ralphie said. "What was the other one, *Kiss the Girls Hello*?"

"Hello and Good-bye," Joey said. "It's a good movie. Ya see it? What is he, a cop?"

"He's a professor," Ralphie said.

"He's a psychologist," said the Unidentified Male.

"This is like a preview of the story," Ralphie explained. "This is a different case."

The gangsters discussed plot development and analyzed motive. One of the female characters attacks her husband with a knife after years of abuse. Joey O summarized this aspect of the movie by stating, "If you're beatin' the dog every day, sooner or later he's gonna attack ya."

They discussed Morgan Freeman's acting career. "Ya ever see *Shawshank Redemption* with him? When he's in jail?" Joey O volunteered. They argued about how cold it was in the room. They critiqued the movie.

"That's North Carolina now?" Joey O asked. "What's he do, he tied her to the tree?"

"He chops her head off," UM said.

"The hair," Ralphie corrected. "Not the head."

The FBI agents sitting in the other room are now in deep trouble. Instead of recording the inner workings of a nefarious organized crime family plotting to take over the world, they had instead a lengthy analysis of a mediocre serial-killer movie. And it was about to get worse.

Here sat a group of alleged and reputed gangsters, any of whom could have been involved in violent criminal behavior. Joey O just the previous week had had a long discussion about "giving somebody a beating." The intended victim owed Joey Cars a lot of money. Joey Cars had torched the guy's van, so the guy bought a new van. Joey Cars then slashed the guy's tires and put sugar in his gas tank. Joey O had suggested he simply visit the victim and beat him senseless every day until the guy paid all he owed. "Every time you see him give him a fucking beating until he comes up with the money," Joey O had said.

Now he was in an air-conditioned Florida hotel room,

discussing the terrible effects of movie violence on the youth of today.

"See things like this really happen, that's the shame of it," he said. "People make movies like that, you know? There's some serial bastards that are in the movie theater, they think about it. And then they're copycats."

"You never know, man," Ralphie said.

"Who had strawberry cake?" UM asked.

"Just put it down," Ralphie said. "We have to fight for it."

But Joey O was not finished. His sense of moral outrage was building. "I'm saying people really do things like this," he said. "And that's the fucking shame of it, you know?"

"They go to the movies," UM said, "and they just get ideas like that. In school. The shooting with these schools."

"That's why it's like a joke now," Joey O said. "When you ever hear all this shit?"

"You know it's a scary thought," UM said. "I have a two-year-old and a three-year-old."

"And it's getting worse," Joey O said.

"Fucking right," Ralphie said.

"Did you get chocolate ice cream?" Joey O asked.

"Will you shut up and watch the movie?" Ralphie said.

"I didn't say a word," Joey O said.

"I gained like five, six pounds," Ralphie said. "Right back in my fucking gut."

"It's your fucking fault," UM said.

"All you wanna do is eat," Joey said. "I never seen a guy eat so much."

"I'm depressed," Ralphie said. "Hanging out with you. I think I'm gonna start taking Prozac."

June 18, 1998

In the afternoon the FBI tape machine whirred away. In Ralphie and Vinny and Joey's hotel room, the guy whose voice the FBI did not recognize—Unidentified Male— was gone. Only Joey O and Ralphie were left. Ralphie sat in a sofa chair right next to the FBI camera, while Joey O sat on the couch directly in front of the camera. Both were drinking beer. Ralphie was wearing a sport shirt and pants, but Joey was wearing only his bathing trunks. Joey kept sitting down and getting up, pacing back and forth across the carpet. His gut hung over the edge of the suit; his gold chain flopped up and down on his sagging chest. As he talked he got increasingly agitated. Obviously something was on his mind. The FBI agents started paying closer attention. Probable cause seemed in the works.

There was some "business" Joey O started talking about. It was why he had been summoned to Florida. It was why Vinny Ocean was already in Florida. It had to do with a kind of corporate restructuring that was taking place within the DeCavalcante crime family. Joey O was vague on the details. All he knew was that the boss of the family, John Riggi, and the alleged consigliere, an old Sicilian named Stefano Vitabile everybody called "the truck driver," had come up with a plan that was becoming increasingly common in La Cosa Nostra. They had appointed a "ruling panel" of wiseguys who would be in charge on the street. This was no easy task. There was always with these panels resentment and animosity. Riggi— who was, by nature, a survivor—tried to choose well. Joey O said Riggi had picked two men he'd known for years—Vincent Palermo and Girolamo Palermo—to serve as his corporate representatives on the street until he could do his time. Both Palermos, who had been active partici-

An FBI surveillance photo of Joseph (Joey O) Masella

FBI surveillance photo

Wiggles, the topless bar in Queens

Photo by Todd Maisel, © 2001 Daily News, L.P., reprinted with permission

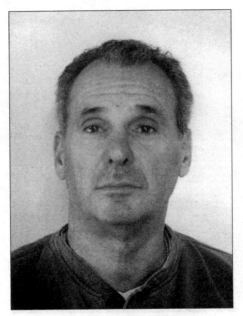

James Gallo, a DeCavalcante soldier

Courtesy of GangLandNews.com

In a recorded conversation,
Joe "Tin Ear" Sclafani wondered if *The Sopranos*
was based on the DeCavalcante family.

Courtesy of GangLandNews.com

Westley Paloscio, a family associate,
otherwise known as "Mickey the Dunce"

Courtesy of GangLandNews.com

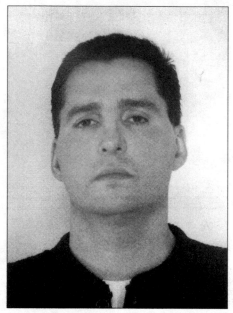

Anthony Capo, the DeCavalcante soldier
who went from contract killer to stool pigeon.

Courtesy of GangLandNews.com

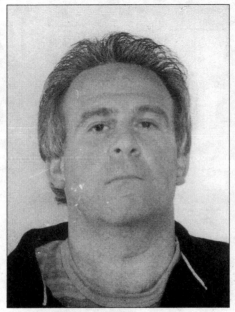

Anthony Rotondo always seemed to disappear
when there was dirty work to be done.

Courtesy of GangLandNews.com

Sam the Plumber in chains on arrival at court in Newark.

Photo by Jim Hughes, © 2001 Daily News, L.P., reprinted with permission

pants in the DeCavalcante family for decades, liked this idea very much. Charlie Majuri—who had also been an active participant for decades—did not. As a result, Joey O had been advised to whack Big Ears.

Joey O was now explaining the murder plot as he paced back and forth in the hotel room in Fort Lauderdale while the FBI videotape rolled. Now here was some probable cause. Joey was going on and on about his problem with the "business." Joey O told Ralphie (and the FBI) that Vinny Ocean had assigned him to monitor the Majuri hit. This was the first time the FBI had any evidence of Vinny Ocean's involvement in a crime of violence.

Joey O told Ralphie that he was supposed to act as Vinny's eyes and ears on the Majuri job, reporting back on all events of note. Vinny, who always retreated to Florida when a "piece of work" he'd ordered was to be carried out in New York, had summoned Joey O to the Sunshine State for an update on the progress of the task. Unfortunately for Joey O, there was no progress to report.

Joey O explained to Ralphie the details of the planned hit, which he clearly felt was turning into a Marx Brothers movie. He paced back and forth in front of the TV set on which a basketball game was quietly playing. He said there were three men involved   himself, Jimmy Gallo, and Anthony Capo. As Joey saw it, both Gallo and Capo were disturbed individuals who were incapable of ordered thought. Joey recounted for Ralphie his conversation with Vinny Ocean about the job. Joey said Vinny told him, " 'I want you to do this. I want you to go there. Joey, I know you. I'm not asking you to do this. You never did it before. You don't wanna do it, I understand.' I said, 'Vinny, I'll do anything for you. If I have to do this, I'll do it.' He said, 'I want you to do it because they're assholes.' "

"They are," Ralphie agreed.

"Anthony has no brains," Joey said.

"I know that," Ralphie said.

"He's Wild West. Jimmy, now, he's worse than Anthony. You know what Jimmy Gallo wanted to do? Ring the doorbell, when he came to answer the door, shoot him. In front of the mother and father."

"No silencers," Joey O said. "With a police captain directly across the street. Four, five houses on the block. It's a deserted area. So if you sit there for three hours, they're gonna see you. What are they gonna do? There's a brown car sitting here for three hours with three guys sitting in it. With a license plate. Fucking cops all over the place."

The day before, Joey O had told Vinny in private about the ludicrous nature of Jimmy and Anthony's crazy plot to kill Charlie Majuri in front of his ancient parents. When they talked, Vinny asked him first thing, "Is it done?" Joey told him he had walked away from the plan. Now Joey O was not sure where he stood with Vinny. He was hearing that another gangster was walking around claiming that Jimmy and Anthony were blaming Joey O for the failure to kill Charlie Majuri.

"They blamed you," Ralphie said.

"Yeah," Joey O said, trying to convince himself that he'd done the smart thing by walking away from the Majuri hit. As he always did when he was upset, he began talking about himself in the third person. "They say when he looks at something he may be a cocksucker, he may do this, he may do that, but I know when he looks at something, he sees the whole picture. Which I do. That's one thing I gotta say, that's one of my traits. One of my fucking traits."

Ralphie said, "That's why Vinny made you go up there."

"If I look at something, I'll tell you it's good, it's bad.

When I seen this, I says, 'That's life in jail.' Too many ifs, ands, and buts."

This talk made Ralphie come to believe that Joey O's relationship with his lifelong friend and mentor, Vinny Ocean, was in deep trouble. Vinny had asked Joey to get involved in the most sensitive of missions, and the mission had been a failure. Now Joey seemed convinced Vinny might no longer protect him from the many people who wanted to do him harm. He didn't actually say this. It was just obvious from the way he kept trying to reassure himself that Vinny was still, in fact, his friend. He began to drink more heavily in the middle of the sunny Florida day. Joey stood on the balcony, letting a blast of Florida air into the air-conditioned suite to fog the room's mirrors. He'd been drinking beer since noon and it was now half-past three.

Ralphie said from inside the room, "You're gonna fucking fall down, Joey."

Outside, Joey stared down at the beach and tried talking about hooking up with two women he'd met earlier on the beach—an older redhead and a younger blonde. Even discussing the possibility of sex, he kept returning to Vinny. They were supposed to meet up with Vinny later, but Joey was now convinced Vinny would simply not show up. This would be further proof of Vinny's disrespect. Again he warned Ralphie not to repeat what they'd discussed.

"No matter how fucking drunk you get, don't ever mention it," Joey said.

"Would you listen to me?"

"God forbid," Joey said. "If he ever tells me to do it, I do it."

Ralphie said he, too, would do whatever he was told. "Do you need me for anything, Vinny? I'll be there."

"This is a serious thing," Joey said, starting in again with a dose of self-pity about his pitiful position within the La Cosa Nostra universe. Joey again began talking to himself. Vinny, he said, was a big enough deal in the Mafia to attend sit-down meetings with other families that resulted in big decisions. "Where do you fucking go?" he asked himself. "Where do you go? You go to put a fucking bet in and then you get yelled at for putting the bet in."

"Come on, Joey, stop."

"You should have made a move like a horse, you should have fucking won the race a long time ago."

"Well, it's not too late.

"You gotta start giving a fuck," he said, again referring to himself.

Ralphie tried to steer the conversation back to the women Joey met on the beach, trying to get him to stop his wallowing. He suggested they would have to decide which one would pair up with the older one and which one with the young one. The two women were getting manicures and massages. Joey suggested the younger one for Ralph.

"Joey," Ralphie said, "I don't know how to deal with young girls."

"Just fuck around with them," Joey said.

"I don't know."

"They like older men."

"Yeah, but what are you supposed to say?" Ralphie said. "At least you got hair."

"I gotta take two Viagras," Joey O said.

"I forgot the redhead's name," Ralphie said.

The FBI agent wrote "END OF TAPE."

8

On the very same day that Ralphie and Joey O discussed weight loss and Viagra inside an air-conditioned Fort Lauderdale hotel room, filming began on the television series about a New Jersey Mafia family. The show was called *The Sopranos.* Three major television networks rejected it because it was too realistic. That meant it had too much realistic profanity and too much realistic sex (although, it was interesting to note, not too much realistic violence). It was to be presented by the "premium" cable channel, Home Box Office, which prided itself on pushing the envelope regarding what was acceptable material for the living-room TV set.

The show promised to present both the personal and the professional worlds of a completely fictional New Jersey crime family. The characters would be shown as they were, sometimes in an unflattering light. They would be vain and self-effacing, mean-spirited and altruistic, loyal and conniving—often in the same episode. The people who put this together went out of their way to do exactly what was not expected.

What was expected, it can be presumed, was Don Vito Corleone and the nostalgic, mythic world created by Mario Puzo in *The Godfather.* Anyone who read or saw *The Godfather* would come away believing that all gangsters were essentially hardworking, noble men born in the wrong century. The characters portrayed in *The Godfather* possessed a flair for the theatrical. There was a dead fish wrapped in a bulletproof vest. There was a gangster shot in the eye because he got too greedy. There was the claim that gangsters only shot one another and always for business purposes. Each of these characters was honorable in the same way, say, as Billy the Kid or Ned Kelley or Robin Hood was honorable. They were outsiders who wished to gain their rightful place at the American table. Wasn't that how legitimate men like J. P. Morgan and William Randolph Hearst and Andrew Carnegie got to own huge corporations? It was true that other movies had undermined this "men of honor" *Godfather* mythology. *Goodfellas* and *Casino* made clear there was little integrity and plenty of duplicity among the pinkie-ring set. *Married to the Mob* and *The Gang That Couldn't Shoot Straight* made fun of these very serious Roman senators and their very serious business. But the image of Marlon Brando mumbling philosophies and applying corporate logic to determine who will live and who will die—this was the image of the Mafia that most people believed. This was the image of the gangster as proud antihero that most Americans believed was real.

This would soon change.

In *The Sopranos,* the protagonist is a fairly intelligent capo named Tony Soprano. He's in the mob because his father was in the mob, and he never wavers from the belief that "the life" is the only way to live. This was all very

Godfather-like. But Tony Soprano also has a wife who runs up credit-card bills, two children who evince all the signs of adolescent angst common to suburban progeny, and a group of gangsters around him who complain more than a bunch of old ladies in slippers playing mah-jongg. He lives in a very nice suburban home and writes down on his tax forms that he is in the waste-disposal industry. He begins seeing a psychiatrist after having a nervous breakdown. He never sits in a darkened room in a tuxedo allowing real working people to kiss his ring and beg favors. He never uses fish to communicate a message. Opera he disdains. He listens to Steely Dan.

The Sopranos, its creator, David Chase claimed, was going to show these people to be just what they were— people. They had families, they had back problems, their hair was thinning, their cars broke down. Yes, they killed one another for business purposes, but sometimes they did it for spite, or because of ineptitude. This was to be the real Mafia, every Sunday night.

Don Vito Corleone would have had a stroke.

The similarities between the real world and the TV world were mostly predictable. Many of the themes and schemes portrayed on *The Sopranos* were based on the Big Four of well-known Mafia activities: murder, extortion, loan sharking, and gambling. In real life and on TV, the mob loaned out money at exorbitant interest rates, then beat their customers with baseball bats if they were slow to pay. They took over businesses by becoming secret partners with entrepreneurs who got in over their heads. They ran high-stakes, all-night poker games for legitimate businessmen. They paid off corrupt cops. They headed to Fort Lauderdale or, better yet, Sicily when word leaked that the FBI was about to show up with arrest warrants in hand. They routinely killed informants, who were inevitably referred to by the all-purpose epithet *rats*. They set up "pump and dump" schemes on Wall Street and beat on brokers who refused to hype bogus stock. They were imaginative with the use of the word *fuck*. All of this predictable stuff that was found in hundreds of mob investigations that had been written about and played out on TV ad ridiculum found its way into *The Sopranos*.

Some of the TV plots seemed to have been lifted straight from the headlines. Take Junior Gotti, for instance. In January 1998, John A. (Junior) Gotti, the son of Gambino crime boss, John Gotti, was indicted in New York on racketeering charges that included his alleged involvement in something known as a phone-card scam. In this version of how to steal from your fellowman, the mob set themselves up as distributors of phone cards by buying millions of dollars of credit from a big phone company. They then sold thousands of bogus cards, refused to pay the company for the credit, and went out of business. The company would then cut off the phone cards, leaving thousands of clueless callers hearing only dial tone. Gotti's phone card was very patriotic. It featured a photo of the Statue of Liberty and could be purchased in poor neighborhoods throughout New York. His name, needless to say, was not included on either the back or front. At the time Gotti was indicted, this was the first time the mob had been implicated in this type of phone-card scam.

Somehow, *The Sopranos* managed to mention this same phone-card scam a year later in a midseason episode.

This occurred again and again. In the case with the phone cards, Gotti was also charged with another new Mafia scheme that had never been revealed before. In New York City, groups of black and Latino construction workers would descend upon white-controlled construction sites and demand jobs. Sometimes they did this by smashing equipment and beating up workers with iron pipes. These so-called coalitions had operated for years, and no one was quite sure how they were allowed to operate in an industry that was allegedly controlled by the mob. The answer, it turned out, was simple—some of the coalitions were also controlled by the mob. In the January 1998 indictment, prosecutors alleged that members of Gotti's crime family had for years secretly paid the coalitions to show up and make threats. The good-hearted gangsters would then step in and and tell the harassed construction-company executive the problem could be "fixed" for a fee, usually substantial. The contractor would pay this protection money and hope for the best, unaware that the gangster would then dole out some of this fee to the coalition leader as payoff for a job well done. That this extremely cynical scam was run by the mob was not known to the general public at all until January 1998—just months before *The Sopranos* episode in which Tony Soprano does the very same thing to a make-believe construction company called Massarone Construction.

It happened again with airline tickets. In November 1999, prosecutors in Atlanta unsealed a racketeering indictment against one of Junior Gotti's associates, a New York businessman named Steven E. Kaplan. Among the many charges, Kaplan was accused of corrupting two Delta Airlines employees by "comping" them at his Atlanta strip club in exchange for dozens of reduced-fare airline tickets. This was the first time prosecutors had charged the Mafia with systematically stealing airline tickets. Coincidentally, *The Sopranos* included the same scheme in a show that was filmed months before these charges were made public.

And then it occurred with Magnetic Resonance Imaging (MRI). In the summer of 2000, the FBI raided a South

Carolina doctor's office and carted away boxes of documents. They were looking into what they believed was the
Mafia's newest scheme. An associate of the Gambino
crime family had set up a company that leased out MRI
equipment. A South Carolina doctor, they were told, got
kickbacks to recommend expensive MRI testing to pa-
tients who didn't really need it. In some cases, they were
told, he'd gone so far as to recommend MRI tests for pa-
tients who did not exist. The doctor then referred the pa-
tients to a company in the Bronx. This company, which
was secretly controlled by a reputed gangster, leased out
MRI equipment. The company would run the patient
through the MRI machine, then submit the bill directly to
the insurer. In this way the MRI company was able to
pocket millions of dollars in insurance fees for care that
was either completely unnecessary or nonexistent.

This new scam had found its way into the Mafia
grapevine shortly before *The Sopranos* went into production and was not revealed to the public until the middle of
the year 2000. The entire scam was mentioned on the
episode of the show that had been wrapped up long before
the public knew anything about the Mafia's alleged involvement in the highly profitable business of MRIs.

In many instances, the activity depicted on television
was remarkably similar to the activity of the real-life
Mafia, activity no member of the public had ever been
privy to. And nowhere were these similarities more obvious than in New Jersey's only homegrown version of La
Cosa Nostra—the DeCavalcante crime family.

Many had whispered about the DeCavalcantes' alleged
connection to the silver screen. It was said that Don Vito
Corleone of *The Godfather* was modeled on Sam the
Plumber DeCavalcante. But many questioned such a connection. Who could imagine a guy offering up unforget-

table philosophical bons mots while sitting in a beat-up heating, ventilation, and air-conditioning office in industrial New Jersey? Whether Mario Puzo took Sam the Plumber into consideration while writing his novel will never be known because Puzo always maintained that he made the whole thing up. No matter. With *The Sopranos,* though, the connection with the DeCavalcante name was obvious.

Events and circumstances that occurred in real life but had not yet been made public made their way into the scripts of *The Sopranos.* Some were innocuous. Most of the names on the show, for instance, came straight out of your average Mafia Yellow Pages—Johnny Boy and Uncle Junior and Philly and Patsy and Richie. One was very unusual—Big Pussy Bonpensiero. No other family had a Pussy, Big or Little, save the DeCavalcante crime family. His name was Anthony (Little Pussy) Russo, a guy who once bragged to an acquaintance about the time he stuffed a murder victim inside a furnace.

Both the TV family and the real family suffered from a persistent inferiority complex caused by the repeated ridicule of the New York crime families, who referred to them as "farmers."

The TV family and the New Jersey family both had bosses in prison who'd designated others to run their operations. At the start of *The Sopranos,* a guy named Giacomo Aprile, known to friends and family as Jackie, is acting boss and slowly dying of stomach cancer. Jackie Aprile's slow death creates a leadership vacuum that threatens to turn deadly. In the DeCavalcante family, the acting boss was a guy named Giaciano Amari, known to friends and family as Jake. Jake Amari was slowly dying of stomach cancer, and his impending demise was creating a leadership vacuum that threatened to turn deadly. This was a fact known only to members of the DeCavalcante crime family and law enforcement on both sides of the Hudson who made it their business to know such things.

One of those agents theorized that the writers of the show were communicating with real members of the De-Cavalcante crime family. "They've got to have somebody over there," said the agent, who did not want his name used as he pointed out other coincidences.

In the TV family, Tony Soprano ends up with a secret ownership interest in a hotel owned by Hasidic Jews. Inside the hotel, Tony runs a high-stakes poker game that goes all day and all night. In the DeCavalcante crime family, a real-life associate ran a high-stakes poker game out of a community center operated by Hasidic Jews.

On the TV show, Tony Soprano the acting boss promoted to capo one veteran soldier named Paulie Walnuts over another named Big Pussy, inspiring in Big Pussy jealousy and resentment. In the DeCavalcante family, Vincent Palermo the acting boss promoted one veteran soldier named Uncle Joe Giacobbe over another named Joey (Tin Ear) Sclafani, prompting scorn and derision in Sclafani.

On TV, the resentful soldier, Big Pussy, is secretly charged with a crime that can put him away for a decade. The FBI then offers to let him walk away with only minimal jail time if he agrees to cooperate and wears a secret device to record inculpatory statements of old friends. In the DeCavalcante crime family, a longtime associate named Ralphie Guarino was arrested on charges that could put him away for a decade. He agreed to wear a wire for the FBI and began recording the conversations of his friends within the DeCavalcante crime family.

On the TV show, the gangsters hang out at a New Jersey strip club called the Bada Bing; in real life, the De-Cavalcante crime family hung out at a strip club in Queens called Wiggles. To make things even stranger, when the makers of *The Sopranos* went looking for an authentic Mafia-owned strip club, they must have possessed special Mafia radar. The actual club on a busy thoroughfare in Lodi, New Jersey, where the show was filmed had once been known as Satin Dolls. According to the State of New Jersey's Commission of Investigation, Satin Dolls was for years secretly controlled by Vincent Ravo, an associate of the Genovese crime family. Ravo, it should be noted, also secretly owned another bar down the road in Garfield, New Jersey, by the highly imaginative name of Goodfellas. One of his front men in that venture was one Daniel Conte, who had a small role as a mob associate in the movie *Goodfellas* and claimed to be a close friend of Joe Pesci.

As the hype started to build in 1998 for the premiere of the show, its creator, David Chase, insisted *The Sopranos* would be anything but predictable. This was a tricky task. Although *The Sopranos* would be realistic, he claimed, it would never be about real people. In an Internet interview published by HBO to help explain how the show was put together, Chase was asked how he managed to accurately portray the lifestyles of the Mafia in his series.

"We try to write about human behavior with all its warts and glories, and we do our research," he replied. "And having grown up in New Jersey helps."

"Are the Sopranos based on a specific person or group of people or just purely invention?" Chase was asked. "Purely invention," was his terse electronic reply.

Not long after Chase gave that answer, a group of FBI agents with surveillance cameras sat freezing off their cannolis inside a van parked on Mulberry Street in New York City's Little Italy. This was shortly before Christmas and the van was bathed in the electric red-and-green glow of the thousands of festive lights that emerge from their hiding places each holiday season in Little Italy. It was parked across from one Mafia social club and three blocks away from John Gotti's former hangout, the Ravenite. Across the narrow street the agents kept an eye on a low-key popular restaurant known as Il Cortile. Inside the exposed-brick-walled classic Italian eatery was focaccia "Puddhica" con Brie for $7.50, lobster ravioli for $25, and a well-attended Christmas party thrown by the Colombo crime family.

The FBI agents—who had not been invited—were interested in the comings and goings of the party's hosts, James (Jimmy Green Eyes) Clemenza, a reputed Colombo capo, and his brother, Jerry, a reputed family soldier. At some point they recognized the two men making their way down Mulberry and into Il Cortile. A few minutes later they got a little surprise. There were two other men—a Frigidaire-size guy with a full head of black curly hair and a smaller but extremely compact guy with a pompadour gone silver at the temples.

Here were mob soldiers Big Pussy and his pal, Paulie Walnuts. Actually it was Vincent Pastore, an actor who played the gangster named Big Pussy, and Tony Sirico, an actor who played the gangster named Paulie Walnuts on *The Sopranos*.

But there was more. Another guy ambled by who was a little tougher to recognize but still within reach for anybody who'd watched movies during the 1970s. It was James Caan, the actor who became famous after playing the volatile Sonny Corleone in *The Godfather,* wandering down Mulberry. He was a guest at the Colombo crime family's Christmas party, too.

At the time it was a significant moment—a vanful of government workers had just made a documentary record of art mimicking life. There now existed a videotape that featured both real live gangsters and real live pretend gangsters, all hanging around the same restaurant around Christmas. It was significant—if not surprising. That's because all three actors—Pastore, Sirico, and Caan—had long known reputed members and associates of organized crime.

For years Pastore had been friends with Danny Provenzano, the grand-nephew of the late Anthony (Tony Pro) Provenzano, a mob-connected Teamsters official who was long suspected in the death of Jimmy Hoffa. Danny Provenzano was also a moviemaker of sorts, hiring Pastore to play gangster-type roles in films with names like *This Thing of Ours*. Pastore would one day show up at a New Jersey courtroom to show support for Provenzano, who at the time would be indicted on charges of using beatings and kidnappings to extort money from more than a dozen men he referred to as "business associates." "I don't know him as a gangster, I know him as a filmmaker," Pastore told the Associated Press after the court hearing.

Caan, who also had a small role in Provenzano's *This Thing of Ours* (English for *la cosa nostra*), long had been associated with a top Colombo family guy named Andrew Russo.

Sirico was in a class by himself.

During the 1970s, he had affected a gangster style that included wearing white suits and getting arrested repeatedly on charges of threatening to do bad things to disco owners if they didn't hand him envelopes stuffed with cash. By 1999, of course, those days were long gone. Sirico was now a respected actor who'd worked in dozens of films, winning praise from the likes of Woody Allen and, of course, David Chase, the creator of *The Sopranos*.

In particular, Sirico was credited for his unusually vivid portrayal of gangsters.

After news of the Colombo Christmas party leaked out, Sirico admitted that he had known the Clemenza brothers forever. "I know them, I know everybody. I've been around." He admitted he had eaten at Il Cortile "maybe five times" in the past few years, often with Pastore. He did not, however, recall the details. There may have been a Christmas party, and then again, maybe not. "I have been to so many dinners and parties and charities, I have no idea," Sirico said, before launching into his shtick about how the things he did way back are things he'd rather forget now and would certainly never repeat.

"I don't want to be mixed up with a lot of bad guys," he said. "All that tough guy stuff went out the window years ago. If I was at a place where there were mob guys, I'm sorry to hear it. I'm sorry for me . . . If I was there, I wasn't hanging out with nobody. I haven't seen these guys in a hundred years. I haven't seen this kid Jerry [Clemenza] in a thousand years."

And clearly he *had* changed. Here was a guy who had been fingerprinted more than once worrying now about a file somewhere deep inside the FBI. "I hope they don't have my name on a list," he said. "I'm an actor. I hope they know that."

But it was easy to get confused. There would be times when these guys would come up to him on the street and make, for lack of a better term, suggestions. These were guys Sirico recognized as being "in the life," as he might have once put it. "I've had guys come up to me, I don't want to tell you," he said. "They say I should have been a little harder in some scene. I don't know what to tell them. What do you say? I mean, what can you say?"

9

GOODFELLAS EXPLAINS IT WELL

When Carmine Sessa was a kid growing up in Brooklyn, he started his climb up the Mafia ladder by shining shoes in clubs and bars in his neighborhood. That was how it all started. It was just like being an aspiring actor waiting tables in a Manhattan restaurant frequented by Broadway casting agents. You were there to be seen. Perhaps you would get lucky. Except instead of casting agents, you had people who made a living by getting over on others, determined never to work a legitimate day in their lives. "That's how I'm meeting these people," he says.

Carmine signed up for the program.

"Eventually I started stealings things and selling them for these people. I also started working in card games and getting to know more people. They got to know me as a good kid, a thief, a tough kid, a stand-up kid. From there the crimes started escalating eventually to murder and seemed never to stop."

He became associated with a well-known gangster from Gravesend named Greg Scarpa Sr. Scarpa was one of the scariest, most devious gangsters the Colombo family or any other family had ever seen. He killed for fun. Then he talked about it, again and again.

Young Mafia wannabe Carmine would spend hours hanging around Scarpa's social club, the Wimpy Boys' Club, scheming and dreaming of being a made man. He was there the time the poodle walked up with the ear in its mouth.

At first Carmine had no idea what was in the little dog's mouth, but then he realized. It made sense, in a way. He and Scarpa had just killed the girlfriend of a mobster who was suspected of being an informant. The girlfriend, it was thought, would also be able to provide the federal government with information that Greg Scarpa and his protégé, Carmine, might not want them to have. So they had shot her in the face inside the Wimpy Boys' Club, not realizing that the blast had blown off her ear. They proceded to cut the girlfriend into small pieces and dispose of the parts. They thought they'd done a great job cleaning up. They missed the ear, which must have fallen down behind a couch. The poodle had found it.

This was the life Carmine chose. He rose all the way to consigliere, committing murders when he was told to. It didn't matter who it was or why. It was part of the job. "I saw friends get killed," he said. "One day you are a friend and the next day somebody said he's got to go, for whatever reason, and sometimes you are a part of it or even have to pull the trigger. You find yourself telling the families, 'We don't know what happened but we're going to find out.' And they believe you."

In the early 1990s, there was a disagreement within the Colombo crime family over who was in charge. The boss of the family, Carmine Persico, who was nicknamed "the Snake" by other gangsters because even they found him to be unusually duplicitous, was in jail for a thousand years. He anointed a loyal minion named Victor Orena as the acting boss to handle matters on the street, but he secretly very much wanted his son, Allie Boy, to step into the CEO suite as soon as Allie got out of jail. When Victor Orena finally realized this, all hell broke loose.

There were shootings on the streets of Brooklyn. Twelve people died, mostly gangsters, but also an innocent nineteen-year-old kid who had the bad luck to be working in a bagel store owned by a gangster. Carmine Sessa participated in this gunfighting, as he was instructed to do. Greg Scarpa Sr. also participated, with enthusiasm and even relish. He shot a guy putting up his Christmas lights. He shot a guy lying on his driveway who said, "What did I do?" He shot a guy sitting in his car, blowing off half his skull. Scarpa would have continued shooting, but he was arrested. Carmine Sessa the protégé somehow managed to get out of town.

For more than a year he remained a fugitive, one of the most wanted on the New York FBI's list. Then he suddenly was arrested outside St. Patrick's Cathedral in Manhattan. Within a week he was cooperating with the FBI and the United States attorney in Brooklyn. Facing the possibility of spending the rest of his life in prison, he had a change of heart about "this thing of ours" called La Cosa Nostra.

"The movie *Goodfellas* explains it well," Sessa said. "Meaning, everybody gets killed by a bunch of animals or so-called friends. This thing I thought I respected so much as a young man had no respect at all, but it did have plenty of disrespect. All the families hate each other and within the families they hate one another. It is a disease that keeps growing and spreading. You cut off the head and a new one grows. You cut off an arm and it grows a new one. To me, the more I wanted to be left out . . . I was pulled in and appointed to a position of consigliere, a position I didn't want. I was looking to keep far away and asked them not to give it to me, but to no avail."

These things he told the judge on the day he was sentenced. He had served seven years in jail and participated in four murders. He had testified in several trials and looked across the courtroom at many of his "so-called friends" and pronounced them murderers and thieves. The government told the judge he was an excellent informant. Now he stood alone in a government courtroom in the town in which he had grown up, and he was letting the world know that the real Mafia wasn't like the movie Mafia at all.

"I hate everything about the life I led," he told the judge in a nearly empty courtroom. "I hope that it ends sometime soon, because it keeps destroying families and young kids who are infatuated with it and can't wait to be a goodfella. I wish I could tell them what it really is and not what they think it is. I don't like what I'm doing putting people in jail. But I don't want this thing to keep growing. I accept responsibility for my crimes and blame no one else—not my associates, not my environment, just me. Thank you, Your Honor."

The judge looked down from his bench and made remarks about how unusual it was to hear such candid expression from a member of organized crime, and then he pronounced sentence: time served. And then Carmine Sessa walked out of court, a new man with a new name, a new social-security number, even a new birth certificate, leaving Brooklyn behind.

May 29, 1998

Every business has a hatchet man. He is paid to be the in-house son of a bitch. He yells at people in front of their colleagues, he relocates them to small windowless offices, he questions their manhood. The hatchet man is an important corporate tool, necessary to maintain order in the chaos of capitalism. In the DeCavalcante crime family, one of the hatchet men's names was Anthony Capo. On this spring Friday evening, Ralphie Guarino was driving through New York traffic on his way to pick up the hatchet man himself.

"I'm going to get Anthony, it's four forty-five, going to the Yankees game, it's a Friday night," he said into the hidden recording device rigged to the inside of his car. "Gonna go to Wiggles to pick up Joey O." He yawned. The radio played. The FBI agent listening in wrote all of this down.

Grinding through the Friday rush hour, Ralphie picked up Anthony in Brooklyn and drove toward Queens Boulevard and Wiggles. Capo was a big pale young man with reddish hair and a look of contempt that never left his wide face. He was a soldier in the DeCavalcante family and the only evidence in public that he paid little attention to the law was his 1985 conviction on charges of performing the job of enforcer for a loan shark named Vincent Rotondo. He was known as a Wild West kind of guy who loved to golf. He was always talking about his game and about giving people a good beating. He sometimes used the same implements for both. On this night he was complaining about the weather. It was headed for summer, but there would be a chill breeze passing through Yankee Stadium.

"I didn't think it was going to get cold like this," Capo said.

"Yeah," Ralphie said, "I was gonna wear a sweater, too."

"My hands are so dry. I haven't been out all week . . . I gotta go to the manicurist tomorrow."

"Best stuff in the world," Ralphie said, sparking up a cigar.

Anthony joined him and soon the car was filled with smoke and complaints. Anthony loved to complain. On this spring evening he dredged up one of his favorite gripes—his boss, a captain named Anthony Rotondo. Rotondo was the son of Vincent Rotondo, the loan shark for whom Anthony Capo had once worked collecting money. Vincent Rotondo, whom everyone called Jimmy for reasons that were never quite clear, was a respected Mafia figure. He lived in a huge house in Bergen Beach, Brooklyn, and made a lot of money for the DeCavalcante family looting a longshoremen's union local for twenty-four years. He had been shot to death as he sat at the wheel of his 1988 Lincoln, which was parked curbside in front of his house. The police revealed that he had just come from a fish store. Beside him on the seat of the car was a container of squid. Jimmy Rotondo was a legend. His only son, Anthony, was anything but.

Anthony Rotondo was known for disappearing when it was time to do the dirty work but showing up when the money was counted. Because Anthony Capo had worked for the legendary Jimmy Rotondo, he was now assigned to work with the less-than-legendary son. Respect, it could be said, was an issue.

"If we got a problem, he has to go home," Capo said about his boss. He then told Ralphie the story of how Anthony Rotondo went home.

"We went to work on a guy," Anthony Capo was explaining to Ralphie. He said "the guy," and he never named

him, came into Capo's bar in Staten Island near the
Verrazano-Narrows Bridge. It was called the Narrows Tav-
ern. The guy demanded payment. Anthony Capo responded by going to the guy's house with a friend named
Victor, whom he described as a bodybuilder.

"I handled myself pretty well. I pat myself on the back.
I hit him good. He gets up and goes, 'I got our number and
your number,'" Capo said. "He didn't die, he didn't die. I
beat him, I cut him, I chopped him up so bad, then I stick
him in the car. I called his brother. I said, 'Here, here he is.'
He said, 'Where's my brother?' I said, 'Your brother's
under the car.' He said, 'Who did this to him?' I said, 'I did
this to him. This is why . . . ba, ba, ba.'"

After Anthony Capo delivered his message to the guy's
brother, he drove to see his capo, Anthony Rotondo, to ask
him for help disposing of the body in the trunk of his car.
The way Capo saw it, Rotondo was a guy who could easily order a murder but would not be willing to assist in carrying out the job. Anthony Capo told Ralphie that his boss
was not interested in helping to do what had to be done.
His capo, Rotondo, had better things to do than bury a
body.

"He said 'I promised my kids.' He said, 'I have problems with a toy. I gotta take it back to Toys "Я" Us.' I said,
'We got a problem. This kid's in the trunk.' Now, I don't
want to throw rocks at the guy, but he's just not my type.
That's why this stays here in the car with me and you."

"Of course. I stand up with all these guys," said Ralphie
as an FBI agent somewhere scribbled furiously.

These were the kinds of stories Anthony Capo loved to
tell, in between talking about golf. He could spend hours
talking about his game. But discussing "going to work on
a guy" really seemed to float his boat. At the time of this
chat on the way to Yankee Stadium, Anthony Capo talked

like this to everyone without fear. The hatchet man was well aware that people were afraid of him. He was practically proud of his extremely short temper. He was happy there were many stories about him. He was involved in this hit, he was involved in that hit. No one was quite sure what to believe, and Anthony Capo liked it that way. Mostly people stayed away from him. In one story, Anthony Capo went to a wedding in Staten Island with a woman who was wearing an extremely revealing dress. The woman began to drink and flirt with several members of the wedding party. Anthony Capo became enraged and threatened to kill one of the recipients of this drunken woman's sloppy affections. One of the man's friends intervened, telling Anthony Capo it wasn't the guy's fault, the woman was hitting on him. This did not amuse Anthony Capo. He made his intentions perfectly clear.

"I will kill you and they will never find your body," he said to the man, who then had to leave the wedding and go into hiding for several weeks.

"There was something very wrong about that guy," said the man. "He was disturbed."

In the spring of 1998, when the boss of the family, John Riggi, was thinking about setting up a panel to run things, no one knew what to do with Anthony. Vincent Palermo was to be promoted from capo to one of three men on the ruling panel, so he would have to reassign all the members of his crew to other captains. "No one wants Anthony," Palermo told his driver, Joey O. "I gotta keep him with me and that's not allowed. I don't know what the fuck to do with Anthony."

Yet Anthony remained. And Vinny was giving him big assignments, such as the order to go out and kill Charles Majuri, another member of the ruling panel. Some wondered why. If everybody hated this Anthony, why was he always around Vinny Ocean? The answer to that question was simple.

Anthony Capo knew something about Vinny Ocean that inspired in Vinny an intense loyalty.

Around 7:30 on the morning of September 11, 1989, three big American sedans with stolen license plates cruised softly through the awakening streets of Staten Island. This was the one New York City borough that had no subway, and most of the people who lived there wouldn't get on a subway car anyway, so even at this hour the streets were filled with the one tool essential for life on Staten Island—the automobile. Even though it was early, the three cars fit right in as they cruised past the huge Staten Island Mall and turned onto Richmond Hill Road. They climbed the hill past one condominium development after another, jammed up next to one another like boxes of shoes on a shelf. This was a neighborhood that desperately wanted to be suburban but somehow could not escape its urbanity. Here one found lawns green as a golf course next to abandoned trucks covered with graffiti. The three sedans turned right onto a dead-end street called Wellington Court, the type of Anglophile name commonly applied to low-rent condos. The sedans drove past a series of complexes dense as tenements, but with nice landscaping. One sedan parked curbside almost immediately at the entrance to Wellington Court. This was the crash car. If the police arrived, the crash car would pull out in front of the cop and cause an accident.

The two other sedans continued until they passed 121 Wellington, a four-story redbrick affair with a glass-brick-and-black-marble entrance that looked like it was built in 1970. It was clearly a place that wanted to be something it could not ever be. They pulled to the end of the road, which emptied into acres of tangled woods pocked with abandoned cars and laced with dirt paths where teenagers went to smoke and drink. On Wellington Court, there was only one way out—past the sedans filled with men.

The sedans turned around to face the way back out and edged close to 121 Wellington. Inside the car closest to 121, Anthony Capo sat at the wheel. It was his wife's car, but he had switched the plates. In the car with him were Jimmy Gallo and Vincent Palermo. Both were making sure the guns they held in their hands were fully loaded and that the safeties were off.

They waited.

At a few minutes past 8:30 A.M., a middle-aged man with a silver pompadour and a rumpled businessman's suit emerged from 121. He had a briefcase in his hand. He was a real-estate developer of questionable reputation named Fred Weiss. He had just spent the night at the condo apartment he shared with his girlfriend. He walked toward his two-year-old dark green four-wheel-drive Jeep parked curbside. He got out his keys.

At that time Fred Weiss was known as a marginally sophisticated hustler who lived at the edge of legitimacy. For a while he worked as city editor of the *Staten Island Advance,* where he was viewed as an up-and-coming hustler who seemed to know everybody on the island. But he wanted to be rich, so he soon gave up the journalistic calling to enter the slightly more mercenary world of Staten Island real estate. "Freddy was the kind of guy who wanted to be a wheeler-dealer," said one of his former newspaper colleagues, "but he wasn't very good at it."

One of the things he wasn't very good at was picking business partners. Weiss hooked up with two men connected to the Gambino crime family, Angelo Paccione and Anthony Vulpis. Calling on all their powers of creativity, they cleverly named their companies W&W Inc. and A&A Land Development. They bought up property by abandoned railway yards in a working-class neighborhood in the Arlington section of Staten Island. At first the neighbors did not complain about the handful of trucks that were rolling in and out of the property late at night. But soon the handful became a midnight convoy. Then the neighbors began noticing rats scurrying about in the woods next to the property. Finally they and their children began to suffer allergic reactions, itchy eyes, rashes they'd never seen before. They complained to everyone they could think of: city councilmen, congressmen, the FBI. An investigation followed, and soon the world knew what the neighbors of Arlington had long suspected—the developers had turned the empty lot near the railyard into one of the biggest illegal dumps in New York City. And it wasn't just any dump. They'd arranged to dump thousands of tons of infectious red-bag medical waste, including, investigators said, human body parts from area hospitals. They had created their very own thirty-five-foot pit of bubbling sewage. The neighbors were furious that the FBI knew this was going on for months before they announced indictments and shut the place down.

In June 1989, Weiss was one of those charged with dozens of crimes that would put him in jail for decades. Weiss was not viewed as a "street guy" who could take this kind of time behind bars. He was viewed as soft. He told his friends he had "nothing to worry about." The then boss of the Gambino family, John Gotti—a man who once declared he would personally sever the head of a gangster who'd shown disrespect to him—thought otherwise.

Weiss knew many things about the Gambino crime family that Gotti wished to keep from the public. Gotti reasoned that Weiss would therefore transform himself from

Weiss the mediocre real-estate developer into Weiss the enthusiastic government informant. He ordered that Weiss be murdered as soon as possible. Because Weiss was a De-Cavalcante associate, the job was theirs to complete.

The DeCavalcante boss, John Riggi, saw this as a positive development. He summoned Vinny Ocean and told him that John Gotti wanted a favor, something big that would put the DeCavalcante crime family "back on the map." Riggi—who'd done well in organized crime by saying little of substance—did not tell Vinny to kill Fred Weiss. Instead he carefully insulated himself from possible future prosecution by doing what any good manager would do—he delegated a subordinate, Anthony Rotondo, to handle the details.

Rotondo told Vinny Ocean that Fred Weiss had to be killed as a favor to John Gotti and specifically told Vinny Ocean that he was to be one of the shooters. This was a big moment for Vinny Ocean—perhaps the biggest moment in his entire mob life. After nearly twenty-five years as a made man, Vinnie was now being ordered to participate in an act the boss of the family believed would put the De-Cavalcante crime family "back on the map." If the job went as planned, his status as a star within the family would be assured forever.

Vinny was given a gun. He was told that Weiss would be lured to another man's home, where Vinny Ocean and Anthony Rotondo would be waiting. Vinny and Anthony showed up at the house to learn that Weiss could not be located.

They went to Plan B.

They knew Weiss had separated from his wife and had for the last few weeks been living with his girlfriend at the condo behind the mall. Vinny Ocean organized three teams—a hit squad, a car filled with backup shooters, and the crash car that could block the way in case police showed up. As it happened, Vinny Ocean and Jimmy Gallo sat in the hit-squad car, designated hitters at 8:30 in the morning.

In the chilly morning light, Weiss apparently did not notice the two sedans filled with men until he was behind the wheel of his Jeep. By then it was too late. Jimmy Gallo and Vinny Palermo exited Capo's wife's car with pistols in hand. Both men fired repeatedly at Weiss, who swung open the sedan door and made a feeble attempt to flee. He fell facedown on the street. He was shot twice in the face and once in the arm. A witness later described Weiss lying on the cold pavement, his dark blue real-estate-developer suit soaked with his own blood. His expensive left shoe had fallen off and lay by the curb.

"The killers," wrote the *New York Times* the next day, "fled unseen."

Within a day of the Weiss hit, Vinny Ocean and Anthony Rotondo met with a capo in John Gotti's crime family to deliver the news. The Weiss matter, they said, was resolved. Weiss's death was seen as a real shot in the arm for the DeCavalcante family because the man who wanted it done, John Gotti, was now a satisfied customer. A potential informant was gone and nobody had been arrested. Those who participated in the killing attained a level of credibility unparalleled for "farmers" of their ilk.

The Weiss killing launched Vinny Ocean, made man, into the ranks of the big time.

It had a downside. In the days that followed, the participants began to understand fully that they would now be linked together in sin by the killing of the former city editor—forever.

Including Anthony Capo.

Vinny knew that Capo had seen what he, Vinny, had

done. In 1989, to the outside world, Vinny Ocean was a legitimate businessman whose only brush with the law involved shrimp theft nearly twenty years earlier. Vinny Ocean wasn't even listed on the intelligence databases of law enforcement that tried to keep track of who was in and who was out of the mob. A murder charge would bring down Vinny Ocean for good. Vinny Ocean knew this; Anthony Capo knew this. Each had much to fear from the other, and they had a good reason for their fear.

Within weeks of the Weiss killing, one of the men in the crash car during the Weiss hit began to act funny. His name was Joseph Garafano. He expressed nervousness about being found out. Again and again he expressed this nervousness. A little nervousness is okay. A lot is not. This inspired other participants in the Weiss hit to worry that Garafano might decide to cooperate with law enforcement to save his own skin. As a result, it was decided that Joseph Garafano had to go. A soldier named Victor DiChiara convinced Garafano to come to his house. There, he told Garafano not to be so nervous, that he was going to be given money in the morning and sent off to Florida to lie low until the police forgot about their interest in the murder of the real-estate guy Weiss. Garafano's birthday was September 21, only a few days away, and he apparently decided that everything was going to be all right. He stayed at DiChiara's house that autumn night, and in the morning DiChiara drove to a prearranged drop-off spot. There Garafano got out of DiChiara's car and into another car with Anthony Rotondo and other members of the DeCavalcante crime family. That was the last anyone saw of Joseph Garafano.

Vinny Ocean and Anthony Capo knew all about Joseph Garafano and the unseverable bond they now had with each other because of their participation in the end of Fred Weiss.

In the fall of 1991, Vinny Ocean knew Anthony Capo was a guy who did not panic when the bullets started flying, and that he could therefore rely on Anthony the golfer to carry out another important job. More often than not, the jobs the Mafia needed done involved making a problem go away. In this case, the problem was one of the biggest ever for the family. The problem was the acting boss.

In 1991, the boss of the family, John Riggi, was in jail. He had thoughtfully appointed a man he trusted to run things from the street as acting boss. The man's name was John D'Amato. There was a problem. Practically nobody liked the man, and nearly everyone agreed that Riggi had become interested primarily in John D'Amato at the expense of the DeCavalcante crime family. To make things worse, John D'Amato was infuriating the other New York families. He was borrowing money from the Gambinos and the Colombos, and he was not paying it back. At the same time he was out partying, spending freely, making it seem as if it was okay for him to spend other people's money and never pay it back. Perhaps worst of all, John D'Amato was reinforcing the image of the DeCavalcante family as a bunch of amateur farmers.

Vinny Palermo and the rest of the DeCavalcante hierarchy decided it was time for John D'Amato to go.

On November 11, 1991, the FBI announced it had recruited a new Mafia informant named Salvatore Gravano, the underboss of the Gambino family. At the time Sammy Bull Gravano was not a household name. He was just a guy who was always seen on the street with John Gotti. Now he was front-page news. The FBI made it clear Sammy Bull was telling them a lot of things they had never

known before. Gangsters across New York and New Jersey—
including John D'Amato—began popping Tums.

John D'Amato had been involved in business with
Sammy Bull, so he figured it was only a matter of time before the FBI showed up at his door. He decided this was an
unpleasant image, and so he hit the road for Florida to stay
out of sight until the Gravano hurricane subsided. While
D'Amato was in Florida, his peers plotted his death in
New York. Shortly before Thanksgiving, 1991, D'Amato
suddenly showed up again in New York. Palermo and the
reluctant capo, Anthony Rotondo, summoned two men to
Rotondo's office—Victor DiChiara and Anthony Capo.

During the meeting, DiChiara and Capo were ordered
to kill D'Amato that very day. In the discussion, the other
captains present—including Vinny Ocean—were willing
to give the order themselves. They were not shy about becoming participants in this particular murder. One of the
captains, however, was not quite as willing. Anthony Rotondo just sat there in silence, not saying one way or the
other whether he wanted the job done. Anthony Capo—
who'd been assigned to Rotondo, but did not respect
him—was not happy about this. He then made it clear that
anyone who asked him to go out and kill somebody would
have to become part of the crime—a coconspirator. This
was insurance. Rotondo, Capo felt, was trying to protect
himself from implication by keeping his mouth shut.

"You're my skipper," Capo finally said to Rotondo. "If
you want me to do this, tell me to do it and it will be done."

Rotondo then reluctantly told him to shoot and kill
D'Amato. In his usual unsubtle manner, Capo had succeeded in making Rotondo an accomplice. And he had
done it right in front of Vinny Ocean. With Anthony Capo,
you were in for it all or you were not to be trusted.

That day Capo was given a gun. He and DiChiara

picked up D'Amato in a sedan at a prearranged spot and drove him to a garage in Brooklyn, There D'Amato was shot in the head. Capo and DiChiara then drove back to Rotondo's office, cruising slowly by and signaling out the window that D'Amato was dead in the trunk of the car. They all met at the nearby home of another capo, where Rotondo helped clean up the car and wrap the body for disposal. Capo asked Rotondo to help get rid of D'Amato's body. Rotondo demurred, although this time it wasn't to return a toy to Toys "Я" Us. This time, he had to go back home and see his wife.

Anthony Capo smoked his cigar on the ride to Queens with Ralphie, expressing his philosophy of survival. He talked openly about "the life" and how he hated "rats" and he complained that his home telephone was tapped and that he couldn't get life insurance because the FBI was always following him. Then he was complaining about another soldier named Vinny, who was owed a debt and was not doing much of anything to collect it, even after the debtor told him flat out he could not pay.

"Vinny said, 'What was I gonna do?' I said, 'Listen to me, did it bother you what he said?' He said, 'Yeah.' I said, 'Then you should do what youse got to do.' He said, 'Yeah?' I said, 'Vinny, you're telling me you didn't like what the guy said to you. If you don't like that guy's shirt, and you tell him to take it off, and he wears it the next day, what are you gonna do? Rip it off his fucking back, right?' "

"Well, you know what?" Ralphie said. "There's an old saying. I grew up in the street. There's an old saying—"

"Put up," Anthony Capo said, "or shut up."

They picked up Joey O at Wiggles. He drove, Anthony got in the backseat; Ralphie stayed in front. The car was bugged but Ralphie was not. That meant the FBI could not hear anything that was said during the entire Yankee–Red Sox game at Yankee Stadium. This turned out to be a long period of time because there was a rain delay of more than two hours. There were several hours of no sound. The FBI had no idea what Anthony was saying to Joey, or what Joey was saying to Ralphie, or what the announcer at Yankee Stadium said to the thousands of fans who braved the unusually chilly May night to watch the Yankees beat the Red Sox six to two.

What the FBI and Ralphie did not know at the time was that Joey O was an endangered species. He owed everyone in the universe a lot of money, and was no longer sure what to do about that. He had gone to his old friend Vinnie Ocean hoping for help. What he needed was for Vinnie— a guy everyone respected—to tell the rest of the Goodfella crowd that Joey O was okay and that, in the end, he would come up with a way to pay off his many debts. Vinnie had known Joey O for years, so surely he'd be a stand-up guy and get Joey out of the hell he found himself in.

That was the plan, anyway. It didn't work out. He went to Vinnie and begged and pleaded, and in the middle of the talk he made a big mistake. He said to Vinnie, "Don't worry, Vinnie, I won't tell anybody about Staten Island."

Those ten words made Vinnie stop his usual manner of listening to Joey O, which was to not really listen, and pay close attention. Vinnie knew well what Joey O meant by "Staten Island." He meant the Fred Weiss killing, the piece of work that made Vinnie a respected member of La Cosa Nostra but also a candidate for a murder prosecution. And here stood Joey O mentioning the unmentionable. It could only mean one thing—Joey O was thinking about becoming an informant.

In the coming weeks, Vinnie Ocean summoned Anthony Capo to a meeting away from his usual haunts. The two men sat down and Vinnie made his wishes known—he told Anthony to start doing "homework" on Joey O, his friend and constant companion. The guy who got Vinnie his coffee and picked up his blood pressure medicine. Vinnie kept the conversation general, but the message was clear. Joey O had to go.

10

June 25, 1998

Joey O was swapping Mafia gossip with Ralphie—who was in, who was out, all the stars in the DeCavalcante constellation—when he made a little joke. He said, "I wouldn't be surprised if I disappear." He made the little joke in such a way that it could be translated as not a little joke. He was beginning to see where he stood in the food chain.

Ralphie was not interested in Joey O's problems. He was trolling for probable cause. By the summer of 1998, just six months after Ralphie Guarino first began taping conversations for the bureau, the FBI had accumulated so much probable cause they were now thinking of doing something that had never been done before—indicting an entire crime family. They would do it in stages, but they would do it nonetheless. Vinny Palermo, the man viewed as most likely to succeed, was now well within the bureau's reach. And by now Ralphie was comfortable asking Joey O just about any question imaginable and Joey volunteered everything. He told Ralphie that Vinny Ocean had been officially promoted to the leadership committee, which meant he had to reassign all his crew members to different captains. He explained how one soldier had been promoted, how another had been passed over, and how nobody wanted a third. Joey even used nautical references.

"Everybody's gotta go to different skippers," Joey said. "Vinny's not supposed to have nobody under him. Nobody wants Anthony."

"What about us?" Ralphie asked.

"No, we're still together. No, anybody who's straightened out guys gotta go to different skippers."

"You mean the guy second-in-command can't have nobody under him?"

"Can't have nobody under him. Well, everybody's under him. But these guys only gotta answer to a captain first, then him."

"So you're gonna be with Joe now?" Ralphie asked.

"No, we're still with Vinny," Joey said. "No, it's not us. It's everybody. It has nothing to do with us."

He was talking as if everything was on track, but uncertainty permeated his every word. It had reached the point where no one knew what he was going to say or do next.

His life was a train wreck waiting to happen. He was living in Staten Island with two daughters from his first marriage, his second wife, Rosemary, and her mother. He now openly referred to his first wife as "the asshole" and his second as "the witch." His older daughter had come to him asking for money for sessions with a psychologist. He refused and told her to move out. He slapped her and she called the police. Then he thought better of it and decided that both daughters should move out. The FBI recorded him talking to a neighbor about his problems.

"I told [my ex-wife] the other fucking night, come and get your daughters," he said. "I can't take it no more."

"What'd she say?" the neighbor asked.

"She said, 'Oh, you gotta understand.' Understand what? You're living nice on a nice lake somewhere, and you left me this responsibility. I'm fifty years old. I can't fucking breathe, I'm dying over here."

He complained to everybody. In one June cell-phone conversation that the FBI carefully recorded, Joey O even complained about his daughter to his boss, Vinny Ocean.

"She came home, I didn't say nothing to her," Joey said. "She didn't say nothing to me."

Vinny the mob boss temporarily transformed himself into Vinny the parent, suggesting that Joey should let the daughter see the psychologist.

"I think you should go with her to talk to this—"

"Wednesday night," Joey O said. "She's got an appointment with this lady. I'm gonna go."

"You gotta go," Vinny said, dropping into his best "these kids today" mode. "I don't understand it. I don't know. I think I'm in another fucking country. Or world."

"Me, too," Joey said. "Me, too."

The agents heard everything. All about his problems having sex, about the debate he had whether or not to use Viagra. The recorded conversations between Joey and his girlfriend, the one whose breasts Joey felt needed improvement. She had asked him to buy her hydroponic marijuana and Ecstasy, and Joey had failed once again.

"You didn't get the hydra?" the girlfriend said.

"No," Joey sadly admitted.

"Or the Ecs?"

"No. Tonight."

"That's what I asked you for, baby."

"Baby, what do you want me to tell you?"

"Damn."

In August, Rosemary Masella threw all of Joey's clothes out onto the lawn. Rumors circulated that he tried to kill himself. He called up his girlfriend on the cell phone and claimed he'd gone out for milk at the corner store and gotten lost in Brooklyn. He said he was disoriented and had just hit a car. He ranted that he was going to kill his wife. His girlfriend begged him to pull over so somebody could come get him, but he refused. He blamed everything on the antidepressants he was taking, and hung up. A few days later he was hospitalized in Staten Island with chest pains, but released when the doctors found nothing wrong.

In one talk with Vinny Ocean, Joey O said, "I just don't give a shit anymore."

"When did you ever?" Vinny replied in disgust.

Ralphie was aware that Vinny was running out of patience with Joey. Vinny now referred to Joey simply as "the asshole," as in "Where's the asshole?" Ralphie tried to cool things down.

"He knows you're mad at him," Ralphie told Vinny the boss. "He don't know what to do. He'd rather kill himself."

"He's a fucking asshole."

"Kiss and make up."

"Yeah," Vinny said sarcastically, "I'll kiss."

In July, the FBI recorded Vinny Ocean practically foaming at the mouth about Joey O. "I listened to him and now I'm an asshole for listening to him," Vinny told an underling. "Even if Joey's half-right, it's a score. But in the meanwhile, I should've figured he's all wrong. He's never fucking right."

"Not one fucking story does he get straight. Nothing.

It's amazing. I can't deal with it no more. I'd rather not see him. I mean I'd fuck him. He's a fucking moron. A real fucking moron. He wants to gamble, ruin his fucking life. You never get even. You get worse."

"This is it. He's a fucking moron is what he is. He's a fucking lowlife. A cocksucker. That's what he is, this motherfucker. I told him, 'You got a lot of money and you take care of your wife and your kids.' "

Ralphie was assigned the task of keeping Joey O on track. Repeatedly he urged Joey to pay off his debts. He played the role of mediator, parent, and counselor, advising Joey that conflict with Vinny the boss was not such a good idea.

"I told you last week, I'll tell you again—don't challenge the man," Ralphie said.

"I don't even want to talk to him," Joey O said.

"That ain't the answer," Ralphie said. "You know why?"

"I can't deal with the man."

"You know what? Put your relationship on the back burner. Just deal with him like on a business level. He's the boss. Don't challenge him."

Ralphie even suggested that Joey O try to get "straightened out"—become a member of the DeCavalcante crime family. For years, Joey O had talked of getting "made." This would involve his swearing his allegiance to the De-Cavalcante family and burning the palm card of a saint in his hand. He would then take an oath of silence, promising to burn just like the saint if he ever gave up the secrets of the secret society to which he had just become a member. Joey O had certainly hung around with wiseguys long enough to know what was involved. He'd watched all the movies. He knew all the famous names and all the famous lines. He had helped beat up loan-shark victims who were behind in their vig. He had firebombed cars. But he had never pulled an actual trigger of an actual gun aimed at an actual head.

Perhaps, Ralphie seemed to suggest, if he were to accept such an assignment, all his troubles with money would go away. Ralphie decided to approach the question directly.

"How come they never tried to straighten you out?" he asked.

"I don't want it," Joey said.

"All the fucking stuff you did?"

"Yeah?" Joey said. "So what's the big deal?"

"You might as well get straightened out."

"And go to jail for the rest of my life?"

"What does that mean, you gotta go to jail?"

"They want to leave me alone, let me be happy," Joey said. "I don't want to get into this shit. I want to go do what I gotta fucking do. I'm very happy the way I am. Who the fuck needs it? I don't want the headaches that go with it."

"If you're gonna live in this life, you might as well fucking live in it."

"The whole fucking life," Joey O said. "Who the fuck wants it? I don't."

June 30, 1998

Joey and Ralphie went for a drive in Ralphie's special FBI-bugged car. Ralphie noticed right away that something was wrong.

"Bad?" he asked

"Bad," Joey replied.

Ralphie knew that Joey had had yet another meeting with the boss, Vincent. The day before Joey met for two hours at Vinny's big house out on Long Island. The house was big because Vinny was making lots of money, some of it because of Joey O's many schemes. But it was clear that the meeting at Vinny's did not end with what one might call rave reviews. Joey went into the meeting knowing that his pulling out of the plan to murder Charlie Majuri had done nothing to improve his relationship with Vinny, and knowing that he owed tens of thousands of dollars to gangsters across metropolitan New York. But Joey had decided to come clean. He'd decided to be brutally honest with his old friend.

He told him straight out that he could not pay his bills. Not to the Gambinos. Not to the Bonnanos. Not to the Colombos. He tried to explain his situation to Vinny, his old pal. Always Joey was just one step ahead—borrowing more and more to put more out on the street and hoping that he hit, but it just never seemed to work out.

"I told him, I says, 'Vinny, I got all fucked up.' I says, 'You always accuse me of drugs and fucking gambling.' I says, 'We're shylocks. Just take my salary and just pay him. I can't do it anymore.' He says, 'You gotta be fucking kidding me.' He says, 'You know this is not my money.'"

Ralphie says, "It's always money, huh?"

"Yeah," Joey said, "that's all."

Joey had then tried to do what Joey did best—provide Vinny with a new scheme. Joey told the boss his aunt was going to sell her house. He said she's looking at three-fifty, they offered three-ten. She'd borrow on the sale and lend him the money. Also he'd get help from his good friend Ralphie.

"Yeah," said Ralphie. "Of course."

And that was that. In four words, Joey described Vinny's reaction. "He went fucking crazy," Joey said.

Vinny had ordered Joey to stop making pickups from the gambling and loan-shark customers in Queens. Vinny would now collect it himself and pay it directly to the Gambinos, who were number one on the "Pissed Off at Joey" list.

"Okay," Joey says. "There went that."

And then, Joey's voice rises a little bit, telling Ralphie what happened next at the big meeting at Vinny's house. He recalls exactly what Vinny said that made Joey's bad heart skip a beat.

"You know," Vinny told him, "by rights, I gotta kill you."

Ralphie stopped talking. Then he said, "Is that what he said? Why? But why would he say that? Why would he say that?"

"I stole his money."

"You stole his money?"

"And I was paying on it. Well, that's the way he looks at it. He'll never get it back. I says, 'You'll get it back.' I says, 'I'm working with Ralph.' I left. I was there for two hours."

"Everything negative," Ralphie said. "Nothing positive."

They drove along, but Joey was losing steam. He knew something had changed with Vinny.

"Let me ask you a question," Ralphie said. "I mean, you've been loyal to him all these years?"

"That don't mean nothing," Joey said. "Money is their God."

"He got that angry?"

"Thank God I went to his house. He woulda shot me right there."

"I can't believe he's like that."

"Oh, I do. I knew that. I fuckin' knew that. I didn't wanna go, but I had no choice."

Ralphie said, "No, you got no choice."

"I have no choice. I have no money to pay him."

Joey owed $50,000, due many yesterdays ago. Or maybe $80,000. He can't be sure. Ralphie suggests that Vinny is just a guy who likes to blow off steam, but Joey is not so sure. He has known Vinny for years, has made lots of money for him in the past. He has been there for Vinny, collecting a thousand here, a thousand there from customers all over New Jersey, Brooklyn, Staten Island. He has been there as Vinny slowly rose through the ranks, from soldier to captain and now to boss. And he is confident that Vinny's star will continue to rise. He knows that Charlie Majuri is history, and that soon Vinny will run the DeCavalcante crime family. And when that day comes, Joey is sure that everything will be okay. He just has to get from Point A, which isn't so great, to Point B.

"It's a sad, sad fucking way to end after all these years," he said. "I'm telling Vinny, I'm putting my life in your hands. Either you kill me, or you help me outta it."

"And what'd he say?"

Joey recalled Vinny's very brief message: "You know what I gotta do."

September 9, 1998

By nine in the morning, Joey O was on the phone trolling for cash and getting nowhere. He was scheduled to take a stress test and he was not looking forward to it. Talking with a bookie named Wes Paloscio, Joey O said the stress test was supposed to be "an all-day affair. They gotta give me some shit. They take pictures. I gotta wait two hours, they take more pictures." He complained that Vinny was avoiding him, perhaps because he knew Joey O wanted to borrow more money off him.

Four hours later, at 12:50, Joey was driving down Kings

Highway in Brooklyn when he called Wiggles on his cell looking for Vinny. During the talk he almost got in an accident.

The manager at Wiggles, Tommy Salvata, asked, "How do you feel?"

"Ah, my fucking luck," Joey said. "I go to take the stress test. The machine breaks. Just my fucking luck."

"What about your eyes?"

"The eyes are three-thirty today. Amazing. Got all the tests, got already to go. The machine malfunctioned. Gotta call the mechanic. He can't come until Tuesday."

"You got no luck at all."

Joey O asks about Vinny and says, "Tell him I said I love him, I'm still alive."

Tommy laughed.

The next night Vinny tracked him down to his home in Staten Island. The two men stood alone in the house, talking about Joey's many problems with money. Actually it was mostly Vinny, yelling.

"You owe this one, you owe that one," roared Vinny, becoming increasingly agitated.

"What do you want me to do?" Joey pleaded. "I'm desperate."

"You got some pair of balls," Vinny said, and then Vinny kicked Joey in the testicles, sending him reeling.

The next day, early in the morning, Joey O called Ralphie in New Jersey. "Florida," he said. "Maybe I'll go to Florida."

"Really?"

"What am I gonna do? I don't want to hang around here. When he kicked me in the balls, I couldn't believe it. After all these years."

"Did he hurt you?"

"Yeah," Joey said. "He gave me a nice kick in the balls."

"I feel bad for you," Ralphie said. "I mean, maybe you don't have anything left. Maybe you should go to Florida."

"Everything's falling apart. I ain't got five cents in my pocket."

"That's terrible."

"It's no way to live," Joey said. "I had to beg him. I says, Vinny, I paid a hundred dollars for these pills. He said, 'I need the hundred. Take it off what you owe me.' "

September 25, 1998

Again Joey O was on the phone first thing in the morning. This time he was howling at Westley Paloscio, who had promised him again and again to hook him up with money. Paloscio was a young man who had recently gotten married to his pregnant girlfriend and lived at home with his mother. He had a nasal twang when he talked, and was prone to making such pronouncements as "I'm fuckin' thirty years old and I never worked a day in my life." He was viewed by some as smart with numbers, but as a bookie he was almost as big a failure as Joey O. He was referred to in some circles as "Mickey the Dunce." On this morning, Joey O started the conversation by calling Paloscio "a major mental fucking retard."

"Hello," Paloscio said. "Why am I a major fucking retard?"

Joey O said the guy Wes had promised would meet Joey at a diner with $3,000 at quarter to eight that morning had, of course, not shown up. "I left you a message five times," Joey complained.

"I told you," Paloscio said. "I was in Lamaze."

"I was with him till nine-thirty"

"I hadda watch pregnancy." Then Wes mentioned "this kid Steve." He said he had a Wall Street guy who gambled and owed him a lot of money, that Joey O could meet with him and get money from him.

October 9, 1998

Joey O was on the go. He'd finally reached a state of positivity. That was important. Positivity meant maybe he could get out of this unbelievable situation he'd gotten himself into. Negativity meant he'd wind up stuffed inside some fifty-five-gallon drum buried deep within that Fresh Kills Landfill in Staten Island. Money was the key to positivity. And his friend Westley Paloscio now claimed to have plenty.

Westley's customer Steve seemed promising. Westley gave Joey Steve's beeper number, and after a few calls that went nowhere, it was looking like Steve was actually going to come through. Joey was on the phone at two in the afternoon on a Friday now that Steve the big Wall Street guy had finally returned the beep.

"Okay," Joey said. "You got my money?"

"Yeah," said Steve. "I'm picking it up now, as a matter of fact."

Joey suggested meeting in the city; Steve wanted to meet on Long Island. Joey finally agreed on Brooklyn. Joey suggested he'd send somebody to pick up the cash. Steve seemed surprised.

"You're not going to meet me?"

Joey needed the money, so he compromised. He agreed to call Steve back for an address in Brooklyn. Joey O got upset only when Steve complained about how much money he had to pay.

"Yeah, well, I don't give a fuck," Joey said. "I don't

wanna hear it. I was promised by Friday I'll have it. Today's Friday."

October 10, 1998

Things were looking up. The old confidence was back. Joey O rushed out of his house on Rhett Avenue in Staten Island, which his forgiving wife, Rosemary, was allowing him to live in for the moment. He was on his way to meet the actual Steve at the Sea View Diner in Canarsie down at the bottom of Brooklyn. Steve had said 7:30 sharp, and Joey could almost smell the $10,000. He'd get his money, he'd give it to the Gambino guy, he'd let Vinny his boss know he gave it to the Gambino guy, and he'd be back on the street in Vinny's good graces making money in no time. He could picture it all. And although he had never actually met Steve and had only spoken to him on the phone just once, he was, nonetheless, brimming with confidence.

It was a mild October evening, temperatures had reached into the fifties; it was a little damp. Joey got in his aging BMW sedan and pulled out of the driveway and headed for the Sea View Diner and redemption. Money was out there in the Brooklyn night, waiting for Joey O to pick it up.

Inside the Sea View, they had giant apple turnovers wrapped in plastic on the counter and plenty of hot coffee in thick white mugs. There were old-style jukeboxes that played Louis Prima and plastic Madonna statuettes next to a mirrored wall. But there was no Steve. Joey looked all around, even heading into the dining room with the fake fireplace. No Steve that he could see. Joey headed back to his BMW. He sat in the lot and waited for a beep.

And waited. The breeze off of Jamaica Bay began to flow in chilly gusts. Here was a place technically within the city limits that seemed as far removed from the glitter and glory of New York as Patagonia. Sitting in his battered car, Joey could look across at the Belt Parkway less than twenty feet away, cars and trucks whizzing by heading out to the Island. Perhaps one of those cars contained Steve. By nine o'clock, it was clear that none of those cars contained Steve.

Now Joey was unhappy. In fact, he was going crazy. He beeped Steve again and again but got no answer. He tried Westley on his beeper, his cell phone, but got no response. Finally, at 9:19, Westley called back at a pay phone outside the diner. Standing there in the chilly wind, the sound of a highway behind him, Joey got the word from Westley that Steve was running behind and would meet him at a parking lot a half mile away alongside the Marine Park Golf Course. Joey jumped into his car, furious but still happy that he was finally going to get paid.

He drove west on the Belt, pulled off at the next exit north onto Flatbush Avenue, and had to make a U-turn to get into the Marine Park Golf Course. As he pulled into the huge parking lot of the municipal golf course, he discovered that there was not a streetlight in sight. He had the place to himself.

As he drove into a corner of the deserted lot, the dark and frigid-looking golf course was on his left. On his right, on the other side of Flatbush, he could make out the lights of the tiny houses jam-packed into the Mill Basin subdivision, which sits perched right on the water. Some had little piers that serviced giant fishing boats. The parking lot he sat in was dotted with broken clamshells dropped by seagulls. The shells made a crunchy sound as he pulled into one of several hundred empty spaces. It was fair to say that he was alone in the world at that moment. All he could hear was the whoosh of cars speeding by on the Belt and the occasional cry of a gull. The water that was no more than twenty yards away was called Dead Horse Bay.

He was there maybe five minutes when a brown two-door late-model Oldsmobile wheeled into the lot and drove slowly toward him.

The car stopped a few feet away. Joey O got out. He began to walk toward the driver's side. As he approached, he could make out Steve—a white man in his forties with heavy eyebrows and a thick mustache, heavyset, wearing a black cap and black leather jacket, sitting alone at the wheel. As Joey got closer, he probably had time to see at least one muzzle flash before he collapsed onto the broken pavement.

As he lay dying, he managed to hear the car screech away.

Motorists on nearby Flatbush Avenue heard the gunshots and investigated. A woman doctor and her male passenger pulled up and saw a man lying on the lot next to his open car door, the lights in the car still on, the engine idling. The doctor called the NYPD, and two patrol officers from the Sixty-third Precinct who were at the station house headed out for a meal got the case. They showed up within minutes.

It was bad. Joey had been shot numerous times, but he was still awake and aware of his surroundings. As he lay on the ground of the empty and dark parking lot, Police Officer Steven Esposito moved in close and began asking questions.

"Who shot you?"

"Steve."

"Steve who?"

"I don't know his last name."

Joey had some difficulty responding, because bullets had pierced one of his lungs, his liver, his pancreas, his stomach, his spleen, and his intestine, not to mention one of his major arteries, which was spilling his life all over the crushed clamshells in the lot.

"Where do you know him from?" PO Esposito inquired. "Where did you meet him?"

"I just have his number," Joey O declared, and recited it. "It's a beeper number." Joey was always good with numbers. He continued giving the cop number after number, being interrupted now and then by Emergency Medical Service technicians, who'd showed up and gone to work on him. They ripped off his shirt and began applying bandages to stop the bleeding. PO Esposito kept asking questions.

"So how come you were down there with Steve?"

"Picking up money for Wes," Joey O replied.

The cop misheard him and asked, "Who's West?"

"A friend." He gave PO Esposito another number and described what had happened in the parking lot in brief terms: "Steve pulled up on the left side of my car. I got out of the car and Steve started shooting. Call my daughter Danielle." He gave out one final number.

This was his dying declaration. People who are dying usually have few reasons to lie. Joey O probably told the cop what he thought was the truth, although he certainly did not provide all the details. A detective carefully wrote all of this down, later, in triplicate.

Joey was transported by ambulance east on the Belt and up Rockaway Parkway to the emergency room at Brookdale Hospital. At no time, while he was lying in the parking lot, lying in the ambulance driving down the Belt, or lying in a bed inside Brookdale, dying, did Joey O say anything about his boss, Vinny Palermo. He did not mention his name even once. He was shuttled into the trauma room, and after the doctors got a look at him, into the operating room he was sent.

At 2:10 the next morning, October 11, 1998, Joseph Masella was pronounced dead of multiple gunshot wounds. His death was ruled a homicide, motive unknown. Joey O was no longer a problem for the DeCavalcante crime family, or more specifically, for the family's rising star—Vincent Palermo.

11

THE GOOD OLD DAYS

Bob Buccino grew up in the streets of North Jersey with wiseguys and wannabes. He knew their names but he was not one of them. He became a cop and ultimately one of the most informed members of law enforcement regarding the crime family of Sam the Plumber. He only met Sam once, and he recalled that he seemed to be a polite senior citizen. He watched the DeCavalcante family for nearly thirty years for the state attorney general's Organized Crime Task Force. He knew where it came from and where it was going.

In the old days, which he would ultimately come to look upon with a certain misty nostalgia, the wiseguys seemed to play by certain rules. The way he remembers it, DeCavalcante would insist that his crews hold legitimate jobs and wear suits if possible. He made sure they didn't kill anybody but one another. When he was boss, DeCavalcante crime family members never broke the oath of silence. Sam the Plumber always insisted that when they were arrested, they would refuse to answer questions, but would do so politely.

"He was a very sharp guy. Always well dressed. I never saw him without a shirt, a tie, and a suit. He was old school. There was strong discipline. He played by the rules. They same thing with drugs. I'm not going to say they weren't involved in drugs, but the rule was if you were involved you couldn't use the family name. When Frank Polizzi [Sam the Plumber's underboss] opened a restaurant, he made all of the family show up and he chewed out one crew for not wearing suits."

After DeCavalcante retired and appointed John Riggi the boss, the adherence to certain rules continued. Buccino remembers his pursuit of John Riggi in the 1980s almost wistfully. At the time Riggi controlled the construction industry in north Jersey. He was a small man who served on governmental boards and attended charity fund-raisers while pocketing millions in extortion payments to maintain "labor peace" on construction sites across Jersey. He once wrote a letter to a respected businessman in Union County, New Jersey, advising him to take up vegetarianism.

Mostly Buccino remembers John Riggi the vegetarian as a guy who almost never said anything that even resembled probable cause. On one occasion, the Organized Crime Task Force got a call from a local contractor who wanted to use nonunion workers and had been contacted by Riggi. The businessman told the investigators that Riggi had summoned him to a meeting for lunch at the Sheraton Hotel in Linden, New Jersey. The task force—which had been surveilling Riggi for months with no success—decided to bug the table in the hotel restaurant where the two would meet. The day of the meeting, they were sweating. The restaurant, which was usually half-full at lunch, was jammed. They couldn't figure out why. When Riggi showed up they weren't sure if the hotel would do the job they were instructed to do and place him at the right table. But the receptionist came through and Riggi sat down to lunch with the contractor as the task force listened in.

Throughout the lunch they waited for incriminating statements. They listened for Riggi to demand cash payments in envelopes. They waited for threats of labor disruption or, even better, violence. Instead, Riggi sat down and said, "I'm John Riggi and I just want to tell you that New Jersey is a very pro-union state."

Then, one at a time, one union leader after another got up from a nearby table and came to Riggi's table. They shook his hand and said what a great guy he was, then returned to their lunch. The leaders of nearly every local in north Jersey did this. It was, Buccino remembers, very impressive. Without saying a thing, Riggi made it clear whom he knew and what he could do. The contractor ultimately opted to hire union workers for his job.

When the task force finally got enough evidence to indict Riggi on racketeering charges in 1989, Buccino went to the boss's comfortable home in Linden early one morning. Riggi opened the door in his underwear and asked the agents if they would let him shave and put on a suit. They complied, then took him to court. He later went to trial and was acquitted of all serious charges but found guilty of the minor charges. Years later law enforcement indicted Riggi on charges of buying off a juror in the case.

Today Buccino thinks what's left of the mob is a spoiled-brat version of the real thing. Today, he says, the younger soldiers are even greedier than their fathers were and far less patient. Half of them have become informants, and half of that number have worked out book deals. The whole thing has become a movie.

He remembers a time when he was listening in on a social club, hoping for incriminating conversation. Agents can spend hours listening to talk about baseball scores and the best place to get prime ribs before hearing a word about crime. Buccino and his fellow investigators had wired up the social club and were listening in when suddenly they heard someone say, "He's a rat! Let's get him!"

They didn't know what to do. They had an obligation to prevent a murder, but the bug in the social club would become useless if they called in the local police to bust in and stop whatever atrocity was unfolding. They heard someone say, "Get the knife." They were about to send in the cavalry when suddenly they heard something that made them stop.

A commercial for dishwashing soap.

"We got all upset," Buccino says. "We thought there would be a murder going down. We got ready to go in when we hear the commercial. It was a movie."

October 11, 1998

The day after Joey O ended his astonishing Mafia career in a dark and empty golf-course parking lot littered with broken clamshells, there was much wringing of hands and second-guessing down at 26 Federal Plaza. The FBI agents who had spent nights and days listening to Joey O were at a loss for words. The constant money problems, the daughter's psychologist bills, the girlfriend's breast implants—all of that was over. In all those hours, it had never seemed that Joey O could emerge as a candidate for a mob hit. True, there were a lot of people in this world who were not happy with Joey O. But he owed everyone money, and if he was dead, he couldn't pay. Or so the logic went.

Now the bureau was confronted with the possibility that they had somehow miscalculated. They had a duty to intervene if there was an indication that someone was about to be killed. And in Joey O's case, there had been some not-so-subtle hints.

In conversation after conversation, it was clear that gangsters across New York and New Jersey were getting seriously tired of hearing Joey O's long list of excuses. The day before he died, he was working the cell phone, trying to keep members of at least two New York Mafia families happy. In a midmorning call it was Joey Smash, a Gambino soldier to whom he owed tens of thousands of dollars. That day Joey O was supposed to deliver cash to Joey Smash, but Joey O didn't show up.

"What happened?" Joey Smash said.

"I can't drive, Joe. It's all fucked up. I tried driving, forget about it. I'm shakin'. My sugar is dropping. And I can't do nothing until I get to this doctor Tuesday. He told me keep it elevated."

"Whoa, whoa, whoa, whoa, whoa, Joey," a furious Joey Smash responded. "Now let me ask you a question. You'll be here Monday for sure, Joe?"

"Hopefully," Masella said. "Most likely."

"Ahhhhh . . ."

Two hours later Joey was on the phone with a Colombo-crime-family soldier named Anthony Stripoli. Stripoli was a hulking man who was involved in several pump-and-dump stock scams without actually knowing much about the Dow Jones Industrial Average. Joey O owed Stripoli and his partner more tens of thousands, and he had once again failed to deliver on time. Joey O was there with the excuses.

"I'm fucking shaking like a bastard," he said.

"Yeah, no, 'cause you know my partner was flippin' out."

"I know," Joey said. "I don't blame him."

"'Cause it's the first week and he just doesn't like anybody trying to take a shot."

"I don't blame him at all," Joey said. "He's got my sugar going crazy."

Then there was Sal the Baker. Sal had called Joey O two weeks earlier screaming into the phone about $40,000 Joey owed him. "I don't want to hear no bullshit," he shouted. "This don't fly with me, Joey. You know what I'm saying?"

The suspects were piling up. And at the top of the heap was one of Joey's oldest and closest friends—Vinny Ocean. The FBI was now going back and reviewing the transcripts of those conversations in which Joey O had the audacity to tell Vinny he simply couldn't pay what he owed. They had all the transcripts and all the actual taped conversations, during which they could clearly hear Vinny Ocean losing all pretense of civility when the topic of Joey O came up. While he was discussing Joey O with one of his subordinates, Joseph Abruzzo, back in July, the fury was obvious in the words and in the tone of voice when he said, "He had the world by the balls and he blew it." And they had Joey O's own words, when he'd told Ralphie all about his confession to Vinny and how Vinny had told him he had to kill him. "You know what I have to do," Vinny had said. Then Vinny physically attacked Joey O, kicked him in the testicles, and told Joey O to stay away from him.

And the fact was that Joey himself was letting just about everybody know Vinny had given up on him. He told Ralphie all about it, and he even told a veteran De-Cavalcante soldier named Uncle Joe Giacobbe. Just eleven days before he died, Joey was on the phone with Uncle Joe, talking about how Vinny Ocean was heading off to Russia to talk about selling cell phones overseas. Joey O was disappointed that Vinny hadn't invited him to tag along.

"He'd probably leave you there," Uncle Joe joked, but the FBI agents heard no evidence that Joey had responded with a laugh.

It was now clear that in the days leading up to Joey O's death, Vinny the boss was furious with Joey. Worse, Joey had made the mistake of letting the world know that Vinny had implied he'd have to be killed. Although this would be merely circumstantial evidence in most criminal murder cases, in the world of La Cosa Nostra, this was not the kind of information one would wish to have distributed on the Internet. In effect, Joey had made a huge mistake. He'd told the rest of gangland that it was okay to kill him—the boss said so.

Adding to the mix was the fact that the FBI had noticed a pattern with Vinny Ocean. Every time he wanted a murder committed, he flew to Florida. The time he ordered Big Ears Charlie Majuri terminated, he'd headed straight for Fort Lauderdale for a warm June weekend. As it happened, Vinny Ocean had jetted down to the Sunshine State just two days before Joey O died. He returned that very day, late in the evening. The idea, the bureau theorized, was that Vinny Ocean could not be tied to the crime because he'd been out of town.

As a result of this second-guessing and reexamination of the taped records and confluence of circumstances, the FBI decided that Vincent Palermo was now the number-one suspect in the murder of Joseph Masella. For the first time in his career within La Cosa Nostra, Vinny Ocean was the subject of a murder investigation.

As a result, the bureau made extra efforts to monitor Vinny's phone conversations. They went looking for implications.

October 13, 1998

On this chilly Tuesday a death notice appeared on page 30 of the *New York Daily News* in between a story about a Rhodes scholar and a terrible accident on the Mexican border. The notice appeared under the name Masella, Joseph N., and it was the only notice to mention a street nickname—Joey O. He was described as a "beloved husband" of Rosemary Abruzzo Masella, and "loving father" of three daughters by marriage, and a stepson and stepdaughter. Joey O was enshrined as the "loving brother" of Marie Beard. It was noted that he was survived by three grandchildren. At the time the notice went into the paper, Joey O's body was in repose at the Cusimano and Russo Funeral Home way down in the Gravesend section of Brooklyn. A 9:30 Mass was set for the next morning at St. Jude's Roman Catholic Church, and there was no need to mention that Joey O would be memorialized under the silent gaze of the Patron Saint of Lost Causes.

Vincent Palermo, who had known Joey O most of his adult life, had spent all day Sunday with his former driver's wife and daughters in their Staten Island home. He had consoled them in their grief and assuaged them of their guilt. He had expressed both shock and remorse. By Tuesday, he was on his FBI-supplied cell phone dialing up his Mafia pals.

At a little past ten in the morning, he called Sacco's Meat Market, the pork store in Elizabeth, New Jersey, that served as unofficial headquarters of Uncle Joe Giacobbe, a veteran DeCavalcante family soldier. This was the real pork store used as a mob hangout that was located a few blocks away from the fake pork store used as a mob hangout depicted in *The Sopranos*. When Vinny called up all he had to do was ask for Joe. The worker knew just who to get.

"How are you?" Uncle Joe answered.

"All right."

"What the heck happened?" Giacobbe asked.

"Hello," Vinny answered. "I can't hear you."

Vinny then went into deep code. He said, "I went to see the truck driver," which was a clever agreed-upon way of referring to Stefano Vitabile, the alleged consigliere of the DeCavalcante crime family. Vitabile owned a sand-and-gravel company and apparently knew how to drive a truck. Vinny then went into an uncomfortable explanation about how he had wanted to visit with Uncle Joe in person, but the traffic on the Jersey Turnpike was too miserable to allow such a thing.

"What'll we do?" Uncle Joe asked, clearly meaning "What do we do about Joey O?"

"Nothing," Vinny said.

"Nothing."

"Nothing," Palermo repeated. "No, I told the truck driver," he said, making it clear he had already discussed the matter with the family leadership.

To the FBI agents listening in, this could be read two ways: either the family had approved of the hit, or the family was now formulating a method of responding to the hit. Either way, it indicated that Joey O's death was clearly family business.

"I'll explain it to you when I see you," Vinny said, and they agreed to meet later that week.

A few minutes later he was on his cell phone with another unnamed man claiming that "a good friend of mine just had a heart attack." Twenty minutes after that he was on the phone with his cousin Eric, making cryptic references to a meeting. "I went over there," he said. "I'll talk to you when I see you."

"Everything all right?" Eric asked.

"No, it wasn't . . . it was that committee, you know?"

"Oh," Eric said. "Okay, good."

The FBI interpreted "that committee" as a reference to the three-man panel appointed to run the DeCavalcante family. The fact that Vinny would even mention it was strange, but there had not been a murder within the De-Cavalcante family for at least two years, so this was a highly unusual moment. Three minutes later Vinny was on the phone with his lawyer, John Serpico, and this time he had a different explanation for Joey O's death. They chitchatted about Serpico helping close on an upscale apartment in a new yuppie neighborhood near the Brooklyn Bridge. Then Serpico brought up Joey O.

"I heard Joey died," he said. "What happened?"

Now Vinny was off the heart-attack story and on to a robbery story. "Somebody tried to rob him," he said. "He went to a diner on Rockaway Boulevard and he took out money to pay the bill—a lotta money—and they followed him and they took all his money, all his jewelry, and they shot him."

"You're kidding?"

"No. Unbelievable," Vinny said. "I got back from Florida Saturday and that's what I came back to. And I'm all day with his daughters, because his daughter, one of them got a problem to begin with. Her boyfriend got killed not long ago. Right in front of her. And we've been going through hell with her. Now this happens, and we were with her all day yesterday, all day Sunday. We laid him out last night and then again today and tomorrow. You know tomorrow we're going to bury him."

"What a shame," the lawyer Serpico said, and the two men finished up some other business and Vinny signed off. Twelve minutes later he dialed up Joey O's grieving wife, Rosemary, a woman Vinny had known for decades. She informed him she was headed off to the hospital in Brooklyn where her husband had been pronounced dead of multiple bullet wounds. She had to "pick up the property. Even though they said it's nothing, but I figured I would get it."

"Aha," Vinny said. "Unnnh."

Rosemary explained that "some guy named Ralphie" called the house. "He didn't even know" Joey was dead, she said. "He was looking for him." She mentioned the death notice in the *News,* and then she wanted Vinny to explain what had happened to her husband, the father of the children. "I just can't make any sense out of it or anything," she said. "They're just saying the same thing over and over again."

Vinny acted as if he never met Joey O in his life and had no idea that poor Joey O actually owed someone some money. He seemed to be talking to himself, or talking for somebody to hear. He said, "What's he owe them money?"

"That's what I don't understand," Rosemary Masella said. "I mean, if I could see if he had money, if he was a big shot, if he was something."

"No, the guy owed him money," Vinny said. "He didn't want to pay him."

"I mean, for nothing," Rosemary responded, obviously not listening to a word he'd said.

"He owed him a lot of money," Vinny continued. "I mean a lot of money." He realized he was making it seem that the mysterious "Steve" might have been justified in shooting Rosemary's beloved. He quickly corrected himself: "I mean, there's never enough for that. I mean . . ."

"I mean you coulda yelled and screamed and made a payment plan or something," she said. "I mean people hung him up before. I can't tell you how many times."

"It's crazy," Vinny said, and the two promised to meet at the funeral home later that day.

At Cusimano and Russo's, he got a call from a man the FBI agents listening in couldn't identify. He was listed merely as Joey LNU for Last Name Unknown. Now Vinny was back on the heart-attack story regarding Joey O. He told a different story depending on who asked. When Joey LNU asked "Which Joey?"—an extremely reasonable question—Vinny responded, "You know, Mozzarella."

"I'm sorry to hear that."

"So," Vinny said. "How you doing? What's going on? How's business? All right, let me get done with all this shit and I'll give you a buzz tomorrow."

"Whatever's good for you," Joey LNU said. "I mean, I know you're busy."

Vinny said no problem and the two made arrangements to meet the next day. By the time the funeral was over, Vinny was back on the job, yowling at the workers at Wiggles about renovations, talking with lawyers about his big deal with Bob Guccione. He was a man of business, and when Rosemary Masella kept calling him about certain things that she wanted to talk about over the telephone, Vinny Ocean tried to walk that thin line between sympathetic and just plain rude. "You know, I wanted to tell you something," she said the day after the funeral. "Do you have a minute?"

He put her on hold, took another call, came back to Rosemary. He had to go, he couldn't talk on the phone about this. They would talk later.

October 20, 1998

Guilt arrived. Vinny called Joey's house in Staten Island and got the machine. Joey's voice was still on the machine. He quickly hung up. He then began calling people to tell them how much he missed his old friend, Joey, what a great guy he was. He sounded very different from the days when he was calling Joey "a sick bastard," kicking him in the balls, and warning him that he would have to have him killed.

"Son of a bitch," he said to his son Michael. "It's hitting me now, you know what I'm saying? Because he used to help me out. I'd say, 'Joey, I need blood pressure pills. My beeper, Joey, my beeper.' Jesus Christ. He would say anything funny. You go away with him, he'd make you laugh all day long. I don't know."

Michael asked if they found the shooter. Vinny made it clear he knew a lot about the investigation. He knew, for example, that before he died, Joey told the police who did it. Vinny said, "And I mean I don't know the freakin' guy. I don't know what Joey was doing, you know what I'm saying?" He even suggested putting together a fund-raising dinner for Joey's family and a $25,000 reward for the capture of the shooter.

During a call to his sister, Millie, he sounded positively weepy. "I'm thinking about Joey. I miss him. All for nothing, all for nothing."

His sister had heard some things. "It must have been more serious than money, is what I'm saying. Money is nothing."

"No," Vinny said. "I'm sure that's what it was."

"What was he, some big shot? What kind of enemy can you make?"

"Who knows? I have no idea. They mention a name. I have no idea."

"If he had confided in you it wouldn't have happened."

"I know."

"Wouldn't have happened," she repeated.

"I need blood pressure pills, or, you know we're going to Florida, get the ticket."

"You take blood pressure pills?" his sister asked.

"Yeah."

"I didn't know."

"Yeah, not strong, but—"

"Yeah but you need something."

"I went for a complete checkup and the only problem I have so far is the blood pressure."

"Well, that's okay," she said, "if you know."

"It's the stress," he said. "You know?"

Over two days, the DeCavalcante crime family paid its respects to wannabe gangster Joseph Masella, who had said "the life" was not for him but could never quite walk away from it. During the wake, Vinny Ocean was balancing his feelings of guilt while working his business deals over the cell phone. Vinny was to set up a corporation called World to World Clothing to distribute women's underwear to the Asians. They even drafted paper, with Guccione's General Media International Incorporated granting World to World Clothing International "exclusive license for the manufacturing, sales and distribution of Penthouse undergarments, lingerie, sweatshirts, t-shirts, blue jeans, sneakers and other apparel in Japan, Hong Kong, Korea, Taiwan, China." They were talking about opening up Penthouse strip clubs and maybe casinos in Russia and New Jersey. They were talking grand scale. Vinny's attorney,

John Daniels, communicated that "Bob"—whom he called "the chairman"—was very pleased with Vinny.

"He said, 'In my opinion, Vincent is the perfect man. I trust him and I like what he has to say and I really have confidence that he can pull it off.' "

Vinny was ready for the sweet life. On the cell phone with his son Michael, he said, "I mean, if this clicks, Mike, you're quitting that job. I don't give a shit. I'm making you a partner, I don't care."

But he stopped midsentence and said, "I tell ya, I really miss Joey." It's was if Joey was Vinny's Jacob Marley—he kept coming back. And the phone calls kept coming. Rosemary Masella called at 1:35 in the morning to say she'd been scrounging through Joey O's sock drawers looking for $40,000 she was told Joey O had picked up the day before he died. She would call to say she went to the hospital to pick up Joey's things but she couldn't find his sports beeper. She was sure the police had it, which meant that the police had every number Joey ever stored in its memory.

Paranoia set in. Everyone knew that when one wiseguy gets executed, all wiseguys have to watch what they say. The police and the FBI start asking questions and listening closer. In a talk with one of his soldiers, a guy from Florida everybody called Marshmallow but whose real name was Anthony Mannarino, Vinny danced around saying what he wanted to say. Marshmallow—who apparently hadn't watched enough Mafia movies to know that you don't say anything of substance on the telephone—tried to discuss the fact that people were talking about him being an informant.

"I'm not, Vinny," Marshmallow said. "Never was and never will be."

"I don't know what you're talking about," Vinny said. "I swear on my kids."

When Marshmallow didn't get the message and kept trying to talk about this subject, Vinny beeped him with another number to call. The only problem was the number wasn't registering and Marshmallow had run out of quarters for the pay phone.

"I'm fucking anxious to hear what you got to say because I have no fuckin' idea what you're talking about, I swear on my kids' life," Vinny yelled. "You're a fucking—out of your fucking mind. Did it come in?"

"No," Marshmallow said. "Yeah."

"Okay, call me on that number."

This was how Vinny had to behave. He had known for months, ever since he saw the FBI agents watching his house from a boat on Long Island Sound, that he was under surveillance. And he knew that the people whose job it was to follow him around every day were likely pretty ticked off that his driver had been terminated right under their noses. He had now entered a new world, where the wrong word uttered in the right context could lead to a dance with RICO. Vinny Ocean now lived his life under the spotlight of the Racketeering Influence and Corruption Order Act.

Joey O was gone, but his ghost remained.

The FBI was going crazy. They now had Vinny Ocean—who for months said nothing incriminating on the telephone and was the sworn enemy of probable cause—twitching like a squirrel. He was speaking in obvious code. The cool and collected Vinny Ocean they had come to know was now a paranoid, amateur prevaricator. Although they were unhappy that Joey O, a living, breathing human being, had been executed on their watch, they knew that the target of their investigation was obviously rattled. And that meant opportunity for the bureau.

They had, by the date Joey O was killed, nearly ten months of taped recordings in hand. Ralphie Guarino had worked his way up the ladder at least far enough to implicate Vinny Ocean in a number of crimes, including a conspiracy to murder Charlie Majuri. He had managed to convince Joey O that he was his friend, and as a result, Joey O had grown comfortable telling Ralphie just about everything he knew or had heard. Ralphie had captured hours of candid talks with Joey about loan sharking, extortion, stealing anything that wasn't nailed down, and murder. Lots of probable cause. And Ralphie's number-one contact with Vinny had consistently been Joey O, who had managed to offer up more incriminating statements about his boss than about anyone else in the entire DeCavalcante crime family. Joey O was practically a repository of damaging information about Vinny Ocean and everyone else in the underworld with whom he had had even a passing acquaintance. And he was history. There would be no more Joey O explaining who was in charge, who was on the ins, who was on the outs. Ralphie was still out there wearing a wire, but his Virgil was dead.

The FBI now sat back and waited. When a member or associate of organized crime dies, the hierarchy has to deal with both his assets and his debts. And if the deceased had been supervising anybody, the supervisee had to be reassigned to a new supervisor. It was all very civil service. Ralphie was now in a position to be reassigned. The options were limited. He was from Brooklyn, and so were most of his loan-shark customers and sports book clients. So it made sense to put him with a soldier in the New York wing of the family. The only question was, who?

The answer came quickly. A week after Joey O's funeral, the family put Ralphie with a fifty-four-year-old old-school gangster from Staten Island who was proud to report to anyone who would listen that once, a long time ago, he had actually known Joe Valachi. His name was Joseph Sclafani, but everyone called him Tin Ear because he was deaf in his right ear. The FBI had a light file on him, listing him as a soldier with a handful of arrests for minor gambling charges and one weapons count. He was not a well-known gangster, but he was Ralphie's.

The fact that Ralphie had been put with a made member of the family was a sign that they trusted him, and that was good news for both the FBI and Ralphie. They now had long talks about where the investigation was going and how to keep Ralphie on the street with his little wire device. They decided to cook up a new "robbery" that Ralphie could take to Sclafani to impress him and gain his confidence. They had no idea how easy it was going to be to do just that.

12

It is a well-known fact that many of the actors who make a living pretending to be gangsters either grew up with or know real gangsters. James Caan, who played Sonny in *The Godfather,* was good friends with a Colombo captain named Jo Jo Russo. Joe Pesci modeled his psychotic Tommy character in *Goodfellas* on a Gambino gangster named Bobby Basciano. And Jerry Orbach spent hours hanging around with Crazy Joey Gallo, right up until the last hours of Joey. Sometimes the relationship between pretend wiseguys and the real thing gets even cozier.

When *The Sopranos* began filming, it would hold daylong casting calls for extras. Hundreds, even thousands of people from New York and New Jersey who saw themselves as looking like members of the Mafia would stand in line for hours, résumés in hand. One such aspiring goomba was a twenty-five-year-old actor from Bensonhurst, Brooklyn, named Thomas Bifalco.

Bifalco was cobbling together a résumé by making

walk-on appearances on TV shows. He'd snagged a walk-on on the show *Spin City* and landed a role in a small production on Long Island with the mysteriously multiethnic title, *Meshuggener Godfather.* He decided to put up with the long line at the *Sopranos* show-up. He endured and landed a walk-on.

But this would not pay the bills. Bifalco had a sideline. He had opened up a boiler room down on Wall Street. This type of operation had become a big moneymaker for the mob in the late 1990s, operating on the principle that where there's money, there's opportunity for larceny. Bifalco's boiler room was the usual setup. A group of young hustlers sat in an anonymous office down in the winding streets near Wall Street, working the phones. In Bifalco's case, there were eight phones. The "brokers" would cold-call unsuspecting victims, usually senior citizens, and try to berate them into buying stock in a worthless company. They would make the worthless company—in Bifalco's case, something called Falcon Marine—seem like the deal of a lifetime. They would then con the elderly persons to invest everything they had saved all their lives. And they had to act quickly because the deal was going to disappear.

In this manner, Bifalco and his colleagues managed to steal $300,000 from thirty elderly victims.

During Bifalco's sentencing on securities-fraud charges, John Panagopoulos, the New York assistant attorney general who prosecuted *The Sopranos* walk-on, tried to make a distinction between the real world and the TV world, but it wasn't easy. "He did not realize this is not *The Sopranos*. This is not television. He cannot shake down real victims and walk away unpunished."

Bifalco got two years in state prison. He will most

likely not be making any more appearances on *The Sopranos*.

November 4, 1998

The courtroom of Administrative Judge Steven Fisher sits far out in Jamaica, Queens, in an aging Tammany Hall–built monstrosity that refuses to enter the late twentieth century. It is one of those ancient structures of New York's outer boroughs that are frozen forever in the past, stuck in a time when political machines rewarded the loyal with jobs for life in obscure municipal backwaters. Here the underachievers of the Democratic Party could file and refile overstuffed boxes of dry, yellowing documents of consequence to few. The whole place was run by dozens of civil servants who could have been characters in *Bleak House*—powerless bureaucrats who knew all the right ways to torture the unsuspecting citizens who ventured into their musty, dusty realm. On this miserable frigid day in November, Vincent Palermo was one of those unsuspecting citizens.

The hearing in question was listed in the civil docket as 16705/98: *City of New York* v. *Din Din Seafood, DBA Wiggles*. The file was impressive. The case had amassed enough motions and replies and memoranda of law that it took up four binders that stacked a good three feet high. Lawyers on both sides had generated millions of words and hundreds of billable hours. The city lawyers said New York Police Department vice-squad detectives had paid the twenty-dollar cover to get into Wiggles, where they discovered adult activity taking place in far more than 40 percent of the club. Lawyers for the club denied it, but the city shut down Wiggles anyway and took its case to Judge Fisher. One by one the city's witnesses took the stand, re-creating for Judge Fisher just exactly what was going on inside the pink walls of Wiggles. As the hearing droned on, Vinny Ocean sat in the back of the room, wondering how it had all come down to this: Was or was not booby pool a violation of New York State law?

Detective Eugene Jung of the Queens vice squad was sitting in the witness chair. Detective Jung was describing a night in October when he was having a little chat with a dancer named Camille. His problem was that he had just had a lap dance in the cigar room, and now he was running out of the money the city allowed him to spend to prove that there was vice in the night. He came out of the cigar room and sat down at the bar, and another dancer named Lena walked over.

"Would you like to play booby pool?" she asked.

This was, for Detective Jung, a new one. He was intrigued. He asked, "What's that?"

"It's a game of pool and the main thing is that when you take a shot, I will try to block your shot with my boobs."

"And did you play booby pool with her?" asked the city attorney with a straight face.

"Yes."

Unfortunately for Detective Jung, in the middle of the booby-pool game a fight broke out in the room outside and Lena the dancer went running out to see what was what. The fight ended and Lena returned to finish the booby-pool game. When Detective Jung would lean down to take a shot, Lena would lean down, too. In the middle of this she asked him if he wanted another lap dance. She said she'd seen the one Camille had provided and was not impressed.

"She was lazy," Lena contended. "She was just lying on you. I can do better."

Detective Jung, however, had run out of municipal funding. He gave her his last five dollars and left.

Next on the witness stand was Lena herself, whose real name was Myan Leroi Masterantonio of Oyster Bay, Long Island. For eighteen months before Detective Jung had showed up, Myan had worked at Wiggles from six o'clock at night to two the next morning, three to five nights a week. She acknowledged playing booby pool but denied touching Detective Jung in any manner. In the cigar room, she insisted that she always wore what she called a "European bottom, which means it has to be basically mainly covered, with a little bit hanging."

All of this amounted to a pretty tough case to make against Wiggles and Vinny Ocean. Lena had denied lap dancing but freely admitted to leaning suggestively over a pool table, and the city had only Detective Jung talking about a single lap dance. There was no pattern to show that the 40 percent rule had been broken repeatedly inside Wiggles, which was the heart and soul of the city's allegation. It was Vinny Ocean's forty-fifth birthday coming up on Saturday, and as the hearing was winding down, he had reason to believe he might get to reopen Wiggles after all. Things were looking up. Then came Frank Stellini, otherwise known as Frankie Pina.

Frankie was being called by Weinstein, the lawyer for Wiggles. The idea was that Frankie would rebut the city's claims that sex was running out of control throughout the entire strip club, instead of being relegated to 40 percent. At Wiggles, Frankie Pina was just another mortadella who got a job because he knew somebody. He called himself the assistant general manager, but two days after the city came in and shut the place down, Frankie became the general manager. This happened because the real general manager, a guy named Tommy, had a heart attack. The first thing Frankie did after taking the witness stand was tell a little joke when they asked him to identify himself.

"They nicknamed me Mussolini because I did not tolerate nothing," he confided to the judge.

He was asked to explain where the rules were posted. He said they posted the rules for all the dancers to see "very inconspicuously—they were right in the middle of the mirrors where they put on the makeup."

Frankie Pina then explained the rules according to Frankie Pina. "Any such activity that does not inquire with the rules is supposed to be reported to the manager."

The lawyer Weinstein did his best to keep Frankie on track. He asked what steps the club took to ensure that the 40 percent rule was adhered to. Frankie replied as best he could.

"We took every step we could possibly take. Sometimes it might look like what you are doing, but they are not doing exactly what they think they are doing. Because in this business, it is imagination more than anything else."

Presumably the judge knew what Frankie was talking about. Frankie allowed that sometimes accidents did happen. "Another dancer by accident . . . maybe a top might come off. One of the girls solicited for the so-called unquote blow job. The girl told me."

But Frankie insisted that these incidents were unusual. He explained that the "industry" was "under attack" and that Wiggles had been forced to do a "configuration of the situation." This meant they started making the dancers sign a set of rules that prohibited prostitution in the club. "So I kill two birds with one stone, as they say."

Then it was the city lawyer's turn. The city lawyer began asking Frankie just exactly what went on inside the cigar room. Frankie was ready with an answer.

"I tell the customer if you want to spend private time with a girl, enjoy nice cheap cigars, it costs this much."

The city lawyer wanted to know how it was that he was selling cigars when he did not have a license to sell tobacco. Again Frankie was ready for him.

"We give them away. That's why they are cheap."

He explained why customers need to spend "private time" with a dancer by contending, "Sometimes they will do anything to hear something nice from a girl which they don't hear from their wives."

The trouble was, the more questions the city lawyer asked, the more times Frankie was forced to confess to another "accident" during this "private time" with the dancers. The city lawyer pressed further, demanding to know how often a breast might "fall out" of a halter top, as Frankie had put it. Frankie explained that he had lived with three girls his whole life and "sometimes it happens."

"So," the city lawyer demanded, "there are times that a breast may be exposed?"

"Sometimes," Frankie admitted. "A big breast, a small bra. It might fall off. It's uncontrollable."

"No further questions," said the city lawyer.

The judge reserved decision and all Vinny Ocean could do was wait. He couldn't be sure if Frankie Pina had simply hurt the case or if he had completely blown it to pieces. He had a lot of deals going and would survive no matter what the judge decided, but Wiggles was a major element of the Vinny Ocean empire. In a way, Vinny benefited from Wiggles's notoriety as much as from its steady stream of crumpled-up five- and ten-dollar bills. He controlled another strip club called Gentlemen's Quarters on Long Island, but who had ever heard of that? Wiggles was in the news. When he was dealing with Bob Guccione, he was able to brag about a known commodity to show the clout he had in "the industry." The closing of Wiggles wouldn't kill Vinny Ocean, but it sure would hurt.

Around midday November 19, 1998, Administrative Judge Steven Fisher made it short and sweet: Wiggles was history. The club, Judge Fisher found, had clearly violated the 40 percent rule and would hereforth be prohibited from doing business. Booby pool and everything else was to cease and desist immediately. The city had won in every way; the residents of Rego Park who had protested in rain, sleet, and snow won in every way. Both groups issued press releases proclaiming victory. Newspaper photographers and TV camera people schlepped all the way out on Queens Boulevard to take a photo of Wiggles's front door with the big orange "Closed" sticker. Vinny Ocean was out of the strip-club business in Queens.

One of his nephews called him to tell him the news at 6:25 P.M., hours after the decision had come in. With the FBI listening in, the nephew said he thought they lost because of Frankie Pina's big mouth. Vinnie agreed. He hung up, and within five minutes he had Frankie himself on the line. Vinny, who usually evidenced a certain modicum of self-control, lost it completely on Frankie.

"You dirty motherfucker asshole moron dirty cocksucker," Vinny screamed. "You're looking to hurt me, you motherfucker. You destroyed my life, that's what you did."

The next day was worse. He must have been stewing in it, turning over certain moments of testimony, recalling the little asides to the judge that Frankie had offered up. On the phone with one of his lawyers he promised to kick Frankie "in the balls."

"This fucking bastard, fucking wiseass bastard greaseball," he added for effect. "They think they know everything."

He called Frankie again on his cell phone and screamed: "I went for a hundred thousand dollars to prove that they're wrong and it don't happen back there and you fucking admit that it does happen! You were trying to make the judge laugh! You think this is a laughing matter? This is my fucking life, man!"

Vinny slammed down the phone.

Over the next six months, Vinny had his lawyers appeal. They lost. He looked all over the city for another storefront to place Wiggles. He found nothing. He immersed himself in his other deals, with Guccione, with the Siemens people in Germany. He had his crew sitting in no-show jobs at T&M Construction, which meant a percentage of all the hotel renovation jobs they were working at the hotels in Manhattan. He had another guy in a no-show job at Barr Industries, the oil company he was fighting over with the Colombo family. He had his other strip club in Long Island and his restaurants in Queens. His soldiers were complaining that he had plenty but never seemed to have enough. Tin Ear Sclafani confided to Ralphie what a lot of the members of Vinny's crew were thinking: "Vinny always says he's broke. He's a multimillionaire." But Vinny had headaches. Both his kids from the first marriage were on their own and doing well, but he was still paying their college bills. And now his three children from the second marriage, Tara, Danielle, and Vinny Jr., were about to enter the college years. Jaw-dropping demands for money were headed his way. Wiggles, Vinny's number-one source of cash, was gone and Vinny Ocean needed money, and he needed it right away.

On Thanksgiving Day, 1998, the sky turned black and opened up. Torrential rain soaked the Macy's Thanksgiving Parade, and Spider-Man had to be deflated in the thirty-miles-per-hour gusts. The temperature dropped, and it was so dark, parade vehicles turned on their headlights. Babe the Pig had to be dragged down Central Park West and Broadway all the way to Herald Square. Out in Staten Island, it was cold and wet when two guys knocked on the door of the suburban home of Westley Paloscio's mother. She was a tolerant woman, but she was tired of the nonsense. Here was her son, in his thirties, still living at home with his new bride and their new infant, and now there were two guys knocking on the door on Thanksgiving Day with all the relatives inside thanking the Good Lord for their bounty.

"Wes," she hollered, "it's for you!"

Wes came to the door and the holiday-induced smile vanished from his face. Standing in the rain was Anthony Capo, official hatchet man of the DeCavalcante crime family. He also was not smiling. He stood there with another guy Westley did not know. Capo demanded that he step outside, but Westley refused. He stood there in his mother's doorway in the pouring rain, looking at two unsmiling visitors who were definitely not invited to the Thanksgiving good times unfolding a few feet away in a well-lighted dining room.

Anthony Capo had a message for Westley: Pay back the money that Joey O owed to Joey Smash. He delivered his message and walked away with his silent but hulking friend.

The next day Westley was furious. Driving on the Belt Parkway in Brooklyn with Ralphie, he ripped into Anthony Capo.

"I'm getting three of my friends and I'm going to leave him dead in his fucking house. I told him, 'You think I give a fuck? You're gonna come to my house? I have a family.

This is my house on Thanksgiving. I got a family. A fucking house full of people.' "

"I can't believe it," Ralphie said.

Westley said Capo had asked him to come outside the house and Westley refused. He was convinced he would have been shot down right there if he had complied.

"This Joey O thing did you in," Ralphie said.

"Listen," he said, "You learn from your own mistakes. The guy happened to be a nice guy, Ralphie."

"Yeah," Ralphie said. "A funny guy."

Three weeks later two FBI agents showed up at Westley's mother's home. They knocked on the door and asked politely to speak to Westley alone. They had something to tell him. What they told him was that Anthony Capo wanted to kill him. They did not say how they had become aware of this information, but they did mention that they had a duty to tell him.

To Westley, this was a plausible scenario.

For a long time Westley had feared and disliked Anthony Capo. He saw him for what he was—an unstable man who saw everything as a personal insult and was happy to commit acts of extreme violence at a moment's notice. The FBI also let Wes know that they knew he'd had a hand in the murder of Joey O. Then they got in their car and left. This was a tactic, and everyone involved in the little dance between federal agents and members of organized crime knew it was a tactic. It happened all the time. The bureau—which pretended to go about its business unseen—would suddenly step out of the shadows and onto center stage as a kind of deus ex machina. The agents would deliver dire messages and leave. The agents returned to their headsets; the gangsters returned to their social clubs. Everybody went back to pretending they were smarter than the other guy. The agents would then listen even more carefully to see if the information they had imparted inspired conversations involving probable cause.

Between the Gambino family and the FBI, Westley was beginning to come undone.

Driving along the Belt, he suddenly admitted to Ralphie, "There was no Steve," referring to the guy Joey O was supposed to see the night he died. Here was Westley admitting to Ralphie (and, by proxy, to the FBI), that Steve was a made-up person. In fact, "Steve" was really Westley. Westley had called up Joey O and disguised his own voice (barely) to lure Joey O to the empty golf course with the broken clamshells way down at the bottom of Brooklyn.

In just a few offhand comments, the FBI decided that Westley had successfully implicated himself as an accomplice to a murder.

For the FBI agents listening in to the Belt Parkway conversation, this admission definitely fell under the category of probable cause. The trouble was, the bureau did not yet possess a smoking gun. Westley Paloscio would not say how he came to be involved in the killing of Joey O. He merely implied things. He implied that the boyfriend of his mother-in-law, a wiseguy wannabe named Anthony, might have been involved in the shooting of Joey O. But he would not say more. Ralphie was instructed to push harder.

In a conversation that took place on December 8, 1998, Ralphie outlined the FBI's theory of the Joey O murder without mentioning the FBI. The theory was that Vinny Ocean—either by explicit order or by the deliberate indifference of, say, Pontius Pilate—had caused the death of Joey O. "Sometimes I would just like to get to the bottom of it, just for my own personal satisfaction," Ralphie said. "Because nobody gets killed over money. But you know what happened here."

"Ralph," Westley agreed, "you don't get rid of a guy over money if he owes it to you."

"I believe that Joey owed fifty thousand dollars to somebody and they ran to Vinny Ocean, because they knew Vinny was involved," Ralphie said. "And Vinny went like this"—here Ralphie brushed his hands together—"and said I wash my hands. You understand what I'm saying?"

"Now—" Westley started to say.

"He owed you fifty thousand," Ralphie said, getting all riled up. "You know Joey O had nothing but bad luck the last two months of his life. Fucking up everybody, robbing people, not doing nothing right. You think they could kill him without Vinny's okay? I mean that's the bottom line."

And then Westley did what any marginally intelligent felon would do—he deflected attention from himself by implicating another criminal he didn't like. "Nobody really knows this guy Anthony," he said, meaning Anthony Capo, the guy who allegedly wanted to kill him.

"Everybody knew he was with Vinny," Ralphie said, interrupting Westley. "This guy, I mean you go to every wiseguy joint anywhere, these guys all knew Joey O. He went to sit-downs. You understand? He was a bum the last year of his life, but prior to that he was a real fucking man. You know he did the right thing. So somebody had to go like this"—Ralphie again brushed his hands together—"and okay that."

Westley was stuttering, talking about how much Joey owed, but he was not going any further. He was very nervous, specifically about his mother-in-law's boyfriend.

"He's the type of guy that he don't shoot to kill you, but he'll shoot to maim," Westley said. "Somebody's going to get shot."

13

St. George Road sits in the heart of Staten Island between the new and the old. To the north lies a popular golf course with grass of a greenness not commonly seen within the confines of New York City. This color seems almost too green to be natural. Men in white shoes and green plaid shorts drive little carts up and down the hills. Just to the south and west of St. George is the old Staten Island, a fully re-created Revolutionary War–era historic site called Richmond Town. It includes a livery, an old wooden schoolhouse, a hoop maker, and none of it is real. All of it was created from drawings and other documents to duplicate what Staten Island looked like in the seventeenth century, long before golf courses and malls and the Mafia.

At the very end of St. George, where it turns a corner and merges with another road, sits a two-story white wood-frame house. It is an old house for this area, built in the 1950s. It is of the faux-Tara variety, with bogus columns at the front door. There is a gazebo and a fake wooden bridge that arches over a manufactured stream to the left of the front door, and a modest-size pool with a curving blue slide in the right-side yard. A plastic raccoon sits near the entrance. What with all these accoutrements, there is hardly any yard left over. It is the only house on the entire block without a name on the mailbox.

As houses go, this one would be extremely difficult to surveil.

There are no houses across the street, just woods leading up a steep hill to the golf course. Any tinted-window van filled with FBI agents would stand out. Any car filled with gangsters gunning for the house's occupants would also stand out. It is, in many ways, extremely secure, and that was one of the reasons Joseph Sclafani had bought it.

He kept a handgun in a sock next to his bedstead. He kept a shotgun in his closet next to his sweaters. Both were loaded.

Sclafani was an old-school gangster. The FBI had a big fat file on him, listing him as a soldier with a handful of arrests for minor gambling charges and one weapons count. He was suspected in several homicides. He was now Ralphie's boss.

Tin Ear knew the FBI had designated him as a made member of organized crime, and in some ways, he seemed proud. "I was on camera before, so it don't make a difference," he told Ralphie. "They know I'm a wiseguy."

Timing, of course, is everything, and Ralphie was assigned to Tin Ear Sclafani just about the same time as Tin Ear learned he had missed the boat. The high priests of the DeCavalcante crime family passed over Tin Ear for promotion to skipper. In his stead, they appointed the seventy-year-old Uncle Joe Giacobbe who lately had been forgetting the names of people he was talking to. To add insult to injury, Uncle Joe was now to be Tin Ear's skipper. All of this left Tin Ear not a little resentful. The Friday afternoon after Thanksgiving he and Ralphie were sitting in Tin Ear's social club, the Bay Club, on Bay Ridge Avenue in Brooklyn. Tin Ear was complaining.

"I'm no left fielder," Tin Ear assured Ralphie, who was wearing a wire under his shirt. "It's just I had a couple of bad breaks. But I'll get out. I always got out. All my life, I had no problem. It's just that it's a little rougher now."

Ralphie was surprised at how quickly Scalafani had come to like him and tell him things that perhaps he should not have told. The FBI agents who were listening in were also surprised. Pleasantly.

"You know what it is," Ralphie said, slipping into his "comfort the afflicted" persona. "You're a little more cautious."

Tin Ear touched on the subject that seemed to haunt his every conversation—how the old-world wiseguys he knew and loved seemed to have been replaced by a new breed of *goombatta* he simply could not understand. "A lot of this is new," he said.

"You know what the thing is?" Ralphie said. "All these other guys you grew up with, you know what? A lot of these guys, they are all settled in their place already. They're all strong. They're all bosses."

"I could of did that," Tin Ear said. "I could of hung out with them. Right now I could."

They discussed Danny Annunziata, a DeCavalcante captain who lived in a $4 million mansion on Staten Island and owned four health clubs around New York that raked in the big bucks. They sounded like envious stock traders discussing Warren Buffett.

"I don't know what the fuck he was worth," Sclafani said. "His house was four million."

"He got off big," Ralphie agreed. "He got rich."

"Rich? Forget about it! They have ranches. They have mansions."

Tin Ear was the old-school guy who came up through the ranks. He hijacked trucks at midnight, he strong-armed officials of union locals, he eliminated informants by order of bosses he'd met only once at a wedding. He was a muscle guy. He didn't go for manicures and pedicures. He was a short, squat guy with a full head of hair at the age of fifty-four, close-cropped and combed back to keep his permanent scowl prominent. Truth be told, Tin Ear was the spitting image of Jimmy Hoffa, without the suit. He had the flattened nose, the boxer's stare, the rolling walk of a guy who could give a fuck. He dressed like a longshoreman and lived with his mother and mother-in-law on Staten Island. He had been a private first class in the United States Army during the Korean conflict, and he went around telling people he'd been in the Special Forces, where he learned how to snap a man's neck. He still collected two-eighty a week army pension. He knew the rules, and he still believed in them.

When he came out of prison in 1974, he was flat broke. He borrowed money from his nephew, a Gambino associate, and put it out on the street. To make his payments up the ladder, he was forced to rob a payroll on West Fifty-third Street in Manhattan. Then he got wise and began targeting warehouses in small towns in New Jersey. He knew that during the night shift only one or two officers were on duty covering a huge area, which allowed Tin Ear and his cohorts to easily break into warehouses and "pop the seals" on containers.

Nothing was too ridiculous to steal.

Totes slippers. Toner cartridges for copiers. Espresso machines. Tiny glass bottles of perfume. Anything that could be carted off in the middle of the night and sold as swag the next day. They hit the Jersey waterfront, they hit Kennedy International Airport. "A pallet of this, a pallet of that," Tin Ear would say. "I was the score guy. We stole mink coats from Jews in Boro Park. We'd sit in a car, see them walking down the street. You ripped it right off 'em, jump in the fucking car, and you're gone."

"You got a day's pay," Ralphie agreed.

Now everything was changing. It was the end of the twentieth century, the Mafia's century, and the New Mafia had arrived. A late-twentieth-century wiseguy had to come up with new, more sophisticated ways to scam and scheme. Wall Street pump-and-dump operations. Internet fraud. Health care rip-offs. These were plots that left Tin Ear Sclafani confused. He was used to using a baseball bat or a .28 to get the job done. He yearned for the old *On the Waterfront* ways in a time when the waterfront was gone. He still operated a social club when nobody went to social clubs anymore. He still openly boasted about his son's involvement in various crimes when most gangsters did not want their sons to get involved in "the life" in any way. He was a Luca Brasi kind of guy in a Tony Soprano world.

He would tell anybody who'd listen that he had "twenty bodies." This was his way of saying he'd participated in twenty murders, which was more than, say, Gary Gilmore or Jeffrey Dahmer. He claimed he'd learned the correct way to garrote somebody from a guy named Tommy Karate. He claimed he'd shot some guy in the head, then buried him in a spot near the Brooklyn end of the Williamsburg Bridge where a police precinct now sat.

Who knew if it any of it was true?

He watched all the movies and knew the lines. He dropped names. "I know Johnny Depp," he told Ralphie soon after the two began working together. "I know movie stars and producers." At times he seemed more interested in the image of the Mafia than in the Mafia itself. Several times during their many months together, Sclafani and Ralphie talked about television shows and movies. The FBI agents didn't always record those talks because they were considered "nonpertinent." But the agents always noted the fact of these talks in their notebooks.

On this day after Thanksgiving in 1998, the agents scribbled in their notes, "JS and CW talk about TV show, talk about old neighborhood."

Soon Tin Ear and Ralphie got up and left the Bay Club, taking a walk through Bay Ridge. The FBI heard no conversation. The two returned to the club, then got into a car and went for a drive. In Brooklyn they pulled over when they recognized a guy they knew, Bobalu. Before they reached the curb, Sclafani told Ralphie that Bobalu was "a hard-on" and that he said he was Italian but he really was not.

Ralphie asked Bobalu what had happened to a man named Jamesie. Jamesie had been run over and killed after stepping out of a Brooklyn bar called Two Toms. Jamesie owed a lot of bad people a lot of money. Scalfani said, "The same thing happened to Joey O. He went out of control betting and tried to beat the bookmakers."

They left Bobalu behind and drove through Brooklyn. Tin Ear pointed out the window at a social club he used to frequent that was once run by Anthony Rotondo's father, Jimmy Rotondo. Jimmy was the guy who was gunned down by unknown assailants sitting at the wheel of his Lincoln at the curb outside his home in Bath Beach, Brooklyn, with a package of squid on the seat next to him. That was back in 1989, and still they were talking about it. Jimmy Rotondo had known Sclafani for years. He'd controlled a New Jersey union local and made a lot of money.

The home he was sitting in front of when he died next to the squid was huge. He'd kicked back money up the ladder and over the river to John Gotti. At the time no one was completely sure why the assassination had happened.

As Sclafani began to talk, the FBI agents listening in hoped he would answer that question. Instead, they got the World According to Tin Ear.

"I know him all my life," Tin Ear said. "There was no reason for him to get hit."

Ralphie said, "He was a gentleman."

"Oh yeah. He was a good guy. A tough guy."

"We still get compliments about him."

"I don't know what the fuck he got hit for, this guy."

"I was in the can when they got him," Raphie said.

"There's no reason for this kid to get hurt," Tin Ear said. "He's not a rat, you understand? I don't believe in hitting nobody if he's not a rat."

"Right."

"Or he fucks around with your wife or kids or something like that. Or your family. You know? That's the only two reasons I go for the guy. Then you can't just turn around."

"Right."

"If you, like, say a guy wants to screw around with your wife."

"Ohhhfff," Ralphie said.

"That's gone."

"Chop his head right off," Ralphie voluteered.

"He's gone," Tin Ear said. "Or he's a rat. That's the only two reasons. For money, you're not going to give it to him."

Suddenly Tin Ear gave Ralphie the scare of his life. "There are agents right there," he said, pointing out the car window.

"Where?" Ralphie said, doing his best to remain calm.

"Right there."

"It's a dealer's car," Ralphie said.

"I don't know," Tin Ear said. "They're driving with two guys. The guy just put his light on us. Fucking cunt. So we'll work it out, Ralphie."

"Let's hope we can do something."

They drove deeper into Brooklyn, and Sclafani seemed to have forgotten about the agents. They talked about this score and that score, about a restaurant in Carroll Gardens, Brooklyn, being controlled by a member of the Colombo family, about a porno magazine being controlled by a member of another Mafia family. They bitched about traffic in downtown Brooklyn and talked about the yuppies moving into warehouses and driving up the real estate. And, as usual, Sclafani talked about the good old days, about how the yuppie neighborhood once belonged to Joey Gallo. They no longer talked about the FBI. Ralpie was glad. The FBI was glad, too.

With Joey O Masella, the FBI had been forced to listen to hours of excuses. With Tin Ear Sclafani, they got a primer in Mafia etiquette. He was the Amy Vanderbilt of La Cosa Nostra. Again and again he would instruct Ralphie in the proper way to do things.

For example:

Ralphie was having problem with Joey Smash, the Gambino captain nobody liked. If you had a problem you didn't go directly to the boss. You went to Tin Ear, and he went to his boss, Uncle Joe Giacobbe, and then he went to the boss, Vinny Ocean, and things got worked out.

"He's sick, I heard," Ralphie said of Uncle Joe.

"Well, he forgets a lot," Tin Ear said. "But he's the best with our reputation. Shorty. They called him Shorty."

"Shorty."

"From uptown. Only Joey is acting. See if Joey—this is between me and you—if Joey wan't like this"—he crossed his fingers—"with Vinny, I'd be the skipper."

"I know that," said Ralphie, always ready with a compliment. "In a minute. I mean, you should."

"But they know I fight," Tin Ear said. "I get in trouble when I fight."

"Excuse me—you know, you should because you're right in Brooklyn. You're right in the action. He's in Jersey. He's looking to go to a farm and retire, Joe."

Giacobbe had been assigned the job of overseeing a small crew that worked in Florida, which to Tin Ear was similar to winning the lottery. Florida was the easy life. "That's where they should keep him, with the Florida guys. They don't have no problems down there."

In all his talks, Tin Ear seemed torn between respecting authority and resenting it. Consistently he knew one thing—he might be out of it, he might be behind the times, but they still needed him around to do the dirty work.

"I'm an action guy," he explained.

Ralphie laughed, knowing it was true.

"Don't say nothing," Tin Ear said.

"Now, come on Joey," Ralphie said.

"But I think you can figure it out."

"I know," said the informant. "Listen to me, you ain't telling me nothing."

During a drive to New Jersey on February 24, 1999, Ralphie was at the wheel and Joey Sclafani said, "You can just drive. I'll talk." They were on their way to a restaurant on Tunnel Avenue in Secaucus, talking about parenting. Tin Ear was very proud of his two sons, both in their thirties, who had grown up and moved out. Ralphie's son and daughter were teenagers still living at home. Ralphie's son was on the edge of leaving home. He was eighteen. He had his son dropping off envelopes of cash to the dreaded Joey Smash.

"The kids are happy, that's all I give a fuck about," Tin Ear said. "That's what it's all about. You can't hold your kids . . . It's gonna happen to you. Your kids are gonna go."

"Absolutely."

"And I got boys. Girls, they stay close. Then when they get pregnant, their mother takes care of them."

"When you get girls, you gain a son," Ralphie said. "When you got boys, you lose sons."

"Now, with girls, they favor the father over the mother when they're younger. Your daughter's probably the same way."

"Yeah."

"But as soon as she gets pregnant, she goes right back to the mother," Tin Ear said. "But she'll always have that soft spot for Daddy."

"No, she's really close to her mother," Ralphie said. "See, I was away all those years in jail."

Joey Sclafani told Ralphie all about his new idea to scam some money—book publishing.

"What kind of a book is it?" Ralphie asked.

"Christianity," he said. "Let me example this to you. We have a guy, a representative who comes in if they're interested in publishing it. Now you got to make your own deal with them. We already got twenty percent."

"All right."

"They're going to try and say, 'Joey got ten percent and whomever he's doing it with has ten percent.'"

"Is it an easy thing to get done or a hard thing?"

"Let me example," Sclafani explained. "This is what it is. They got forty million followers."

"What group is it?"

"Christianity. Born-again Christians. They got tapes. Wiseman's souls. I got to show it to you. When we go to the restaurant, I'll show it to you."

"Somebody wrote this book and now it has to be published?"

"Right. It's got to be published. They got forty-three million. If each one of them buys the book for a dollar, we have twenty cents each."

"This is a big group."

"They have lawyers and everything."

"And they can't get nobody to touch it."

"Nope," Sclafani said. "It's religious."

"If Barnes and Noble's passed on it, it's big money," Ralphie said.

They talked about other schemes. Ralphie mentioned that somebody named Paulie knew Bill Cosby, Joey Sclafani mentioned once again that he knew Johnny Depp, and then Joey, without warning, started explaining in detail that the DeCavalcante crime family had been secretly involved in an internal war for the last year. The FBI had some idea that this was going on, but the details had never been made clear. Never one to hold back, Joey Sclafani proceeded to provide the bureau with a play-by-play.

What had happened, according to Tin Ear's version, was the New Jersey faction of the family—headed by Fat Charlie Majuri—decided the New York chapter of the family was getting too powerful and had to be eliminated. The New York guys, headed by Vinny Palermo, learned about this before it happened. They learned of it because one of the players, Jimmy Gallo, had been approached by Majuri to do the job. Gallo promptly told Vinny Ocean and the big plot failed. Much of this the FBI already knew from the tapes of Joey O Masella. Now they were hearing for the first time what happened after the Majuri "coup d'état" died with a whimper.

Sclafani made it clear that the majority of the alleged three-man panel—Vinny Palermo and Jimmy Palermo—along with the alleged consigliere, Stefano Vitabile, had decided that the New York chapter was earning more than the other chapters, and thus its elimination would be foolish. This occurred despite the fact that both Jimmy Palermo and Stephano Vitabile were Jersey guys whose power remained ensconced west of the Hudson. They had seen clearly that in order for the DeCavalcante family to survive, they needed the New York guys.

From Sclafani's conversation, it was clear that things had gotten pretty ugly for a while. Sclafani himself had been the target of a hit.

Ralphie asked, "Why would they do something so stupid when things are going so well?"

"'Cause they would get all the money."

"'Cause of the money," Ralphie repeated. "So how do you forget this? How do you put this behind you?"

"You don't."

"You keep it in the back of your head."

"No."

"You forget about it?"

"I ain't forgetting about it."

"That's what I'm saying," Ralphie said. "How do you forget about it?"

"Time," Tin Ear said. "They put a hit out on me, and then I'm going to eat with them? Say bye-bye."

But the war was officially over and the DeCavalcante family was still up and running. In fact, Sclafani was convinced it was stronger than it had ever been. By the end of the decade, the leadership of all five New York families, which were under siege by the federal government, was in doubt. Sclafani mentioned that no new members were being allowed into any of them "on the other side of the border in New York."

"You told me that," Ralphie said. "Why?"

"Because they're too scared over there. They name good guys over here. Everybody wants to go where we are. The whole fucking world wants to come where we are. We have no rats, nobody knows fucking nothing."

"I fucking love it," Ralphie said.

With this talk of Jersey as the promised land, Sclafani had dropped all resentments and animosities. He was now strutting. "You got a real street guy here," he told Ralphie. "Let me tell you something, how you expect a guy to make money here? Guy's got to be a hoodlum. I don't want a guy who's going to be scared of a fucking cop. I want guys who fight these motherfuckers."

"I agree with you," Ralphie said.

"I'd always rather go with a hoodlum."

"If I'm rich or poor, I act the same," Ralphie said.

"Our time'll come," Tin Ear answered.

"It's gonna come."

"We're gonna get it."

July 29, 1999

The Biscayne Bay Marriott was not the most expensive hotel in Miami, but it certainly wasn't the cheapest. At this time of year, with the temperatures hovering consistently near the hundreds, it was easy to book a two-bedroom suite. That gave the FBI plenty of opportunity to enter the suite Tin Ear Sclafani and his new best friend, Ralphie Guarino, booked for a series of "business meetings" and install a special video-camera system that could record for hours at a time. This time they hid the device directly across from the couch in the main room so anyone who was sitting talking would be heard clear as a bell on tape in some courtroom someday. As it happened, Joey Sclafani and the associates he was to meet all liked to sit around on the couch for hours at a time, hatching plots.

The room itself wasn't so bad, with its sweeping view of the ocean and the pool. It was air-conditioned and had the nice balcony, a big color TV. It was late afternoon and Tin Ear was standing outside looking down at the scantily clad crowd. He was providing commentary, like the guy on ESPN. "Look at that one," he called in to Ralphie and his—Tin Ear's—son Anthony. Anthony was a tow-truck driver in his late twenties who spent a lot of time at the weight bench. He considered himself one seriously good-looking goomba. He was of a different time and place from his father, who had gained a little extra around his middle and ate too much red meat and drank too much booze.

"We're not eating that much, really," he had said to assure himself.

"No," Ralphie said. "What did we eat today—eggs? A hamburger?"

"And I still gained weight," Tin Ear said. "Anywhere I go, everything I eat, I gain." Then he had walked out onto the balcony and commented on the beach crowd.

Ralphie soon joined him.

Anthony began talking about a guy named Louie who worked out with weights and got huge. Joey was sensitive about this. He said, "I'm in good shape."

"Yeah, Pop," Anthony said. "You look great, honest."

"Listen," Ralphie offered, "not everybody could be thin, not everybody could be rich."

"I know I look good," Anthony said. "That's it."

"Ha, ha, ha," his father said. "And I look bad."

"I did not say that," Anthony said. "But that booze is no good for your health."

"What's no good?" Tin Ear said. "I do a hundred push-ups a day."

All day Anthony had been talking about different ideas he was working on. His father kept telling Ralphie that Anthony was "a fighter." He was proud of his boy. His boy was insisting that the way to make money was to open a trendy club in South Beach, like the one called Liquids run by the Colombo crime family. The club was written about all over the country because people like Madonna showed up and got to hang around with the wiseguys and the wannabes and everyone was happy. "All they got is money" was how Anthony put it. He was explaining the need to get the big celebrities and pro athletes into the club, which would attract the suckers who would pay ridiculous prices for watered-down drinks just to say later how they sat a few seats away from Madonna. He was speaking a language that was totally foreign to his father.

"It's a hot joint," Anthony was saying. "It's the flavor of the month. They have no loyalty. Boom, whatever is on the radio. You gotta spend money on the radio. You got Hot Z100. They got Jennifer Lopez to come. Sylvester Stallone. They all go there and people want to go see them. They're not going to drink. It's going to see the highlights. I heard at Liquids, they pay a movie star two grand to come and hang out. The attraction is the bait."

"No doubt," Ralphie said.

"You know what's even bigger down here?" Anthony asked. "Fag joints."

"You gotta have a fag for a partner, that's the problem," Ralphie said.

"You gotta have a fag running the joint," Anthony said.

"Yeah, so?" Tin Ear said. "I'd rather have a fag running the joint, making all that fucking money."

"All they got is money," Anthony said. He then suggested opening a topless club under the name Whisker Biscuit.

"Wiskaskit?" his puzzled father asked.

"Whisker Biscuit," Anthony explained. "That's a modern nickname for twat . . . Stupid money. There's the Booby Trap, the Cheetah. They're all making money down here. Hand over fist."

"Can you find a place that's zoned for it?" Ralphie asked.

"Reynolds is looking for that," Anthony said.

Reynolds. Reynolds Moraglia was the reason they were stuck inside a hotel room on a beautiful Florida day. He was an associate of the Colombo crime family, a veteran wiseguy who was now living in Florida and helping to run things for what was left of that family down there. The De-Cavalcante family was hoping to consummate several deals with the Colombo family, which meant that they had no choice about talking with Reynolds. He'd been around forever, and he was one of those guys who could not wait to tell you just how smart he really is. He had a habit of turning any dialogue into a monologue, and for a guy like Tin Ear Sclafani, who was already having doubts about his place in the universe, the sound of Reynolds's voice was like the sound of fingernails on the chalkboard. It was annoying, but it was temporary, and then they had plans to have dinner at a nice crab house in South Beach.

"Should I wear a jacket?" Joey asked his son Anthony for the third time.

Reynolds finally showed up. To make matters worse, he was now talking about the Internet. At this point in his life, heading straight into his sixties, Tin Ear hadn't given much thought to the Internet. He didn't know a dot-com from a Web site. And now here he was, stuck inside a hotel room on a beautiful Florida day with this windbag going on and on about how you had to get on the Internet pronto or that was it for you, pally. His idea was to sell things over the Internet that maybe people couldn't get on the street.

"I got more things going on with Viagra," he said.

"Viagra," Tin Ear said.

"Everybody wants Viagra," Reynolds said. "Everybody."

"I want it today," Tin Ear said.

"Selling it over the Internet," Reynolds said. "We're gonna open a Web site, sell it right over the Internet, I'll make four or five million dollars a week. We're gonna do it, I got the kid write the program on the computer. What's goin' on is unbelievable . . . That's the whole thing. If you're not, if you're not in this world right now, in this fuckin' life that we live every day; if you ain't like a chameleon, if you can't change—"

"You're finished," Ralphie said.

"If you wanna keep thinking like this, fuck you, you're done, you're finished, you're never gonna earn anymore. These fuckin' kids, twenty-five, twenty-six years old, will teach you things you could not ever believe."

"They—they make money with the computer?" Tin Ear asked.

"They're going in banks," Reynolds said. "They got kids that go like this, they go into the banks, they're robbing the banks from their computers, send them the money from the banks to Switzerland. Before they know what's goin' on, they want ten million from them."

"This is the thing today," Tin Ear said.

"They can't stop it," Reynolds said.

Ralphie said, "They can't stop it."

"You gotta be able to change," Reynolds said. "The world's constantly changing—that's why, you know what?"

"I'm old school, you know that," Tin Ear said.

"Change," Reynolds said. "You gotta change."

"I can't change," Tin Ear said. "How the fuck, after all these fuckin' years?"

"Let me tell you something," said Reynolds, using his favorite phrase. "A good guy, you can get any good guy you know, any fuckin' guy you know. A man's man. Goes and does fifteen years, comes home. How long is he home?"

"Three months," Ralphie answered, knowing just where Reynolds was headed.

"How come?" asked Reynolds the teacher.

"Because he's the old school," Tin Ear answered, trying to learn.

"Because he don't know the fuckin' street no more," Reynolds said. "The street has changed."

"Well, I'm changing," Tin Ear promised. "It's hard."

Later that night, after dinner and a visit to a strip club, Ralphie and Tin Ear had a conversation in which they critiqued a new TV movie about Joseph Bonanno, former boss of the Bonanno crime family. Bonanno was now living in Arizona, where anyone who needed to find him could do so by opening up the phone book. He had written a book about himself and got himself a TV-movie deal to boot. The book and movie essentially glorified the good old days of the Mafia, spent much time discussing the "men of honor" myth, and presented the story of Joe Bonanno in a particularly self-serving manner. It was also the first time a boss had confirmed the existence of "the commission," the ruling panel of bosses that controlled Mafia life in the United States. Because of this, an ambitious prosecutor named Rudy Giuliani used the book to indict the bosses of all five New York families in what came to be known as "the commission case." Not surprisingly, the book and movie were not exactly viewed by the wiseguy set as positive developments.

"You've been on the street since you were thirteen years old," Ralphie said to Tin Ear. "Big difference, no?"

Tin Ear: "Well . . . I robbed apples when I was fuckin' seven, eight years old from the pushcarts. Elizabeth Street, Mulberry Street. There was no fuckin' food. We had respect when we were kids. I was born into this fuckin' life. I dream of 'em . . . makin' a movie. If I ever get the chance, I'm the right kinda guy. I don't mean one of them fuckin' Bonanno movies. I wonder what they said about that movie, anyway."

"That fuckin' movie, boy, it's all over the place," Ralphie said. "But, ah, that guy."

Ralphie was referring to Reynolds; he wasn't sure about him. He was speculating about the possibility that Reynolds was an informant. This was an interesting subject for a guy who was himself an informant to discuss.

"Did you hear what Reynolds said?" Ralphie asked Tin Ear. "He didn't give up one guy on Bath Avenue. I thought he gave up everybody."

"He's a fucking rat," Tin Ear said.

Tin Ear and Ralphie noted that becoming a rat did not necessarily mean that one's career was over. In fact, fame and fortune could be involved.

"They're making movies and television," Tin Ear said. "And he appeared on it, am I right or am I wrong? I didn't see it."

"I didn't see it either," Ralphie said, and then he started to discuss Salvatore (Sammy Bull) Gravano, the Mafia hit man who became an informant, testified against John Gotti, wrote a book, and then went on prime-time TV.

"That's the name of your family, he's on TV telling them about us," Tin Ear said, outraged that Gravano could name names and describe specifics and even dare to confirm that there was, in fact, a Mafia. "We're not supposed to say that there is anything," Tin Ear said. "I'm gonna start believing in the movies."

In the movies and in real life, everybody knew that if you started talking about a contract hit with someone else, that person automatically became a coconspirator. By simply listening to talk about a planned murder, you entered into a contract. You became vulnerable. Ralphie had been wearing a recording device for the FBI out on the street for nearly a year and a half and he had discussed his own participation in many crimes—loan sharking, gambling, stealing pallets of Totes slippers. He had never been asked to commit a murder. Now, on this late evening, Tin Ear Sclafani changed all that.

There was a "piece of work." There was a guy, though Sclafani wouldn't say who. Ralphie was going to have to help in some way. Ralphie said of course, knowing in the back of his mind that the FBI would allow you to participate exclusively in so-called crimes of nonviolence but never in anything resembling a murder plot. Now the genie was out of the bottle. Tin Ear had chosen to talk about this planned hit with Ralphie. Ralphie was now part of the crime.

For the first time since the investigation of the DeCavalcante crime family had begun in January 1998, Ralphie was in a situation.

14

In Walker Percy's 1961 novel, *The Moviegoer,* the protagonist, John Binkerson ("Binx") Bolling, describes a process he calls "certification." He had concluded that movie life was more real than real life, a phenomenon he first observed while watching a movie at a small neighborhood theater in New Orleans. He was watching *Panic in the Streets*, a 1959 film noir starring Richard Widmark as an earnest navy doctor trying to stop an epidemic of plague before it races through New Orleans. Binx notices that the neighborhood shown in the movie is the same one he's sitting in watching the movie. The movie had "certified" Binx's neighborhood. He extrapolated certification further, arguing that a real-life street one traversed daily became certified as real if it appeared as an on-location shot in a movie. Sitting in a movie theater watching your street on the screen made the street real. Life had no meaning until it was part of a movie.

The season premiere of a television series called *The

Sopranos took place on January 10, 1999, almost a year to the day since Ralphie Guarino first strapped on a recording device for the United States government. As it unfolded, the show took unprecedented steps to knock down the wall between what was real life and what was purely fictional.

To recapitulate: It was well-known that James Caan had grown up with members of the Colombo crime family and he was, in fact, good friends with Anthony Russo, acting street boss of that family. Russo himself had been convicted of shaking down a producer of *Raging Bull.* Joe Pesci had also grown up with gangsters. Mickey Rourke, who played a gangster wannabe in *The Pope of Greenwich Village,* had visited Gambino boss John Gotti's trial in 1991 and kissed the alleged godfather's ring. And the legendary Joey Gallo, it was said, had spent hours watching gangster films and modeling himself on Richard Widmark in *Kiss of Death* and Paul Muni in the original *Scarface.* In the 1960s, the story goes, an actor who will remain unnamed visited Gallo to learn the correct way to be a gangster. Gallo quicky imparted the wisdom he'd learned from a previous generation of actors.

The Sopranos carried on this tradition. Dan Grimaldi, who played a wiseguy named Patsy Parisi in the TV show, had a sister named Louise Rizzutto who was the girlfriend of Anthony Spero, the acting boss of the Bonanno crime family. When Spero wound up on trial, Grimaldi the actor who played Patsy the wiseguy showed up in Brooklyn Federal Court to lend his support. When *Daily News* writer Mike Claffey asked Grimaldi about the irony of a fictional gangster showing up in court to lend support to a real-life gangster, the response was typical of the show's public-relations line.

"It's just a coincidence," he said.

But *The Sopranos* went a step further. It was hyped for

its extreme realism, but the hype never made clear just *how* real it all had become. The line between fact and fiction disappeared. Real-life gangsters auditioned for parts and got them. The FBI had videotaped two TV actors known for playing gangsters attending a Christmas party thrown by actual gangsters. And more remarkable, real-life gangsters started viewing the show as a kind of justification for their behavior. The characters on *The Sopranos* became heros to the underworld. They were names to be dropped. Santo (Buddy) Sirico, a Gambino associate, started telling people that Tony Sirico, the actor who played capo Paulie Walnuts in the television show, was his cousin. He did this to impress people. Sirico the actor denied the relationship up and down, but the deed was done. TV gangsters had become the ideal to which real wiseguys aspired.

The "certification" was complete.

March 3, 1999

The name Barr Industries appeared stenciled of the sides of Dumpsters from the east end of Long Island deep into the heart of Brooklyn. It was a waste container company owned by a man named Anthony Marcantonio. There were offices near Red Hook in Brooklyn and Ronkonkoma way out in Suffolk County, Long Island. It was a going concern, with one exception. A growing dispute had emerged between Barr and a company called Madison Oil over a $450,000 "debt" Madison claimed it was owed by Barr. Barr was refusing to pay. Usually such matters are hashed out in litigation, with both companies agreeing to settle and at least two law firms walking away with sizable commissions. In this case, that was not to be.

The problem was Chickie Leto. Chickie was a soldier in the Colombo crime family, and he, along with his Mafia supervisor, a capo named James Clemenza, were the secret owners of Madison Oil. And the "debt" they claimed Barr Industries had to pay was simply protection money. Now, Barr was willing to pay protection money. Barr, after all, was in the waste container business in New York, which had long been an open piggy bank for organized-crime families. The trouble was that the owner of Barr, Marcantonio, had decided that $450,000 was too much. Through his father, he reached out to a member of the DeCavalcante crime family whom his family had known for years— Joseph Sclafani, better known as Tin Ear.

The owner of Barr had learned a disturbing thing in January 1999—that Chickie Leto wanted to kill him as soon as possible. He called on his friend Tin Ear, who agreed to help out in any way he could for his good friend, as long as Barr put him on the payroll in a no-show job for a set weekly fee that would start out low and surely rise. Tin Ear, in turn, went to a captain, Anthony Rotondo, who arranged a series of sit-down meetings with Leto and Clemenza. The two families, the DeCavalcantes and the Colombos, then began negotiating who would be picked to suck the lifeblood out of Barr Industries for as long as possible before Marcantonio had to file for bankruptcy. It was purely mercenary, and Marcantonio clearly had no clue what was about to happen to him.

One of the meetings took place at a diner in Queens where Rotondo and Sclafani were supposed to meet with Leto and Clemenza. They'd heard the Colombos were going to bring two more guys, so they did the same, taking along Ralphie and a low-level hanger-on named Billy, who was always joking around.

On the drive to Queens, the DeCavalcante family members felt comfortable complaining about the Colombo family and all their arrogance. There was not a high level of trust evident on either side. Tin Ear had met before with his Colombo counterpart, Leto, and Leto had told him they would have to wait for two other men to show. Tin Ear, who had been all by himself, refused to wait. Now they were driving to Queens for another meeting and already they were hearing that the Colombos wanted them to get in another car and go someplace else when they arrived.

"You know I ain't going," Tin Ear told Rotondo. "They ain't going to do nothing anyway. What are they going to do? They have to be out of their fucking minds if they have something on their fucking minds."

As both Sclafani and Rotondo saw it, the Colombo family was acting as if they were the big-name sophisticates from Brooklyn who were not impressed by the farmers from New Jersey. There was a possibility that the entire meeting was a setup and that they would arrive and shots would be fired. This was just a possibility. Cooler minds on both sides believed that this violence would simply be bad for business and that there was enough of the Barr Industry pie to go around.

"They make rumors about the Jersey guys, that they're farmers," Sclafani said. "That they don't know." He paused. "Now they know."

"Now they know," Rotondo agreed.

As Scalfani was about to make clear, something had happened recently that had made the DeCavalcante crime family a little more respectable in the eyes of the New York families.

"Hey," he said, "what's this fucking thing, *Sopranos*? What the fuck are they?"

"You ever watch it?" Ralphie asked, not sure if it was a good idea to admit to such a thing.

"Is that supposed to be us?" Sclafani said, implying

that he'd watched but not saying whether he paid close attention.

"You are in there," Rotondo said, and Ralphie laughed. "They mentioned your name in there."

Tin Ear—hesitating between belief and suspicion—said, "Yeah? What did they say?"

"Watch out for that guy, they said," said Billy, a knock-around guy who thought he was pretty funny. "Watch that guy."

"Every show you watch," Rotondo said. "Every show you watch, more and more you pick up somebody. Every show."

Clearly Anthony Rotondo—highly respected capo in the DeCavalcante crime family, a man whose father had been murdered by the Mafia when he was just a young man—was a fan of the new TV Mafia show. He began talking about the many similarities between people and places he knew and the TV show that claimed to be so authentic. The first name he mentioned was Gaetano Vastola, but he called him by his street name—Corky. Corky Vastola was a legendary DeCavalcante captain who was six-foot-two and weighed 260 pounds and who once broke the jaw of a loan-shark victim with one punch. He was a big, tough muscle guy who got the job done and never complained. He was, Rotondo felt, the model for Paulie Walnuts, a big, tough guy who got the job done without complaining.

Then Rotondo mentioned Jake Amari, the onetime acting boss of the DeCavalcante family who had died, slowly, of stomach cancer. By the end of the first show, *The Sopranos* had presented Jackie Aprile, an acting boss of the TV family who was dying, slowly, of stomach cancer. To Rotondo, he was "the guy that died and had stomach cancer."

"They had a guy die with stomach cancer?" Billy the club owner asked.

"Yeah," said the still-skeptical Sclafani, "but where do they get that information from?"

"Ah," Rotondo said. "Where."

"Joey," said Billy. "There's somebody close to you there, Joe."

"Huh?"

Rotondo was clearly a *Sopranos* fan. He had found out that parts of the show were actually filmed "right on Third Avenue" in a bookstore. Third Avenue was a reference to Third Avenue in Elizabeth, New Jersey, where Sacco's meat market was located. As the FBI noted in one of its many memos written during the second month of *The Sopranos*'s debut season, "Uncle Joe Giacobbe and other members of the DeCavalcante family regularly held meetings inside Sacco's meat market." In the first episode of the TV show, the members of the Soprano crime family meet inside Centrani's pork store, a few blocks away from Sacco's. In later shows the name would be changed to Satriale's and the filming moved elsewhere, but the idea stayed the same.

"Sacco's," Rotondo said.

"No," Sclafani said. "That's not Sacco's."

"Oh, it's supposed to be," Ralphie said.

"Is it?" Sclafani asked, clearly impressed.

"That's the block," Billy answered.

"They always sit outside," Rotondo said, either of the make-believe gangsters in the show who sit on chairs on the sidewalk in front of the pork store, or the real-life gangsters like Uncle Joe Giacobbe who did the same.

"Yeah, they do," Billy said. "It's Sacco's."

Rotondo was so into the show he'd noticed that a taco joint that appeared in one of *The Sopranos* episodes shots near the fictional pork store mimicked a taco joint located near Sacco's.

"Jesus," Ralphie said.

"Really?" Sclafani asked.

"I'm telling you," Billy said. "You gotta watch."

"So what do they say?" Sclafani said, continuing his futile effort to convince his peers that he was't terribly interested in any of this.

"Aren't they funny?" Rotondo said. "I'm telling you, you ever watch that, Ralph?"

"Yeah, I caught it one night," Ralphie said. "I didn't think it was really that bad."

"What characters," Rotondo said. "Great acting."

"Is this the car?" Ralphie asked, bringing them all back into the real world.

"We're supposed to meet them over there," Sclafani said.

The meeting took place at the appropriate Queens diner without anyone pulling out a gun or even a baseball bat. Nobody walked away happy. The basic problem was insurmountable greed. Everybody wanted everything from Barr Industries. They could not bear to think of the company as a going concern with real customers and employees that relied on a weekly paycheck. They simply saw it as a big pile of cash that rightfully was theirs for the absconding. Neither side was willing to budge, yet. Tin Ear Sclafani in particular walked away from the meeting disgusted with the Colombos and their arrogant attitude. The Colombo family was aware that the FBI had been actively pursuing a case against their boss, Allie Boy Persico, for years, since the day he was acquitted of a racketeering indictment that came out of an internal family war. The war had resulted in the murder of fifteen people, including a nineteen-year-old bagel-store clerk whose only sin was that he worked in a store one wiseguy assumed (incorrectly) was owned by a rival. This is one of the many instances in which the myth that the Mafia only kills its own was exposed for what it is—pure fiction. Because the boss, Persico, had walked out of court a free man, the FBI was in full attack mode to charge him again. The entire Colombo family was under constant surveillance, and thus when they met with their DeCavalcante counterparts, they talked in riddles and avoided declarative sentences. They were maddeningly sparse with detail when discussing who was going to do what to whom. They kept referring to a Jo Jo, whom the DeCavalcante crew figured was Jo Jo Russo, a ranking member of the Colombo hierarchy. But there were so many Jo Jos these days, it was hard to know. Rotondo finally figured out the Colombos were simply and derisively referring to Joseph (Tin Ear) Sclafani by a name he had never been called, not even by this mother.

"He says that's the only way I know how to meet Jo Jo," Rotondo said. "How do I know who Jo Jo is?"

"Me?" Sclafani asked.

"Yeah," Rotondo said.

"They call me Jo Jo now. First I was Little Joey, then Joey Blue Eyes, now Jo Jo. Where the fuck do they get all these fucking names?"

Dilemma begat dilemma.

Tin Ear or Jo Jo or whatever Sclafani was called—his dilemma was simple. His boss, Vincent Palermo, had ordered the murder of a veteran capo named Frank D'Amato, and he had specifically asked Sclafani to get the job done. But D'Amato was an experienced gangster who trusted no one. "He's a hard captain," Sclafani said. "He's good, he's sharp, he works. Very smart." This was Sclafani's problem.

To solve it, he asked Ralphie to help out. Ralphie could not refuse without inspiring great suspicion in his new mentor. And Ralphie and his FBI handlers faced a dilemma as well: how to extricate Ralphie from the plot to murder, which was surely not allowed in any FBI handbook, without tipping their hand and losing their insider informant. Losing their informant would have been a very bad idea at a time when Tin Ear Sclafani was providing them with so much probable cause.

Much of the probable cause came out of Tin Ear's obsession with killing D'Amato. This was a kind of puzzle to the FBI. They couldn't figure out why anybody wanted this guy dead. He earned for the family and he had been around for a long time. True, he was the brother of the one-time acting boss, John D'Amato, who'd been killed by orders of the family hierarchy in 1991. But that was a long time ago. And from what the FBI could pick up, it was clear that Vincent Palermo really did not like Frank D'Amato. Whatever the reason, when Vinny gave the "piece of work" to Sclafani, Tin Ear immersed himself in the details like a lawyer with a new deep-pocket client.

And so, in the spring of 1999, Tin Ear Sclafani enrolled Ralphie Guarino in the Sclafani School of Mob Technique. He overwhelmed Ralphie with stories about this wiseguy and that wiseguy. He distinguished between real wiseguys and pretenders. The truth was that Joey Sclafani seemed to like Ralphie, the way a father takes a son under his wing and teaches him, say, the correct way to tie a trout fly or the perfect stance to assume when hitting a curveball. In this case, Joey Sclafani was teaching his newfound protégé the correct way to kill a guy. And throughout the lessons, there was a hint of resentment over not being appreciated. At times Sclafani sounded like a government worker complaining about how so-and-so won a promotion in clear violation of civil-service rule such-and-such. Always he was there with the longevity business.

"I'm here over forty years," he would whine. "I did things for them."

The lessons were daily and Joey Sclafani never seemed to tire of them. They would talk about everything—about Sclafani's failed efforts to quit smoking, about his recent experimentation with Viagra. They talked in Ralphie's car, in Joey's social club on Bay Ridge Avenue, during trips to Florida to check in with the DeCavalcante branch office. But in the spring of 1999, Tin Ear mostly talked with Ralphie about the best, most convenient way to kill Frank D'Amato.

He seemed to rely on movies to guide his way.

During a March 20, 1999, conversation, Sclafani—intentionally or otherwise—kept referring to scenes from *Goodfellas* as he discussed his plans. He said that when a guy was murdered on orders of the bosses, the guy's name was simply never mentioned again. "Like our Joey O," he said. "If they take you, you'll never hear of him no more. They had a guy. I says, 'What happened to that guy?' 'Oh, we don't talk about him no more.' "

"Don't they okay it with everybody first?"

Joey Sclafani gave the ultimate Brooklyn reply: "Yeah. No. No no no no. It's okayed. It's sanctioned. But they don't want John Doe to know. Like, me to know. If you took a guy, I'm not supposed to know it. They pack 'em up, and say go to a farm or something, like five miles away or wherever the fuck it is. They don't know where the body is, except one guy. They dig the hole. Somebody digs a hole first, and that's the guy that takes it. He just dumps it in and covers it. Nobody knows but that guy."

"That's the right way, Joey."

"Unless you and me did it. We could both dig the hole and put it in. That's the way they do it."

"That's terrific," said the chronically enthusiastic Ralphie.

Then Joey brought up the motorcycle plan. He had decided that Frank D'Amato was an extremely difficult old guy to kill. Frank had been around forever and knew everybody, and because his brother had been murdered, he trusted no one. He would be a tough job. Which was how Joey Tin Ear came up with the motorcycle plot. He was going to pull up alongside Frank's car as he was driving along the highway and blast away. Then he'd speed off into the night while Frank careened off the road, perhaps into a busload of septuagenarians headed for Atlantic City, but you couldn't worry about things like that.

The motorcycle plot had many problems. For instance, Tin Ear did not own a motorcycle. He had been bugging Ralphie to get one from an acquaintance in Florida, and now he was pestering Ralphie again.

"Why are you bringing the motorcycle back up?" Ralphie said. He was clearly not convinced that the plan was a good one, plus he had been instructed by the FBI to delay Joey Sclafani from carrying out his plan for as long as possible. The idea was to collect as much incriminating information while still preventing a death.

"I want it to whack that guy," Tin Ear said, and Ralphie laughed.

"I know, I know."

"I'm dying to whack him."

"I know, I know. Well you have to take me with you."

"I'll get that cocksucker. Even if you ain't there. I go by myself sometimes."

"Yeah, but you got to take me," Ralphie said.

"No, I know, you'll be there. If I got to put him in the

trunk half-alive and bring him to you and say, 'Here, finish this guy off,'" Tin Ear said, and they both laughed.

There was another problem with the motorcycle plan. Tin Ear Sclafani—who claimed he'd been in the Mafia forty years and had twenty bodies—had never ridden a motorcycle in his life.

"They got to teach me how to do it," he confided.

"No, no," Ralphie said. "You just sit on the back."

"No, I want to learn how to ride. God forbid you get shot at, too, and get hit in the leg. I got to learn how to ride."

"One guy in the front and one guy in the back," Ralphie offered, "and you just drive up next to him and 'bango!'"

"We'll get him," Joey Sclafani said. "This guy has got to be gone."

During the next week, Joey Sclafani told Ralphie he had tried four times to kill Frank D'Amato. This was one tough piece of work. The two were told to meet with Vinny Ocean on a street corner outside à diner in Brooklyn. The FBI was very excited about this meeting. There was a good chance that Ralphie—who would be wired to the gills—would be involved in a conversation with Vinny Ocean and Tin Ear about the ongoing unsuccessful attempts to kill Frank D'Amato. This kind of talk would constitute what the government liked to call an "overt act" and would be of use in the conspiracy case they were trying to cobble together against Vinny Ocean. Why they termed it an "overt act" was a mystery. None of the "overt acts" committed by the Mafia were ever "overt."

Nevertheless, on the day of the meeting, they got a disappointment. Tin Ear told Ralphie to stay in the car while he walked over and had a little chat with Vinny the boss. Ralphie waited in the car, and Tin Ear returned a few minutes later, smiling. "We are all right with him, believe me," he told Ralphie as Vinny drove away in another car.

"What'd he say?"

"You hear me talking to him? Well, I could tell you a little bit," Sclafani said, and the FBI leaned forward and turned up the volume. "He says, 'Joey, did you go for the guy?' 'Yeah, I went four times. Yeah, all right. I didn't get him.' "

Ralphie asked, "Did you tell him you were with me?"

"I didn't say nothing."

"Oh, okay."

"Nothing about you. When it's done, I'm going to say, 'Okay, me and Ralphie. Nobody knows, only him.' "

"He wants it done when?"

"Well, I got to do this."

"So let's get the motorcycles."

Joey Sclafani made it clear that killing this Frank D'Amato would not be an easy task. He pointed out, for instance, that nobody else in Anthony Rotondo's crew had assisted in any of the previous attempts. "All four, five guys, I'm the only one who went. By myself I went three times."

"If he gives us a mission, we'll take care of it," Ralphie said.

"We got permission," Sclafani said, demonstrating why they called him Tin Ear. "I got it."

"No, I said mission," Ralphie said. "We'll take care of it."

The problem was not only that familiarity bred contempt, but in the case of the suspicious Frank D'Amato, it also bred high paranoia. This was a familiar Mafia phenomenon—the closer you got to the people with whom you do business, the less you trusted anybody. Tin Ear knew he could not get close enough to D'Amato to kill him because D'Amato knew him too well.

"I got to get a stranger," he told Ralphie, "because he knows it. He stays away. You follow me?"

But with the FBI listening in, Tin Ear Sclafani made it very clear that despite all the little details, despite all the little problems—none of that mattered. His boss, Vincent Palermo, had consulted with the other bosses and the consigliere of the family and there was now no question about what had to be done.

"Vinny said, 'I don't give a fuck, he's got to go,'" Sclafani said. "He's gone. This motherfucker is gone. Like a fucking spaceship."

In the spring and summer months that followed, the FBI began piling up the evidence for probable cause. There was talk of murder, there was actual murder. There was loan-sharking galore. And plenty of extortion. Extortion seemed to be a daily occurrence in Tin Ear Sclafani's life, especially complicated extortion. In the case of Barr Industries, the complexity of shaking down a hapless and frightened businessman had risen to new levels. With the DeCavalcante and the Colombo families bickering over who would obtain the bigger pound of flesh, the owner of Barr, Marcantonio, had decided it was a good time to get out of town. He and his wife bought tickets, boarded a plane, landed in Miami, and then pretended that no one would find them there. This pretense lasted only a few days before members of both families found out where Marcantonio was hiding. They were not pleased. The guy claimed he wasn't running away, that he was just on vacation. But there was the discovery that he had emptied out some of his bank accounts just before his plane took off for the Sunshine State. And then there was the glaring fact that he had sold his house in New York and bought a new house in Florida. And he opened a restaurant, which by happenstance was listed only in his wife's name. For a guy who owed gangsters hundreds of thousands of dollars and who was claiming he was broke, these were considered brazen acts.

Sclafani was explaining all this to Ralphie while he waited for Marcantonio of Barr Industries to beep him. "I'm trying to get straight in my mind what to tell him," Tin Ear said. "But there ain't nothing to tell him. The guy, he's out of order. He's talking too strong. I don't like the way he's talking."

He said he had talked to DeCavalcante capo Anthony Rotondo, who effectively washed his hands of the matter. The decision had been made to leave the owner of Barr Industries to the mercy of the Colombo crime family and Chickie Leto, who had already made it clear that he was going to kill the guy because the guy owned him $450,000.

"He says let them do what they want," Tin Ear said. "They got a free hand with him."

For Ralphie, the conversation about Barr was complicated by his inability to participate in or contribute in any way to a murder plot. His job was to convince Sclafani not to hurt the guy, or at least postpone things long enough for a case to be made against everybody involved in the plot.

"You know what I'm thinking?" Ralphie asked. "What if they look to hurt him and then he comes back and says, 'You know, you were right, Joey. I didn't do the right thing. I apologize.'"

"Then I go back to them and we can make a deal," Sclafani said. "I'll say, 'Well, what are you gonna do here? You came off, you robbed this money, you robbed a half a million dollars. Right after you robbed it, these guys start threatening you, then you put me on the books. You never even came back with fifty thousand, a hundred thousand. You never came back to take care of anybody. You took off to Florida, where you bought a house. You canceled all your businesses here and everything and you said nothing to nobody. You never called me, but you put me on the books so I could keep these guys away from you.' "

Tin Ear was not happy with the position this put him in. Here he was, brought in for protection by a guy who then hit the road and bought a house. In a way, this Marcantonio seemed to be mocking everyone involved. Tin Ear was nearly finished with him. He was considering telling the Colombo soldier Chickie about another piece of property and another business the guy owned.

"I gotta give him all the help I can give him, because he's a wiseguy, you know?"

"I think that works, Joey," Ralphie replied. "That's the right move."

"I gotta do it this way," Joey said. "This kid is too cocky. I really don't know how to handle him but to hurt him. Because he's a legit guy. He's not a street guy. I could go there with a couple guys, break his fucking head. I could say, 'Ay, you gotta listen to me.' But that ain't gonna accomplish nothing. Whatever he's doing, I want guys close to me to work with me. You know what I'm saying? I don't want them to fear me. Well, fear me in the sense that they know if they fuck me they're gonna die."

July 29, 1999

The hardened gangster with twenty bodies on his underworld résumé sat on a hotel sofa in his underwear drinking a beer. He wore a sleeveless white T-shirt, a pair of print boxer shorts, and dark socks. He looked like any man in his middle fifties beaten down by a life of hard living—his whole body slumped a little, as if it was running out of gas. His hair was disheveled, his gut was inching over his belt line. When he talked he sometimes seemed distracted by events taking place inside his head. He sat splay-legged on the couch facing Ralphie Guarino, who was wearing a polo shirt and shorts and looked ready to hit the beach as long as he could stay out of the sun. The men were sitting around chatting, and only one of them was aware that the United States government had hidden a camera in a wall fixture. The camera faced Joseph Sclafani head-on, and Ralphie sat next to him in a cushioned chair, sneezing from the air-conditioning. A cooking show played quietly on the hotel television with the volume low enough that the agents could hear every word as Joey Sclafani explained how wonderful it was to be a member of the Mafia.

"You can never get killed here," he said to Ralphie. "To get killed, you got to fuck a guy's wife. You got to be a rat, or you got to do something really bad. Like, say, I took your money, fuck you, I'm not paying you, I don't give a fuck what you do. But they take care of it their own way. No bullshit this way."

"I believe sometimes guys go because other guys are just jealous," Ralphie said. "But that's all the other crews. Not this."

"No, they're not jealous over here. Well, there's jealousy in every crew. But it's different over here. It's not the—"

"They are more civilized."

Sclafani sat in his underwear and complained about his septuagenarian captain, Uncle Joe Giacobbe. Uncle Joe had recently committed a major-league La Cosa Nostra faux pas—he asked about a guy who'd been killed. Sclafani was implying that Uncle Joe, who had been collecting Social Security for a decade, was beginning to lose it. He said Uncle Joe had asked not once but three times about the whereabouts of a guy who'd been murdered, which was essentially like Martha Stewart forgetting to set out the salad forks. It was simply not done. He was recalling the entire conversation for Ralphic.

"Don't you know you haven't seen him in two years, and you're asking about him? Nobody here, Joey. You asked about him three times already. Every time you opened your mouth, they look back and walk away. He says, 'Yeah, I was wondering why.' What do you mean, wonder why? He says, 'Oh, oh, all right.' Now you know. Don't ask about him no more. You understand?" Once again Sclafani launched into his "why me" shtick, complaining about less capable people being promoted to captain when obviously he should have gotten the nod.

"This is what I'm saying. He may be older than me—he's seventy-five, seventy-six—but he ain't got as much as I got."

Sclafani was beginning to sink into his old war stories mode. The more difficult it was to think about the present, the easier it was to drift back into the past. He began telling a story about a plan to rob an armored car on the west side of Manhattan near Greenwich Village. "My score again," he said. "I always come up with the score." The driver on the job was a gangster named Joey Farrone. They decided to do a dry run. Sclafani instructed Joey Farrone to drop him off on a corner of Varick Street, then drive around the block several times until an appointed time. The problem was Joey Farrone could not handle even the simplest of instructions.

"Joey's got no mind, you know? He always gets lost," Sclafani said. " 'All you have to do, I don't give a fuck what you do, just keep making right turns. Just make right turns, Joe. If you make a right turn, you gotta come back here.' " Ralphie was, by now, laughing out loud. "I'm serious," Sclafani said.

The day of the dry run, Sclafani packed away a pistol with the intention of doing the job if the conditions were right. If they were not right, he would simply check out the details, walk out of the building, and get picked up by his driver, Joey Farrone, for a clean getaway. As planned, Joey Farrone dropped Sclafani off on the corner of Varick and immediately got lost in the winding streets of Greenwich Village. Meanwhile, Sclafani and another gangster walked into the building and right up to the two armored-car guards carrying sacks of money. They did not make a move, but instead saw what they needed to see and walked out of the building. When they got outside, Joey Farrone was nowhere in sight.

"I just keep going around the block," Sclafani said. "Do you believe he left me on the corner for three hours? He just couldn't find me. He took the car home to my house in Brooklyn. Three hours I'm in New York, and I'm calling my wife. She said, 'Joey? Yeah, Joey's here. He dropped the car off and he says he got lost. He says he couldn't find you.' She says, 'It happened again, Joe.' My wife, she knows."

Ralphie was still laughing when Sclafani said, "I had to take the subway home."

The phone rang and Ralphie said, "Who the fuck?"

"Keep it fuckin' ringing," Sclafani said. "I hope they ain't listening to us."

"Oh no," Ralphie said, picking up the phone. When he was done, Sclafani brought up something he'd obviously been thinking about for a long time.

"I'm gonna put you up," he said. "I'm gonna propose you."

For anyone who knew anything about La Cosa Nostra and the secret society and the history and the mythology and everything else, this was a huge moment for Ralphie Guarino. Joseph (Tin Ear) Sclafani had just said he was going to propose Ralphie Guarino for membership in the DeCavalcante crime family. This meant he would be formally inducted into the family. There would be a ceremony and everything, where they'd burn the picture of the saint in his hand and warn him that he would burn just like that if he ever informed on his brothers in crime. He would swear allegiance to the DeCavalcante crime family above all others, including his own family. He would be a made man, a button man, a man of honor. He would have to pay a percentage of his earnings each week to his captain, but no one could touch him without permission from the family hierarchy. His name would grow in stature in certain circles. The fact that Sclafani was willing to do this showed how much he trusted his friend and protégé. It also showed the success of the FBI's daring ruse. They had planted a listening device in their secret informant, and somehow he had thrived. It was rare indeed for someone to be proposed as a made member of organized crime. Some Mafia associates work for years hoping in vain for that magic moment. Here was an FBI informant being proposed for membership. Scalfani was putting his reputation on the line. He was vouching for Ralphie. He had no idea how wrong he was.

"I want to do it," he said.

"Well, thank you," Ralphie said.

"Now, when you're proposed, you're like a wiseguy."

"I know, I know."

"You know what that means? That it's just a matter of time." He explained that he had the support of the three bosses, Vinny Palermo, Jimmy Palermo, and Charlie Majuri. "Though Charlie can't say nothing anyway."

"I can't believe this," said Ralphie, playing his role.

Sclafani then began talking to Ralphie as if he were a bride getting ready for the big day: all the do's and don'ts. "First of all, you're not supposed to get in no trouble, no fights. No problems with wiseguys. But we'll keep you out of that anyway." He was very excited about the whole thing. He warned Ralphie it could take some time. Another associate named Vic, who'd been proposed months before, still had not been inducted into the family. But Sclafani was enthusiastic about getting moving quickly. He was confident he had made the right choice.

"I'd rather you get proposed right away," he said to Ralphie, and to the FBI agents listening in. He asked Ralphie if he wanted another beer, but Ralphie said no.

They discussed heading down to the pool, then Ralphie talked on the phone with his wife and told her he bought white T-shirts and confided that he only wore black underwear but that he bought a white pair so he would wear them under a white outfit.

"You wanna talk to me or you wanna call me back later or something," he said to his wife. "You seem like you're involved in something. I heard the bathroom flushing. Are you finished now? Are you feeling better or are you still hungover?" Pause. "Boy oh boy. What'd you take, mean pills this morning? Hold on." He took another call from Joey Smash, who demanded to talk to him in person. He came back to his wife and said good-bye.

The two men then put sunscreen on each other.

"That's why I do it in the room, because I don't like doing it down there," Ralphie said.

"Why?"

"Because people look at you. You can't put it on right,

you know? I put it on my head," Ralphie said, rubbing lotion on his growing bald spot.

"You should of bought a fucking hat," Sclafani said. "Should I put some of that stuff on my leg?"

"Sure," Ralphie said. "Otherwise you'll cook out there, Joey. I tell you, I can't believe how fucking fat I got. I can't believe how fat I am."

"I need that little bag," said Sclafani, the trained killer.

"What do you gotta bring the little bag down there, right? I don't have a bag. You go down there with bags, they'll think we're shopping-bag ladies. Joey, do me a favor," Ralphie said. "Put this on my back. Yeah. Now the shoulders. This is good stuff."

"Yeah?" said Joey.

"Bain de Soleil. Now I'll do your back. That's where you get it, on the back. You don't realize it. The front, you know it when you're hot. The fucking back, you got no control."

"Nope," said Tin Ear Sclafani, veteran soldier of the DeCavalcante crime family.

"I don't believe how fat I got," said Ralphie, gangster in the making. "Fucking fat."

15

Sometime in the summer of 1999, the DeCavalcante crime family became aware there was a rat in the ranks. The FBI, of course, did not yet know this.

By the summer of 1999, in fact, they were quite pleased with themselves. They had collected thousands of hours of secretly recorded conversations implicating numerous high-ranking members of the DeCavalcante crime family. They had enough, in fact, to bring an indictment. But they faced a dilemma. In the middle of their investigation, one of the key players, Joey O Masella, had been murdered right under their noses by persons unknown. With that in mind, they had pressed Ralphie Guarino to get back out there and see what he could see about the murder of Joey O.

After his many months of wearing a wire, Ralphie had by now grown quite comfortable in his role as secret agent. He had worked his con to such so effectively that he was about to be proposed for membership in the mob. The FBI and Ralphie both felt Ralphie could ask aggressive questions in order to figure out who killed Joey O. The problem was, with Tin Ear Sclafani, it was difficult to know what was actual knowledge and what was inference. Ralphie had grown weary of Sclafani's stories. It got to the point where he began his work day by talking into his recording device before he headed out to meet Tin Ear.

"Going to meet Joey Sclafani," Ralphie would say into the tiny microphone. "See what his story is today. Every day he's got a new story."

On this day he was again trying to find out who killed Joey O.

"If somebody killed your nephew, wouldn't you like to know what happened?" Ralphie had asked Tin Ear in one FBI-monitored discussion. "What'd he do wrong that he had to be killed?"

"I know who did it," Sclafani said. "I have the best idea who did it."

Ralphie said it had to be Vinny who ordered Joey O murdered. "He got mad," Ralphie said.

"No, it wasn't Vinny," Sclafani said.

"No? No? I thought it was."

"Possibility."

With Sclafani, nothing was clear. He said Westley Paloscio knew more than he was saying, but that was all he would say. The bureau sent Ralphie to talk with Westley. He found him in a state of pure terror, convinced that someone was going to kill him, though he wouldn't say who. All he would admit was that the Steve who called Joey O the night of the murder wasn't Steve, that he was Steve and that he had pretended to be Steve to lure Joey O to the deserted parking lot at the bottom of Brooklyn. That was as far as it went. The more questions Ralphie asked about Joey O's murder, the more nonanswers he and the FBI received.

Then Vinny Palermo stopped using the free cell phones Ralphie had been providing. In fact, Vinny Palermo seemed to stop talking on any phone. Somehow getting information was becoming more and more difficult, and the FBI did not know why.

Inside the DeCavalcante crime family the guessing game was under way: Who was a rat?

Every gesture was scrutinized. Every question was second-guessed. Innocent comments became infected with nefarious intent. Allegiances were formed, lines were drawn. Who could be trusted? In a world where lying was an everyday event, this was not a simple question.

Everybody had their favorite suspect; usually it was the guy you hated most. Tin Ear Sclafani, for one, had decided Anthony Capo had to be the rat. He hated Anthony Capo because he believed that in his world of criminality Capo was a man you could not trust. He had heard that Capo wanted to kill Westley Paloscio because of the murder of Joey O Masella. Westley was considered "with" Sclafani, so, if proper Mafia etiquette was followed, Anthony Capo should have approached Sclafani and explained his reasoning. Perhaps Sclafani would have given him permission to do what had to be done. But Capo had ignored Sclafani, and Sclafani was furious. He sought a meeting with Vinny Ocean and Vinny had instructed both men to work out their differences. Sclafani felt that Vinny was protecting Capo because he needed Capo around to do his dirty work. Vinny wanted proof. Sclafani kept going back to Vinny, warning him that Capo was trouble, but Vinny stood by his guy: "If my guys did something wrong, I'll kill them tonight. Before the sunrise, tonight, there'll be two dead bodies there. You got proof they did it?"

Other culprits were found.

By midsummer, it was decided that Thomas Salvata, the front man at Wiggles, was an informant. Salvata was a silver-haired middle-aged wiseguy wannabe who'd served for years as Vinny Ocean's eyes and ears at Wiggles, watching the money and making sure Vinny got his fat envelopes of unreported cash every week. He had also been involved in collecting loan-shark payments from T&M Construction. After Wiggles closed and he recovered from a heart attack, Salvata had been put in charge of Gentlemen's Quarters in Babylon, Long Island. Then he went off the radar screen. This was out of character for the doggedly loyal Salvata, and whenever a wiseguy did anything out of character, he immediately became suspected as an informant.

A new suspect was picked in November 1999. His name was Frank Scarabino, a hulking DeCavalcante associate who had acquired the nom de wiseguy Frankie the Beast. There were actually several Frankie the Beasts in various families. This particular one had been sitting in a backup car when Vincent Palermo and others shot the would-be Staten Island real-estate mogul Fred Weiss in 1989. Frank Scarabino had been around a long time. Now, with word of an informant circulating faster than police gossip through a doughnut store, the bosses of the family decided that this particular version of Frankie the Beast was acting funny. This Frankie had been asked to show up to a meeting, and he had refused. He had even gone into hiding. As a result, a hole was dug in a remote urban wasteland section of northern New Jersey that was just big enough to encompass Frankie the Beast's enormous frame.

•   •   •

On a September day in 1999 Vinny Ocean and his trusted and hard-of-hearing soldier, Tin Ear Sclafani, stood on a street corner on the Brooklyn waterfront chatting. They were down near the bottom of Fulton Street in the shadow of the Brooklyn Bridge. This was the site of the old Brooklyn ferry that had inspired Walt Whitman to write his famous poem. This was also a spot seen in a thousand movies and TV shows—the swirling edge of the East River, the most beautiful bridge in the world, the Manhattan skyline in magnificent display on the far shore. This was a popular spot for tourists in buses and braver tourists who'd taken the subway over from Manhattan and wandered down to water's edge. It was not an easy spot to find.

At this time Joey Sclafani was doing the best he could. In the past year he had made a few thousand here and there selling "a pallet of this, a pallet of that" stolen from tractor trailers and warehouses on the Jersey and Brooklyn waterfronts. There was the 2,250 cases of stolen Due Torri Pinot Grigio wine, 1,630 cases of stolen Gucci clothing, 29,000 packages of stolen Centrum vitamins. Joey and his cohorts would take anything. A truck trailer filled with Kraft food products. A load of 56 Minolta copy machines and accompanying toner cartridges.

The theory was, somebody would buy this stuff.

At that moment Sclafani was not swimming in money. Much of the time the FBI sat listening in on his many lengthy conversations with Ralphie, Sclafani whining about how broke he was. Sometimes he would complain that Vinny the boss was a multimillionaire and didn't pay attention to the needs of his soldiers, but usually he remained loyal and willing to do whatever had to be done. Lately there had been a lot of missions but little action. The Big Ears Charlie Majuri hit had been nixed when all sides agreed Big Ears Charlie wasn't worth killing. The Frank

D'Amato hit was not succeeding because D'Amato was too difficult to kill. None of this had resulted in the boss being in a better mood. Of late, Vinny Ocean was as unpredictable as, say, the ocean. One moment he would be asking about a person's family, how everybody was faring; the next minute he'd explode into a tirade about respect.

On this day the two men were meeting on a street corner to discuss business. Vinny was getting an update on the lack of progress in the continuing effort to kill Frank D'Amato, a guy Vinny Ocean really did not like. Tin Ear Sclafani was making it clear the job was not going to happen anytime soon. They were unaware that the FBI was watching from a van parked across Fulton Street right in front of the building that once housed the old *Brooklyn Eagle* newspaper and its intrepid scribe, Walt Whitman. The agents could not hear what was being said, but they could see what was going on.

They saw two men, one in his fifties and one nearly sixty-two. The younger man, Vinny Ocean, gesticulated and talked on and on in an agitated manner. The man in his sixties, Joey Sclafani, nodded patiently but said nothing. As the two men talked, a hapless tourist wandered up and asked for directions.

The flustered Vinny Ocean broke away from his conversation about homicide, stepped back, looked at the tourist, and suddenly began frisking the tourist down, right there on the street.

The tourist, unfamiliar with the customs of the New Jersey Mafia, backed off quickly and headed away from the agitated man. He seemed baffled yet grateful to be walking away. The FBI watched as Vinny Ocean and Joey Sclafani walked away in different directions. The agents watching this were aware that Vinny and other members of the family knew they were being watched. Twice in the last few months agents had been forced to warn members of the DeCavalcante group that they were targets of intended hits, as they are required to do when they learn of any potential homicide. But usually it was all a little game—the good guys watched in secret, knowing the bad guys knew they were being watched. The bad guys went about their business, fully aware they were under surveillance but pretending nobody could see what they were up to. Rarely did either side acknowledge the other. Vinny's loss of control on the street corner indicated that the game had changed. The FBI was not yet sure how.

September 3, 1999

"I don't like to talk on the phone no more," Tin Ear told Ralphie. The two were discussing a sample of counterfeit Tommy Hilfiger jeans Ralphie had obtained from fellow DeCavalcante schemers. They were waiting for Wes Paloscio to show up with the truckload that Ralphie estimated could be worth $20,000.

Sclafani asked, "This could be a steady thing?"

Of late, Sclafani was scrounging. His plan was to sell the jeans and put the money on the street at usurious interest rates. "I know I gotta steal in the street. I may have to do a stickup or something pretty soon."

Ralphie had been kicking around a plan to rob a payroll delivery at an office building in Times Square. He had talked it up as a huge score, leaving out that it was just an FBI setup designed to keep him on the street. Joey Sclafani was very interested in the score and impressed with his protégé. He was more confident than ever about proposing Ralphie for membership. He said he had both Palermos—Jimmy from New Jersey and Vinny Ocean—on his side, which should seal the deal. "They love me, so if they love me and they like you, where you gonna be?"

Ralphie wanted to know if they should accept Vinny Ocean's invitation to visit his new gambling boat. This was Vinny's replacement for Wiggles, which had been closed for almost a year. Vinny was a secret partner in a casino boat running out of New York. The idea was to take advantage of the fact that if you cruised two miles offshore, you were in international waters and no longer subject to the laws of New York State that prohibited casino gambling. Vinny's casino boat sailed through the strict approval process for two reasons—Vinny was not listed on any paperwork as the actual owner, and Vinny had hired a former judge to handle the matter. The ship was an instant success, which inspired Tin Ear Sclafani and Ralphie and just about every other low-level gangster in the DeCavalcante family to believe that Vinny was rolling in the green.

"He's got money all over the place. He could cover anything. They close one joint, he opens a boat. He's covered. I'm not covered," Sclafani said. "Imagine a two-million-dollar boat, a three-million-dollar boat. Where did they get this money?"

But there was a problem with this boat. Sclafani said Ralphie could visit the boat but he could not because the FBI was watching the boat. "They're taking pictures of it already," he said. "Like a wake. Who's going in there, who's going out." He laughed. "You know what they're going to do when they find out he owns that fucking boat?" The FBI was everywhere. They were on Long Island taking pictures of Vinny's boat, they were in New Jersey watching Jimmy Palermo. "They came there to break his balls," Sclafani said.

Clearly Sclafani knew the FBI was getting closer, but he felt so comfortable around Ralphie that he began, for the first time, openly talking about the hierarchy of the De-Cavalcante crime family. He was practically sketching out a diagram of corporate structure. He did not bother with code.

"For five years he was number two over there," Sclafani said of Jimmy Palermo.

"Why didn't Jimmy Palermo take over everything?" Ralphie asked, pressing for more probable cause. "Why did Vinny?"

"He got lazy, so they took him down. He wasn't active enough. You need somebody running around," Sclafani said. He kept referring to John Riggi, the actual boss of the family who was sitting in a jail cell in Fort Dix, New Jersey, as "the other guy." As in "When the other guy went to the can, nobody knew how to run the company. When you gotta run the company today and you're a made guy, and he's in the can, they put in a committee of three. That's the deciding vote. You got three guys, and the consigliere picked three guys. That's three guys to run the family."

He went on to disclose more rules and regulations, and expressed increased confidence that Ralphie would be accepted as a made member of the family and that he himself would soon win his promotion to skipper he'd been seeking practically since 1982, when he first became a soldier.

"If I become skipper, you'll be with me," he said, and grumbled again about where Wes was with the Hilfiger counterfeits. Wes was, as usual, late. Then Sclafani got weepy. He made it clear that he was proposing Ralphie in order to leave behind a legacy. He seemed convinced that he was going to die.

"God forbid I get killed tomorrow, they know you're all right," he said. "I put my life up for you already. I want you to be with me all the way."

"This way we can go together, do things," Ralphie said.

"Let me explain something to you," Sclafani said. "This is very important. You can't get into no trouble right now. No fights. I mean, if your back's against the wall . . ." He was referring to the $40,000 Ralphie owed to a soldier in the Colombo family, who was not happy of late with Ralphie.

"I'm gonna go slow," Ralphie promised. "I'm not gonna lie."

"I'm gonna say you're over here with me," Sclafani said. "I'm your guardian knight. You're established. The main thing is make money. Don't bother them with no money problems."

One of Wes Paloscio's friends showed up and said Wes was stuck in traffic with the truckload of counterfeit goods. They agreed to reschedule for the following Tuesday. The score was off for the moment.

October 27, 1999

The devices were small and could be hidden. Their sole purpose was to secretly record conversations. Four days before Halloween, a customer walked into a local Radio Shack somewhere on Long Island and bought two. The customer in question was Vincent Palermo, ranking member of the DeCavalcante crime family.

Things had been going so well for him. He was about to reopen Wiggles after more than a year. He'd managed to convince the city that he was now meeting the 40 percent requirement. His daughter from his first marriage, the schoolteacher who was headed out of her twenties and was still single, was about to get married. The ceremony was set for Thanksgiving weekend. One of his daughters from his second marriage, Tara, had just started college at a nearby university. But there was a dark cloud. Word was out that there was an informant walking around with a wire. Vinny Ocean knew this because one of the family's soldiers had told him. The assumption was that the informant's earnest efforts would ultimately result in the arrival of federal agents and the unveiling of multipaged indictments with numerous references to organized crime.

Vinny Ocean decided what was said was said.

All he could do now was damage control. His solution was to fight fire with fire, or more specifically wire with wire. He went out and bought two little microcassette recorders small enough to fit in his pocket. He figured that if he recorded his conversations, he could collect what lawyers called exculpatory evidence. In simple terms, this means proof that he was really just a modestly successful business guy from Long Island who had a couple of restaurants and was working on selling Penthouse lingerie to the Chinese. His name could be found on no documents. In addition to all the cash he took in, he also had plenty of traceable income from legitimate businesses, like the restaurants. He looked the part of successful businessman. He did not look like a guy who shot Fred Weiss in the face on a Staten Island morning exactly ten autumns ago. He could pull it off. The trick was to secretly record dangerous people without anyone discovering he was walking around with a wire. Naturally, if he was discovered, this could prove to be very dangerous to his well-being.

On this October day, he tried out his new machines on a deli owner named Joseph. He'd loaned Joseph $15,000 to pay his mortgage, which Joseph had agreed to pay back at a rate of interest that could crush small animals. When he was unable to pay, Vinny put one of his people in a no-show job at the man's deli. The man's salary went to Vinny. Now Vinny met Joseph at his restaurant in Queens,

Sea World. He had the tape recorder turned on, and he said hello. It was an odd moment in the history of the American Mafia, an acting boss of a crime family sitting in a Chinese restaurant secretly recording a loan-shark victim to prove his innocence. Imagine Don Vito Corleone secretly recording the words of the undertaker promising to "use all my skills" to patch up the body of his assassinated son. It was difficult to picture.

The idea was to have a conversation in which any action that could be interpreted as an act of extortion or loan sharking could instead be explained as an act of extreme altruism by a charitable soul and all-around great guy. Vinny got right down to business.

"Did I ever give you any money?"

Joseph's answer was unintelligible. The tape was turned off, then back on. Vinny continued, abandoning any pretense of subtlety.

"Did you ever give me money?"

Again the answer from Joseph was unintelligible. Vinny was an amateur in the James Bond game.

"Did I ever put that guy in the deli? Did I ever extort you?"

"No," Joseph said, keeping it simple.

"No," Vinny continued, helping Joseph out. "I never extorted anybody in my whole life. You hear what I'm telling you?"

"Yeah," said Joseph.

"Never," Vinny said. "Today is October twenty-seventh, 1999. They could look till October twenty-seventh of two million, they will never, never, never find anybody to say that they gave me one penny. Never. I never did that in my whole life."

"I agree with you," Joseph said helpfully.

With the tape running, Vincent Palermo tried to explain

himself. At times he seemed to be talking directly into the microphone, as if Joseph was not there. "Maybe it's on their mind, the question I asked you with the deli. Did I know that guy?" He didn't say who "they" were. He seemed to have lost his train of thought. "I mean, I always treat you like my brother."

"I know," Joseph replied.

"The problem, the one time you were behind on your mortgage, remember? You needed the fifteen thousand dollars. I borrowed under my name from the business where I was working to help you with that."

Joseph's answer was unintelligible. Cars beeped in the background.

"You know what I'm saying? And I told you, Joe, don't worry about paying me back. Whenever you have it. And you came to my house and said, 'Why are you doing this? Don't you understand? My own family don't do this.' I said, 'Joe, I like you.' What could I tell you? 'I like your family, you're a family man, I see you work hard, you're a good man, and I helped you.' Huh? What's wrong with that? Everybody should do that."

Joseph, who by now was an active participant in the little one-act play, said, "I agree with you." This clearly was his favorite line.

"As far as taking a penny, I never, ever took a penny from anyone in my whole life," Vinny said. "Ever. Okay?"

"I agree with you."

Then the tone of Vinny's little chat took a turn toward the slightly menacing.

"It makes me angry that certain people mention certain things that's not true," he said. "And they listen to some asshole who's maybe jealous. You know what I'm saying, Joe?"

Before it got ugly, the wife of Vinny's partner in the

restaurant walked over to the table and said hello. He called her Mrs. Kim. Vinny asked her how she was, said his wife was asking for her as well, then began using her to augment his argument. He told her he was about to reopen Wiggles the following Monday. He was headed over to the club to supervise preparations for the big reopening of the legitimate business that he secretly owned.

"If I start now, I'll be done at five, five-thirty in the morning," he said, launching into his favorite bootstraps monologue. "I worked my whole life. Eleven, twelve years old. Two jobs. All my whole life. I love to work. People see that you have a nice house, a nice car, they figure maybe you did something wrong. My whole life, Mrs. Kim, never never did I do one thing wrong. That I know of."

Mrs. Kim laughed nervously.

"Because I don't have to. I like to take something, keep moving up. Understand? My house, I bought my house, my car. Nobody gave me these things. All my life I've been a workaholic. Three jobs, four jobs. Even now, I put in fifteen, eighteen, twenty hours sometimes a day, all week long. Working. Some people are jealous, some people are stupid. They say, 'Oh, nice house, uh-huh, there must be something wrong.'" He began to get angry. He assumed the persona of the furious taxpayer. "That's bullshit! I worked, I pay my taxes. I don't do nothing wrong! Some people have big, big mouths, that's the problem. Everybody keeps quiet, you wouldn't have a problem. It's all bullshit."

The tape continued to play, but there was no more chatter, just the background sounds of the restaurant. As he headed outside, he stopped by to make one more comment to Mrs. Kim.

"Just wanted to stop by and say hello," he said, and then the tape went dead.

November 28, 1999

The wedding reception was held at a banquet hall on the South Shore of Long Island and it was well attended. Renee Palermo, New York City schoolteacher, was to wed Emil Onolfi. She was about to receive her master's degree. He was a heavy-equipment mechanic for the county of Nassau on Long Island. It was a late-blooming romance. They had been dating for two years. He had two children from a previous marriage. They were planning on moving to the south shore of Long Island.

The father of the bride, Vincent Palermo, had five children from two marriages, but this was his first daughter to get married. He invited his family, and with seven siblings, that was a lot of people. He also invited all his friends, including the entire hierarchy of the DeCavalcante crime family. They all showed up with envelopes of cash for the bride and groom. For Vinny Ocean, it was supposed to be a happy day.

And it was. Until he happened to spot the men outside the banquet hall with telephoto-lens cameras. The men were walking from car to car, jotting down license plates— just like in *The Godfather.* Everyone knew this was part of the little dance with the FBI. They wrote down your license plates and took pictures of your guests; you pretended they weren't there.

But the pressure had been mounting.

The service was over, the guests were eating dinner, and Vinny was boiling like a teakettle. He could not believe they had the cannolis to show up at the wedding of his daughter. Was there no honor? Was there no respect? Despite warnings from his associates, Vinny suddenly broke away from the crowd and ran outside.

The agents were taken by surprise. There they were,

doing their jobs, playing their parts, when all of a sudden this crazy person came running out of the banquet hall in his tuxedo, frothing and fuming. He waved his arms passionately and shouted epithets that the priest from Sacred Heart Roman Catholic Church who was inside probably did not hear.

"Enough!" he shouted. "Enough!"

The agents backed away but did not leave. They moved across the street and continued to do their jobs. Vinny Ocean walked back inside to his daughter's wedding reception and that was that for the rest of the day.

The day after Thanksgiving, the Christmas season kicked off in New York City officially, although it had been up and running for weeks. The crowds grew heavier at Rockefeller Center and along Fifth Avenue. Vinny Ocean's wife went about her usual business of shopping and keeping house. The two youngest kids went to classes at their private schools, and the oldest daughter continued her freshmen year at Fordham University in the Bronx. Everything seemed normal, with one exception. The agents who staked out Wiggles weren't seeing any sign of Vinny Ocean. He had stopped using the cell phones Ralphie Guarino had given him and they hadn't heard his voice in a long time. Ralphie asked around, but nobody could say for sure where he was. After a few days of searching, the agents reached a conclusion.

Vinny Ocean had disappeared.

16

DO YOU OWN *THE GODFATHER*?

There was a time in the 1960s and 1970s when prosecutors had to spend a good amount of time educating jurors about the ways of the Mafia. They would bring in expert witnesses to explain a little history of the secret society, talk about the difference between a capo and a soldier, shed some light on the concept of *omerta*. There would be charts and graphs and other visual aids. In those days this was new territory. People had to learn the language before they could even consider the case itself. It was all a little mysterious, even exotic. By the end of the twentieth century, the mystery was gone.

The change was best illustrated by jury selection in *United States* v. *Steven Kaplan*. Kaplan was identified as an associate of the Gambino crime family who was running first a nightclub in Boca Raton, Florida, and then a nude club in Atlanta, Georgia. He was indicted by federal prosecutors in Atlanta on racketeering charges for allegedly paying protection to the Gambino family. In exchange, they let him use the Gambino name to get what he wanted. It was an unusual case in that most of the big traditional organized-crime prosecutions take place in New York and New Jersey, where people are somewhat more familiar with the quirks and jargon of the genre. The presence of the family run by John Gotti south of the Mason-Dixon presented both sides with a challenge: How would the Mafia play in mainstream America?

It was difficult to know going into the case what the people of metro Atlanta knew or thought about the Mafia. During jury selection, the defense attorneys and federal prosecutors haggled over what questions to ask to weed out potential prejudice in either direction. They questioned people about their feelings regarding strip clubs ("Do you have any particular feelings toward nude dancing establishments which may interfere with your ability to be impartial in this matter?"). But they spent a lot of time inquiring about the Mafia and, more specifically, Mafia movies.

"Do you or your spouse have any specific interest in or fascination with the Mafia?" was one of the first mob questions. It assumed that everybody knew what the Mafia was. Jurors were then asked if they had known anyone associated with the Mafia. They were then given a Mafia primer, and asked if they were "familiar with the terms 'La Cosa Nostra,' 'made man,' 'soldier,' 'captain,' or 'LCN'?" Specifics about the real-life Mafia followed: "Have you ever heard of John Gotti?" "Have you ever heard of the Gambino crime family?"

Then came questions about the pretend Mafia of TV and movies and even the Internet. They asked jurors if they watched *The Sopranos* or visited Mafia Web sites. They asked which books jurors had read "on the subject of the Italian Mafia." They asked jurors to list all the mob movies they'd watched in the last five years, and specifically whether they'd seen any of *The Godfather* movies. "If yes, how many times and do you own any of these movies?"

During jury selection, most of those who were asked these questions had some familiarity either with the TV show or the movies. One woman admitted she was a big *Sopranos* fan, which prompted concerned questioning by Assistant United States Attorney Arthur Leach, who was afraid she might be a kind of Mafia groupie. *The Sopranos* presented the capos and soldiers and their families as somewhat sympathetic figures, which was a concern to a prosecutor who was about to present the Gambino crime family as the epitome of evil. Leach thus found himself asking this juror about totally fictional gangsters in his effort to prosecute real-life gangsters. He asked about Tony Soprano, the fictional mob boss, and the woman said she liked him. A bad sign for Prosecutor Leach, but perhaps not reason enough to justify kicking someone off the jury as being prejudiced against the government. He decided to ask about another TV character named Big Pussy, a soldier who becomes an informant against the people he'd grown up with.

"Oh, him," the potential juror responded. "He's a rat."

The juror was summarily removed from the panel.

December 1, 1999

The sixteenth-floor office of DMN Capital Investment looked like hundreds of other small investment firms located deep in the heart of capitalism. It was located right on Hanover Square a few blocks from Wall Street, and it included all the trappings of high finance, which is to say legitimacy. If an investor took the time to check out DMN, he would find oak wainscoting, fake masterpieces, and ersatz walnut furniture in the hallway and DMN CAPITAL in gold block letters on the polished oak doors. Inside the office there was plenty of blond wood furniture, green-blue carpet, and two dozen plastic telephones trilling away. A smart conference room with a door to shut out the trill-trill-trill looked out on the old Farmers Insurance building, one of the premiere landmarks of lower Manhattan. If the diligent investor had the time, he would watch and listen as a dozen brokers and stock promoters worked the phones, cold-calling senior citizens culled from specially prepared lists. The investor would hear the hard sell, as aggressive young men hyped over-the-counter chop stocks, stocks that allowed the willing investor to bet on the fortunes of tiny companies nobody had ever heard of. Companies that owned health clubs in the American Southwest. Companies that sold in-home nursing care or recycled roofing shingles. Companies that claimed to operate Web sites. And those phones were humming, with the biggest bull market in the nation's history charging forth to make everybody rich. Everybody—not just the descendants of the *Mayflower*'s original passenger manifest. Everybody! Taxi drivers. Toll collectors. Chinese-food deliverymen. And DMN was right there at 5 Hanover Square, surrounded by the happy drone of capitalism, ready to make some money.

The FBI was there, too.

On this day, as money was being made, microphones hidden inside the walls of DMN Capital picked up every word spoken, every curse uttered. The Dow was cruising back toward 11,000, the government was cranking out reports that made everyone feel good about dumping their life savings into the stock market, and the FBI was taking notes about the events unfolding at DMN. The dozen brokers and promoters sat at their desks amid stacks of papers and lists of names, hammering away, keeping those customers confident, unaware that somewhere, documents were being drafted.

DMN, after all, was really just a branch office of the Bonanno crime family. It was controlled by a Bonanno captain named Robert Lino, who was called the Little Guy because he was, in fact, little. He was a young man with a Julius Caesar haircut who stood about five foot two inches tall and spoke quietly and deliberately. Every week he showed up to pick up his fat packages of money. In exchange, he lent his name and the prestige of the Bonanno family to DMN. This made DMN an unusual place.

For instance.

A few months earlier, a Colombo family associate who believed DMN owed him $40,000 stormed into the office, pulled out a .38, and shot up a computer.

A stock promoter who wasn't doing what he was told was sucker-punched in the head and knocked out cold in the company's conference room. His colleagues then stripped off his shirt to make sure he wasn't wearing a wire.

The three DMN partners—Jeffrey Pokross, Sal Piazza, and James Labate—were actually Bonanno associates. Pokross had actually once been a broker but had his license revoked for making unauthorized trades. Labate and Piazza couldn't tell yield burning from short selling, but they liked to make money. As the lunch hour ticked by and the Dow crawled north, the DMN partners sat in the conference room. They were not talking tech stocks or bitching about blue chips. They were discussing another investment they had made in a New York Police Department detective named Stephen Gardell.

Detective Gardell, a decorated veteran of the New
York City Police Department who looked exactly like a
decorated member of the New York City Police Department, lived on Vineland Avenue in Staten Island. He had
snow-white hair, a ruddy complexion, and the look of a
man headed straight for the pension board at age fifty-
two. He'd solved many of the city's toughest cases as a
member of the Brooklyn homicide squad and his name
had appeared in the paper under the heading HERO COP.
He'd risen through the ranks to collect an $80,000 salary.
This did not make him a millionaire, but he did all right.
He lived in a rented house with a $3,000 aboveground
swimming pool in the backyard. The pool had been con-
structed expressly for his use, though it was built on land
owned by someone else. This was not a problem for Detective Gardell, because he had not paid out a dime. A
friend of his took care of the whole thing. The friend was
his neighbor from down the street, James Labate, who
everybody called Jimmy. As it happened, Jimmy Labate
was an associate in the Bonanno crime family of La Cosa
Nostra.

In Staten Island, this was considered normal. After all,
somebody has to live next door to the Mafia.

Because Labate and Detective Gardell were neighbors,
they had come to know and like each other. Gardell both
knew and did not know about Labate's "affiliation." Labate said Gardell once asked him "a funny question: Am
I a gangster? I said, 'Do I know people? I know a lot of
people.' "

Ultimately, each realized he had certain things to offer
the other.

Gardell had been with the NYPD for twenty years and
still had to struggle to pay his rent. He wanted a little
something more. Labate was glad to help. He had a friend

of his build Gardell the big backyard pool. He arranged to have the veteran detective comped at a nice casino in Las Vegas and Atlantic City, and sent Gardell and his girlfriend to San Francisco for a weekend. They found him a stolen mink coat, and special computer chips for his TV to snag DVD programs from the stratosphere.

Detective Gardell was to provide a little something in return.

He had worked his way up into the top offices of the Detectives' Endowment Association, the union that represents police detectives in New York. He was the treasurer of the union, which made him aware of the immense size of the union's $175 million pension fund. Labate and his friends at DMN decided that the pension fund should begin investing some of its money through DMN Capital Investments, for a fee.

"If this fund works out right and you can open up doors for more funds," Labate told Gardell and his girlfriend, Sharon Kilcoin, "you won't have to work as long as you live."

"I know," Gardell said.

"That's a hell of a parachute," Labate said.

"I won't have to work Monday, Tuesday, Wednesday," a gleeful Gardell gushed.

"Will I have to work?" his girlfriend queried.

"No," he said.

"I know what I want," she said. "A Mercedes truck."

Besides helping gangsters get ahold of the pension funds of New York City cops, Gardell provided other little favors when he could. He got Labate a permit to carry a weapon and, perhaps even more important, eight special New York Police Department parking permits that allowed Labate and his Mafia friends to park anywhere they felt like.

Sometimes though, Labate felt there was more give then get.

"I'm very annoyed," Labate said. "He got a three-thousand-dollar pool we bought."

Sal Piazza, Labate's partner at DMN and a Bonanno associate, defended the investment: "I was happy to set the guy up. If I need the guy, I would expect him to be there."

Labate said, "I didn't say I don't like him, I just keep saying the same thing. I think that we give, give, give, give, and get very little back. It's an observation."

But Labate knew there was potential with this investment in Gardell. "He knows a lot about everything. He knows all of this business. If you think not every phone, every cop is feeding him information, every detective is feeding him information, you're out of your mind. If you think there's no half a dozen wiseguy rats talking to him, you are out of your mind."

Labate's partner at DMN, Pokross, a small, balding man with a rat-tail thin mustache who looked like an accountant with an attitude, frequently mentioned being "with some fellows from Avenue U." This was a street in the heart of Brooklyn where gangsters were known to collect their mail. Pokross liked hanging around guys from Avenue U, but he was smart enough to know that you had to be discreet. Pokross mentioned that Gardell was boasting he had made charges against a Bonanno associate named Michael Grecco disappear. Grecco had beaten up a recalcitrant stock promoter with a pool cue, and the promoter had actually filed charges. After three weeks, the charges suddenly disappeared. Gardell was walking around openly claiming credit. Pokross worried that this boasting could bring attention to Gardell, just when he was providing information the Bonanno crime family needed.

"I don't come to work with black turtlenecks," Pokross

said. "We don't need him to interface with the other half in Brooklyn. It will be obvious I don't want to look like a mob social club when he comes in."

The three men at DMN were obviously very interested in preserving Gardell as their very own leak at One Police Plaza. Labate asked Lucille, a secretary, to call Gardell on the office phone. Gardell was supposed to be checking into the new Paris Hotel in Las Vegas, the one with the fifty-story half-scale Eiffel Tower, the faux Opera House, the bogus Louvre, and the ersatz Arc de Triomphe. There, Detective Gardell was to spend the next few days, comped by the Bonanno crime family. Lucille got the hotel and Sal Piazza got on the line and left a message for Gardell: "Stephen, it's Sal. Jimmy and everyone want to know how you got there and if the room's okay."

The FBI agent recording this conversation noted the time in his logbook—1:18 P.M. They had to be wondering exactly what was going on in the mind of Detective Gardell. He was giving the Mafia parking permits and claiming credit for a disappearing assault charge and all he got out of the deal was a lousy $3,000 swimming pool? Aboveground? What else was he giving them? They were very confident they would find out, because they had one tremendous advantage over the Bonanno crime family. One of the men in the room talking was actually secretly cooperating with the government. Jeffrey Pokross, who didn't wear black turtlenecks but liked to mention Avenue U, was actually at that moment a government informant, steering the conversation. And now he said something that surprised even the FBI agents who were monitoring his every word.

"What's the story with this Gardell thing for tomorrow?" Pokross said. He wanted to know about the impending arrest of members of organized crime that was scheduled to take place the following day and whether Robert Lino, the Little Guy, was on the list.

"Who's getting pinched?" he asked. "It don't involve the Little Guy?"

"Not at all," Labate said, and that was the end of the conversation.

Pokross seemed to think the arrests involved the Bonanno crime family, but the stunned FBI agents listening in knew better.

For weeks, the FBI's New York office and New York City Police Department detectives assigned to the Organized Crime Task Force had been secretly planning a massive arrest of forty members of the DeCavalcante crime family. The sweep was to take place at dawn on December 2, 1999, and it involved hundreds of federal agents and city cops. Several law enforcement personnel would be assigned to each arrest. They would meet at a prearranged spot, then approach the suspects' homes just before six in the morning. This was a tried-and-true method for arresting members of organized crime, who were known for sleeping late. Usually these Mafia arrests went smoothly. For reasons that are not entirely clear, many of these men who think nothing of murdering their best friends are extremely polite when the FBI comes calling. Nevertheless, any agent or police detective assigned this task is aware that sometimes things don't go as planned.

Sometimes people have guns, and sometimes they get funny ideas. Big arrests are thus viewed as big headaches.

They are also viewed as difficult to keep secret. The more people who need to be arrested, the more police and agents need to be involved, the more potential there is for a leak. In this instance, Detective Gardell, who was well known and liked by most of the city's major-case detectives, was in a position to know who was going to be arrested and when. A list had been drawn up, which was supposed to be confidential. It was not. Somehow Gardell must have got a look at it and the information was transmitted to the parties concerned.

This was somewhat distressing to the NYPD and the FBI. They had intended for the DeCavalcante arrests to come off with as much secrecy as possible. If members of the DeCavalcante crime family knew about the arrests, they might want to try to leave the country. Several times in the last decade the gang's members had tapped into a pool of funds saved for fugitives and fled the United States for obscure villages in Sicily. One of the family's veteran capos, Pino Schifiletti, had gone on such a trip with his wife a few months earlier. The FBI knew this because other gangsters had discussed it with Palermo.

Now that the list was out, the FBI had to move quickly. The bureau first had to get its prized informant, Ralphie Guarino, off the street as soon as possible. They were worried that some of the brighter members of the DeCavalcante clan might notice that Guarino—who knew nearly all of the people on the arrest list—was not on the list himself. This could present certain problems, since the FBI was also aware that the DeCavalcante family had suspected for weeks now that one of their own was an informant.

Hours after learning that the sweep had been compromised, the FBI quickly made arrangements for Ralphie, his wife, and two children to get out of their Staten Island home and into the witness protection program. United States marshals were sent to the home to escort the family out. The family was given only a few hours to pack as much as they could.

Next, the lead agent in the case, George Hanna, went

through the logistics of arresting forty people in sixty minutes across Brooklyn, Staten Island, and New Jersey. Each suspect was expected to be at a certain spot. *Expected* was the operative word. Some suspects were more predictable than others. Tin Ear Sclafani, the soldier, spent most nights at home with his wife in Staten Island, and Uncle Joe Giacobbe, the aging capo, woke up every morning and drove to his usual table at Sacco's meat market in Elizabeth. Sal Calciano, the World Trade Center maintenance employee who had helped Ralphie in the Twin Towers robbery, lived in an apartment building in Brooklyn with his mother- and father-in-law. Others would be more complicated. People like Jimmy Gallo and Anthony Capo could be anywhere. For years, Vincent Palermo religiously had returned home each night to his second wife and their three children. Since the screaming incident at his daughter's wedding, this was no longer true. For days, the agents had tried unsuccessfully to find him during surveillance runs. He was off the radar screen.

On the night of December 1, the case agents in charge of the case did not go to bed. They stayed up, making last-minute preparation, getting ready for that moment when they had to knock on a stranger's door. On TV, thousands stood in Rockefeller Center to watch the lighting of the big spruce and it was apparent from all the flushed faces that it was going to be a cold dawn.

December 2, 1999

Sunrise was still an hour away and the temperature was in the middle twenties when the agents came knocking on the door of Anthony Stripoli in Brooklyn. He was a big young guy with a full head of black hair who played football long ago and now worked as a bookmaking and loan-shark collector for the Colombo crime family. When he felt like golfing, he drove out to the best country club he could find, pretended to be a member, signed in as Tom, and played a few rounds. Nobody bothered him. At 6 A.M. a half-dozen agents stood on his doorstep and one knocked on his door.

"What's the charge?" Stripoli asked, standing there in his underwear as the agents swarmed past him and into his home.

"Shylocking," the agent replied.

He called up to this wife, "Get dressed! I'm getting locked up!"

She called down,"What do you mean 'locked up'? How do you know that?"

"Believe me, they're not here to play golf," he said. "Ding ding bang bang, they come early to catch you off your guard." He turned back to the agents, one of whom was wearing a shirt that read RUSSIAN ORGANIZED CRIME TASK FORCE.

"You got the wrong shirt on," Stripoli said, making a little early-morning joke.

The agents told him he was under arrest and to go up-stairs and get dressed. One of Stripoli's daughters woke up from all the commotion and started crying. One of the agents, playing Good Cop, told Stripoli, "Listen, she's up there crying. I want you to go upstairs and tell her it's going to be all right. It'll make it a lot better."

"No way," said another agent, playing Bad Cop.

"Listen," said Good Cop. "I'm taking him up there."

Good Cop escorted Stripoli upstairs and he sat on the bed with his daughter, who was sobbing. He told her, "It's all right. I sold bad fish to somebody I'll be home tonight. I don't want to go, but I have no choice." He told his daughter not to cry, that she didn't have to go to school that day. He said, "I'll be home tonight."

"You better be home tonight," his daughter replied.

The agents asked him if he had any guns. He said, "They're all over the house." He claimed he had a license for each one, and he helped them find them. They asked him about a safe; he told them where it was. They asked him for his loan-shark records; he said he didn't have any.

"Then sit down," said another agent, a woman, promising to go back and get a search warrant to check the entire house. "We're going to be a while."

Stripoli made a decision on the spot. He decided to help them find whatever they needed to find but not tell them anything. They found a book with a list of names in it, including Robert Lino's. Stripoli did what he could because he did not want to delay the search too long. He had this image of a thousand FBI agents in jackets that said FBI in huge letters swarming around his home and him being hauled off in handcuffs just as the school bus pulled up to pick up his daughters for school.

Stripoli quickly got dressed and was in the car by seven. The agents turned on a tape recorder and started asking him questions. They asked him if he knew this guy and that guy.

"I'm not going to talk," he replied. "No disrespect. You do your job and I do my job, but I'm not capable of doing business with you."

"Don't worry about it," an agent said. "We've got thirty-five of your friends. You'll all be together."

SCLAFANI

He wanted to hit a big score. He'd been talking about robbing somebody just for a quick score. He didn't want his wife of thirty-five years to work anymore. He'd lived in the same small home on St. George Road in Staten Island for nineteen years, his wife's home. He still liked to sleep late. Before dawn on a winter morning was not a time of day he wanted to see.

The agents came into the house and they told him to change, he was going down to New York FBI headquarters at 26 Federal Plaza in lower Manhattan. They followed him upstairs into this bedroom, where he began to change into jeans and a sweatshirt. While he was changing he opened a closet door. An agent happened to notice something long and cylindrical wrapped in a ratty old towel. He asked what it was.

"Oh, that," Sclafani said. "That's my brother-in-law's gun."

It was a fully loaded .22 rifle rigged as a semiautomatic. They asked if there were any more guns. At first he acted as if he did not understand the question, simple as it was. Then he recalled that there might actually be another gun, just a little one, tucked away somewhere over there near his bed. The agent found a cabinet next to the head of Sclafani's bed and began pulling items out of it. He found a brown paper bag, and Sclafani said, "No not those." The agent then reached inside the cabinet and pulled out an unusual object, a sock into which was stuffed a loaded .380 semiautomatic handgun still in its holster. Sclafani seemed surprised at the sight of the gun. The agent asked him why he kept a gun near his bed.

"In case they come to get me," he said, "I'll be ready." The agent asked him to describe what he meant by "they." Sclafani stopped talking and continued to get dressed. As he dressed, he told the agents that he did a hundred to a hundred and fifty push-ups each day. He let them know that if he were a younger man, there surely would have been a disturbance when they knocked on his door at six o'clock in the morning. He told the agents how he was with the Special Forces when he was in the United States Army from 1955 through 1957.

The agents nodded and remembered what they could without writing it down. They then escorted him out of his home and his Staten Island neighborhood and took the sixty-two-year-old pensioner into the city to face a list of charges that could put him in jail for the rest of his life.

VINNY OCEAN

The agents first visited Vinny Ocean's isolated waterfront palace in the suburban town of Island Park. It was located in an island accessible by only two roads and was surrounded by the man-made channels that lead to the natural Broad Channel, which funnels into the Atlantic Ocean. It was a neighborhood that would clearly know when a stranger was driving through. It was a difficult place to get into and out of. The house itself lay behind an ornate six-foot cement wall with an eight-foot wrought-iron gate. In the dawn chill, the agents broke through the gate, drove past the basketball hoop in the driveway, and knocked on the front door. Palermo's wife, Debra, and son Vincent Jr., came to the door. Debra informed the agents that she had no idea where Vinny Ocean was or could be. This would be the same Vincent Palermo she'd been married to for more than a decade who came home nearly every night. The agents left, in search of Vinny Ocean.

They did not have far to drive. Palermo and several other members of the DeCavalcante family were known to hang around a certain beach house in nearby Long Beach when they wanted to avoid detection. The agents took the bridge into the popular beach resort town and drove to the beach house just as Vinny Ocean and one of his most trusted soldiers, Jimmy Gallo, were walking out of the house. Vinny Ocean was carrying two bags. One was packed with clothes, as if Vinny was considering taking a little trip. The other contained the two recording devices Vinny had used to create his own record in the event he was arrested by agents of the United States government, as happened to be the case.

PRESSER

By noon, thirty-three of forty defendants had been rousted out of bed in their underwear. FBI agents and New York City cops showed up with arrest warrants in towns across New Jersey, Long Island, and New York City. They found one gangster in an apartment in Scranton, Pennsylvania, and one in a house trailer in Las Vegas. All the locals were shuttled to windowless holding pens inside the upper floors of the FBI's New York headquarters in lower Manhattan. They were herded into the same room so they could all get a look at one another. Some knew others well. Others had never met. In a few cases, low-level associates got to meet the bosses for the first time. Appropriate respect was shown, though discussion was kept to a minimum. One soldier of the Colombo family, Anthony Stripoli, recognized one soldier from the DeCavalcante family, Anthony Capo. He knew him from youth football on Staten Island. They talked about football. Another asked Stripoli about his uncle Jerry Lang, a Colombo capo sitting in jail. Stripoli looked at the guy like he was asking about the color of his sister's underwear.

"Jerry who?" he growled.

The newly assembled group of friends and strangers began the tedious and mysterious practice known as "intake," in which they would be fingerprinted, photographed, and interviewed by low-paid Justice Department employees with checklists of questions about their jobs and wives and prior experience with the criminal justice system. Usually they would all be presented to a federal magistrate who would hear them plead not guilty and assign them a District Court judge. Because there were so many bodies to process, nearly everyone involved— from defendants to prosecutors to defense attorneys to court workers to the judge himself—dreaded the day ahead.

A press conference was set for 1:30 P.M. in the lobby of the office of Mary Jo White, the United States attorney for the Southern District of New York. The television people set up their bank of cameras, facing a podium with a blue curtain and the Justice Department seal as background. Blue, it was said, worked best on TV. Stacks of indictments were made available. At a little past the appointed time, White walked out and faced the gaggle of television, radio, and print-media representatives who usually showed up for her press conferences. This was a slightly smaller gaggle than usual. Lewis Schiliro, the head of the FBI's New York office, stood nearby, along with a posse of FBI agents and detectives with the New York City Police Department. Many of the cops and agents looked like they hadn't slept all night, which in fact they hadn't. It was a time-honored tradition—the prosecutor faces the camera and says that she has struck a blow, hammered a dent, put the fear of God into organized crime. Inevitably there would be much discourse on the fact that all the different law enforcement agencies involved—the New York Police Department, the Federal Bureau of Investigation, the police department of the Port Authority of New York and New Jersey—all had worked together, cooperating with one another. Inevitably someone would note that the indictment would "send a message" that "law enforcement will use any means necessary" to eradicate organized crime.

Prosecutor White, a veteran of this performance, laid out the details and revealed the numbers. She referred to "the cooperating witness" or "CW." She called Vinny Ocean an "acting boss" and Tin Ear Sclafani a "veteran soldier." She mentioned that Joe O Masella had been killed in a golf-course parking lot. She never once mentioned the name of the real star of the show, secret informant Ralphie Guarino. She assured the public that "nearly" all of the $1 million stolen so long ago from the World Trade Center had in fact been recovered. She made the usual statement about how the indictment would hurt but certainly not kill the DeCavalcante crime family and organized crime throughout New York.

"This investigation proves that those who declare the death of the mob do so at their own peril," she warned. "We are not there yet, but we have done much in terms of progress."

The reporters were drifting out when White announced that nearly all of the intended targets picked up that morning were at that very moment being arraigned over in magistrate's court. That got the reporters' attention. With the speeches over, the gaggle quickly shut down their cameras and hustled out the door, headed for court and the chance of a good "Mafia shot."

COURT

The classic Mafia shot is known to anyone who watches television news. The shot usually involves a large man in a nylon jogging suit or black turtleneck running either away from or at photographers trying desperately to make the shot. Sometimes the men hold carefully folded newspapers in front of their B-movie faces. Sometimes they throw coats over their heads. Sometimes they throw gestures at the photographers, who snap eagerly away in response. There are famous incidents associated with the Mafia shot. James (Jimmy Brown) Failla is the best example. Here was a seventy-four-year-old troll of a man walking down the sidewalk, a metal cane affixed to each arm. As the photographers approached, Brown produced a string of curses in his best guttural Sicilian and started swinging the canes like golf clubs, aiming for the faces of the startled shutterbugs.

On this day, the photographers assembled outside the United States District Court, confident that at least some of the alleged and reputed members and associates of the De-Cavalcante crime family would surely leave the building at some point. When they did, the cameras would be ready.

Inside on the fifth floor, life was not nearly so dramatic. The suspects had been brought into court by van and now sat in the holding cell next to the magistrate's chambers. They had been sitting for a while. It was Thursday—Part One day. That was the day when all indicted defendants were brought in one by one to the magistrate to be assigned to District Court judges. It was a day when all experienced lawyers and defendants brought along paperbacks while waiting for the welter of institutions to come together in what no one ever described as ballet. It was taxpayer-funded chaos, every Thursday. With dozens of new DeCavalcante defendants brought in, the system quickly began to fall apart.

Defendants were ready, but lawyers were not. Lawyers were ready, but defendants were still out of the building. Defendants and lawyers were ready, but the magistrate was not available. On and on it went, all afternoon.

At one point, Westley Paloscio—the Mickey the Dunce bookmaker who lived at home with his mother—was brought in, shackled to four others. He had been charged in the conspiracy to kill Joseph Masella. That meant he could face the death penalty. He shuffled in, looking like a small animal trapped in the sudden glare of an oncoming tractor trailer. As the magistrate asked Paloscio's lawyer if his client had read the indictment, Paloscio glanced around the court, nodding to his buddies and assiduously avoiding eye contact with his mother. The prosecutor, Maria Barton, was trying to convince the magistrate to keep Westley locked up because, as a participant in the murder of a fellow human being, he had demonstrated that he was a danger to the community.

Westley's mother began to pace in the audience. "Westley," she kept saying in a stage whisper that got louder as the hearing unfolded. She was a small woman in her fifties wearing a winter jacket and new walking shoes. Her eyes seemed sad, and she alternately shook her head in disbelief and muttered in anger. The muttering grew in volume. Finally it was all too much. Mrs. Paloscio stood up in a rage and approached the wooden railing that separates the officers of the court from the people who pay their salaries. She started waving her hand to get the magistrate's attention.

"My son has a new job!" she cried. "My son has never been in trouble in his life. He just started the job. He's not a murderer." She was yelling. "He's going to lose his job! He's not a danger to anybody." She was shouting; the United States marshals were moving closer to her. She began shrieking. "He finally got a job to get away from all this shit!"

The marshals asked Mrs. Paloscio to step outside the courtroom. She complied slowly, walking out and watching as her son was led away in handcuffs, still studiously avoiding her eyes.

Anthony Stripoli was with the group attached to Westley, but the prosecutor had not called him a danger to society and so he was allowed to leave. He stood up and smiled at his relatives, who clapped him on the back as he walked through the rail on his way out of court.

"Look at you," one of the relatives said. "You're a movie star."

DMN

Six days after his arrest, Anthony Stripoli the movie star and Colombo family soldier sat in the conference room of DMN Capital in the heart of Wall Street. There sat Jimmy Labate, Bonanno associate, and Little Robert Lino, Bonanno captain. Everybody knew what was what. Anthony had been arrested and charged with bookmaking, a charge he could live with. Mostly he was there because he needed money, and he needed to convince his friends to pay him what he felt they owed him for a pump-and-dump scheme that hadn't worked out as planned. That way he could pay his lawyer. Mostly Labate and Little Robert wanted to know what was happening now that Anthony was busted. They seemed concerned.

"What's up, Anthony?" Labate asked. "How'd you make out?"

"Six rats in the case," Anthony said. "They just wrecked that whole family."

"It's up to six already?" Labate asked.

"Six rats. I don't know any of them. They think I know them all."

"You're guilty by association," Labate offered. "Your name could have just been mentioned in passing."

"No," Stripoli said. "My name was mentioned from Joe with the cell phone that got killed."

Stripoli was referring to Joey O. The very night Joey O was killed, Anthony Stripoli was supposed to meet him near the golf course way down in Brooklyn. He was not charged with killing anybody, never mind Joey O. But he was convinced he would soon be dragged into that part of the case, where the death penalty was lurking. He mentioned the death penalty several times.

"I had been beeping him all night," Stripoli said.

"That kinda only shows you didn't kill him," Labate said.

"I just called him," Stripoli said, his voice beginning to rise. "I was freaking out—"

"He's already dead!" Labate hollered.

"And his daughter answered the phone and said, 'My father died,'" he said. "I was supposed to meet him at eight."

"On the golf course," Little Robert said.

"On the golf course."

Little Robert tried to assure him that everything would be okay, and although he seemed happy with circumstances, he needed some reassurance himself. "They got surveillance on you or me or anything like that?"

"They didn't tell me that," Stripoli said. "They got my phone book with your name in it."

This did not make Little Robert happy, but he and Stripoli worked out a deal where Stripoli would get $40,000, most of which would wind up with his lawyer.

Labate tried to be helpful. "Eighteen months federal," he said. "When you come out, you're like a fucking champ."

"Oh yeah," Stripoli said. "I'll be fuckin' working out every day."

17

April 5, 2000

A little past two on a sunny spring Wednesday, United States District Court Judge Lawrence McKenna strolled into his well-funded courtroom in lower Manhattan. He wore shirtsleeves, not bothering with his black robe. Judge McKenna began chatting with his deputy and clerks and the defense attorney and prosecutor who had come to argue in front of him. He was a tall, friendly man with snowy hair and a hesitant manner that seemed almost shy. His informality disarmed nearly everyone who came before him. He was considered one of the nicest men in the building. His court was fifteen stories above the city of New York. Far below, the city sparkled silently in the spring sunshine. Here no street sound could be heard. The criminal justice system went about its business in an orderly world of its own, high above the chaos.

Here in the Southern District of New York, prosecutors

were used to winning. They had a conviction rate of 96 percent, and when they stood before a judge and asked that a defendant be tossed in jail as a danger to the community, more often than not they got what they wanted. This was the case because most judges would rather be run over by a bus than be labeled soft on crime. A judge who's called soft on crime is like a hockey player who is said to be afraid to brawl. Overcompensation is inevitable. A judge labeled soft on crime metes out extreme sentences and denies bail as a matter of course. In the Southern District of New York, Judge McKenna was an exception to this rule. While most of his colleagues usually gave the prosecutors the benefit of the doubt, McKenna tended to take that position with the defendant. Defense lawyers called this open minded. Prosecutors dreaded walking into his court.

McKenna's deputy got off the phone and told him the defendant had been brought up from the holding cell and was ready to be presented. The judge nodded and retired to his chambers. The informal chat was over, and the two adveraries—prosecutor and defense lawyer—took their appointed places. In a moment the United States marshals led in the prisoner of the moment, Joseph Sclafani.

Sclafani had been sitting in jail for four months. He entered the walnut-walled courtroom without handcuffs, dressed in the baby-blue togs of federal pretrial detainees. He wore sneakers without laces and his pants were secured at the waist by elastic. In prison, shoelaces and belts were forbidden. He sauntered in with a kind of rolling strut of the seasoned wiseguy that conveyed the message "Who gives a fuck?" He nodded to his wife and two sons, who were the only spectators sitting in McKenna's court besides a lone newspaper reporter. The Sclafani progeny smiled and waved at their father; the wife looked like she was about to burst into tears.

The defense attorney, Francisco Celedonio, bent in close to Sclafani and began whispering. Sclafani pointed at his ear and Celedonio got up and switched sides. Judge McKenna appeared in his robes and took the bench. The prosecutor, Lisa Korologos, a small, quiet young woman whose voice never seemed to rise above the level of benign conversation even when she was furious, quickly rose and smiled at the judge. She stood at a table in front of Sclafani and his lawyer, her back to them.

Celedonio the defense lawyer paid no attention to the judge or the prosecutor as he continued to whisper to his half-deaf client.

"*United States* versus *Joseph Sclafani,*" said his deputy. "Is everyone ready?"

Celedonio stopped whispering and averred that he was ready. Judge McKenna got right to business.

"I guess I will begin by asking Mr. Celedonio: I am aware of the background in this case; would you just put on the record the package you're proposing?"

The package at hand involved the set of circumstances Celedonio the lawyer could present to convince all concerned that the release of Tin Ear Sclafani would not place the Republic in jeopardy. At least that was the way he saw it. He was there to get his client out on bail. Sclafani had been sitting in jail since the morning the FBI agents showed up at his house on St. George in December 1999, and he wanted out. The package would include collateral he could raise toward that cause combined with conditions that would assure the judge that Mr. Sclafani would be there for his next court appearance. Sclafani's lawyer, Celedonio, proposed $30,000 cash and a bond of considerably more, backed by the faux Tara in Staten Island Sclafani called home. He suggested that the FBI could bug all of Tin Ear's phones. He agreed that his client would wear an electronic bracelet that would set off an alarm should Tin Ear venture away from St. George Road. Sclafani would be confined to Tara and his gazebo with the fake bridge and the plastic raccoon, and would be allowed to meet only with his immediate family and his lawyer. If he needed to go someplace else, he would have to get permission. That was the package Celedonio earnestly presented.

"I believe, Your Honor, these are all the elements that I am proposing," Celedonio said.

"So the real issue is the weapons," Judge McKenna said. "Let's talk about them."

In the federal system, a judge must hold the accused in jail if the prosecutor demonstrates that the person is a danger to the community. In Joseph Sclafani's case, the fact that the FBI found loaded weapons in the man's bedroom did not help Sclafani's argument that he was a danger to no one. Celedonio knew this, but he had a plan. He began an unusual argument—one that had never before been proposed in the history of the American Mafia—to get his man out on bail.

It would not be easy. The government had alleged that Tin Ear—at the age of sixty-two, deaf in one ear, suffering from various stomach ailments, etc.—was a danger to the community because besides all these things, he had been a made member of organized crime for forty years. Many gangsters did not live that long. He had sworn a blood oath to live and die for the mob when the prosecutor, Korologos, was not yet born. When the FBI had come for him, they had discovered not one but two loaded guns in his bedroom. He volunteered to the agents that he needed the guns in his bedroom just in case somebody came to get him. No particular somebody, just somebody. The government lawyer, Korologos, had reminded Judge McKenna of this statement on several occasions.

Celedonio asked Judge McKenna to have an open mind.

"Aside from the weapons that were found in his home, it is important to note that despite this assertion—that he is an active member, that he is engaged in violence, that he has been a member of this alleged crime family for thirty-five or forty years, my client has never been accused—prior to this indictment—of participating in any crime family."

Korologos the prosecutor turned back to look at Celedonio. She tried not to display a trace of emotion, but her face betrayed her. She seemed to have produced, just for a second, a smirk.

Celedonio, an impassioned veteran of lost causes who claims never to have read *Don Quixote,* argued on. "The weapons, although they were found in his home, were not his weapons," he said. "They were his brother-in-law's weapons."

Prosecutor Korologos practically snorted out loud at this one, and she clearly rolled her eyes. She jumped right in, noting that the brother-in-law had been dead for nearly three years, and reminding Judge McKenna that Sclafani had been caught on hours of tape—both video *and* audio—discussing murders and extortion and loan sharking and gambling and just about every criminal option available to a soldier of the DeCavalcante crime family. Or as the defense lawyer might put it, the "alleged" DeCavalcante crime family. And now he was blaming his brother-in-law.

Celedonio barely flinched. He had just begun. He now attacked the argument that Tin Ear was a member of the Mafia. Long ago, in the 1960s and even 1970s, defense attorneys often argued with a straight face that the Mafia did not exist. Celedonio tried a new approach.

He argued that the Mafia was now just a movie.

"The disclosures that the government refers to, that certain murders are alleged to have been sanctioned, is no great piece of information that requires extensive surveillance or extensive investigation," Celedonio said. "Just from watching the movie *Goodfellas* one knows that with people alleged to have involvement in crime families, the assassinations may or may not be sanctioned."

Prosecutor Korologos nearly turned completely around. Even Judge McKenna of the open mind smiled a little bit. He wasn't sure he was hearing what he was hearing—that Sclafani was blaming a movie for his troubles.

"You don't necessarily believe whatever is in a movie," Judge McKenna said. "But on the other hand, the United States against Locascio, in the Court of Appeals' opinion—the testimony of the FBI experts in that case was to the effect that may or may not be in *Goodfellas* or something else—that killings had to be sanctioned by the boss. In that case, I believe it was John Gotti. So you can find these things out more reliably than by only seeing *Goodfellas* or *The Godfather.*"

The prosecutor, Korologos, now mentioned again the hours and hours of Sclafani going on and on about this murder and that murder. There was Sclafani describing how he would happily kill anybody he even suspected of being an informant for the government. On a motorcycle even. There was Sclafani talking about all those rules about killing people who slept with wiseguys' wives and so on. She waved a transcript as she said this, and Sclafani shook his head as if saddened by the whole state of affairs.

Celedonio the lawyer was unfazed. He now argued that his client—in his many hours of recorded conversation with the FBI informant Ralphie—was merely trying to get the informant to pay him money owed. He was, in effect, conning the con man with his *Goodfellas* dialogue. Or so Celedonio claimed.

"You don't have to be a member of any crime family," he pleaded. "The Gambino crime family, the DeCavalcante crime family. You don't even have to be a learned individual to know that if there is such a thing, if someone becomes a cooperator, then yes, there is likely going to be some level of retribution."

He claimed Sclafani told Ralphie what Ralphie wanted to hear. "In exchange for money, my client gave Ralphie an elaborate story based on nonsense, based on nothing more than what I can speculate on by watching television, by watching *The Sopranos*, by reading a novel by Mario Puzo. There is nothing to say that my client's assertion that someone who sleeps with someone's wife can be a candidate for an assassination. The assertion itself doesn't make it so and it doesn't imbue anyone with any specific insight into what these alleged crime families do or don't do." He was on a roll. No one interrupted. The prosecutor's face by now had changed from puzzlement to amusement. She wanted this to go on.

"I could have told Ralphie if someone is a member—or alleged member—of an organized crime family, and that person becomes a cooperator, like Sammy the Bull, then he is going to be a target." Celedonio dropped in Sammy the Bull without mentioning his last name, as if he were a movie character familiar to all. "That doesn't imbue me with any specific knowledge as to this alleged crime family. It just means I read the newspapers, I follow the news and watch TV."

The argument went on for a few more minutes. Celedonio tried the sick-client approach—mentioning Tin Ear's tin ear, listing the names of several pills Sclafani was taking. The prosecutor countered by arguing that Sclafani claimed he could do one hundred push-ups, although she was uncertain on the exact number.

"As you can tell by looking at him, he is somebody that either lifts weights or does a hundred or a hundred and fifty push-ups a day," she said.

"I can't tell from here," the judge said. "You may be right, you may not, but I can't tell. He has got a shirt on."

But the momentum was gone. The movie defense had collapsed. Celedonio the defense lawyer was merely dancing in an empty auditorium. His audience was gone. Even Judge McKenna wasn't buying at this bake sale. The government prosecutor, Korologos, now literally brought out both guns—the .380 semiautomatic pistol and the .22 rifle—two magazines of bullets, the ratty old sock the pistol came in. She offered to pass them up to the judge, after promising not to wave them at his deputy. He declined, and said he would reserve decision on whether to release Tin Ear Sclafani on bail.

Throughout this performance Tin Ear continually fiddled with his hearing aide and shrugged his shoulders, implying that he wasn't hearing anything. His family in the spectator row waved as he was led off. He gave them another shrug and walked away through the side door into the holding cell, a marshal on each side, just another wiseguy headed back to the pen.

The hearing was over. Joey Sclafani would be shuttled back through a series of halls and tunnels to the Metropolitan Correctional Center behind the courthouse. There he would be placed back into the prison's general population. The Sclafani family surrounded the lawyer, pelting him with questions about when their Joey would be getting out. The lawyer Celedonio said he did not know, it was up to the judge. He said it in such a way that it was clear Joey Sclafani was not going anywhere.

The two Sclafani sons glowered at the prosecutor and the newspaper reporter; Mrs. Sclafani looked at the floor, defeated. The three Sclafanis then shuffled out into the hall, took an elevator to the lobby, and walked outside into the glorious spring afternoon, knowing that they were not in any movie and that they might not see their Joey again for a long, long time.

February 21, 2001

The temperature had dropped below freezing on Sixth Avenue as the black limousines pulled up to the curb outside Radio City Music Hall. The group of photographers did their job with frozen fingers as the celebrities strutted quickly into the warmth of the ornate theater. It was a premiere, but it was most definitely not a normal premiere. It was a Bridge and Tunnel premiere. The celebrities looked like they had come straight out of the neighborhoods of Brooklyn and Staten Island and New Jersey. You had your Gravesend representatives, your Todt Hill contingent, your Elizabeth crew. It was the season premiere of HBO-TV's *The Sopranos,* and the phony wiseguys were out in force.

Inside Radio City, the room was filled with gindaloos and gindalettes, mamaluks and mortadellas. Men wore black turtlenecks with black suit coats. Some wore black leather jackets and sunglasses indoors. There were many guys who looked like they came straight from the social club and were more comfortable in jogging suits and wraparound shades than suits that seemed just a little too small. One girlfriend had the big hair and a backless gown the color of swimming-pool water at night. Guys built like home appliances walked down the aisle wearing actual pinkie rings. One guy had on a black leather knee-length jacket perfect for hiding large-caliber weaponry. A gaggle of gindalettes screamed out in unison, "Vinneeeeee!!" from the balcony as "The September of My Years" played loudly off ornate art deco walls the color of gold and bronze.

"When I was twenty-one," Frank Sinatra sang, "it was a very good year."

All the cast members of the TV show were present, dressed in expensive suits and evening gowns, looking just like they did on TV except shorter. The only one who seemed not to fit in was the guitarist-turned-actor, Steven Van Zandt. He strolled toward his reserved seat wearing his usual bandanna and a black leather jacket and waved to the crowd. The crowd cheered.

In a middle seat, Robert Funaro sat with his brother-in-law watching in awe. Robert had snagged a job playing Eugene, an associate who works with the character Ralphie in controlling the carting industry in New Jersey. He was a tall, bulked-up guy with blue-black hair, wearing a light suit with dark shirt and tie. For the crowd assembled, this was very conservative attire. Nevertheless he had the look. The look was hard to describe. You knew it when you saw it. It was partly in the walk and partly in the talk. In Robert Funaro's case, it was also in the childhood.

He had grown up in Bensonhurst and knew both made guys and wannabes. He was working booking acts at Caroline's Comedy Club in Manhattan when James Gandolfini, the star of the TV show who pretends to be a Mafia boss, came in and suggested he audition for the show. At Caroline's, he'd booked Goomba Johnnie. "I don't know him by any other name," Funaro said. "He had a date that he had to cancel once because of that problem."

Goomba Johnnie was actually John Anthony Sialiano.

That problem was Sialiano's arrest in January 1998. At the time Sialiano was living a rather colorful life. He was handling the morning-drive time slot at WKTU-FM in New Jersey, where he cultivated his wannabe gangster shtick as Goomba Johnnie. Goomba Johnnie had come to realize that gangsters can be funny guys. He was trying to break into comedy, and was working on a TV show with his partner, Sean (Hollywood) Hamilton, dubbed *Let's Get Stupid.* He had also been a bodyguard and bouncer at strip clubs around New York for years, including a club called Scores in midtown Manhattan. There, it was alleged, he got involved in extorting the owners for the Gambino crime family. He was indicted with John A. (Junior) Gotti and others on charges of pocketing $230,000 from shaking down Scores and gambling. The day after his arrest, Goomba's legitimate employer, WKTU-FM, issued this unusual statement: "John is an exemplary employee. The matter being investigated is related to a second job."

At Caroline's Comedy Club, where Robert Funaro booked the acts, Goomba Johnnie had to cancel at the last minute due to indictment. Some of his Goomba buddies showed up anyway, demanding to know where their paisan was.

"There's guys who talk about it and guys who don't talk about it. The guys who talk about it, you know they're not the real thing. These guys come in the night Goomba Johnnie didn't show. Some of these guys showed up, saying 'Where's Goomba Johnnie?' They had the rings on, the suits, the whole thing. They weren't the real deal."

Now Robert Funaro sat in Radio City Music Hall, surrounded by anything but the real deal. There were pretend capos sitting next to pretend soldiers hanging out with pretend associates commenting on the pretend boss. Funaro prepared to watch himself on a giant movie screen pretending to be a gangster. He described his role cryptically, the way a real gangster might describe his. "I'm going to play Eugene and I'm going to be working my way in to the family more and more," he said. "I can't really talk about it."

The room went dark and two episodes of the TV show played on Radio City's huge screen. When it was over Funaro stayed to see his name in the credits for one last time. Some guy called out, "We love you, Paulie!" and Tony Sirico, the actor who plays Paulie Walnuts, waved to his unseen fan. Slowly they filed out into the frigid night air, walking a few blocks to the big party for cast members and their guests that would surely resemble a scene from a Staten Island wedding.

Three years had passed since the first day in January 1998 when Ralphie Guarino strapped on a federal recording device and began talking to his friends. On the day the FBI convinced Guarino to work with the bureau, no member of law enforcement involved in the case could have imagined what damage he would do. Ralphie's tapes set off a chain reaction that resulted in seventy arrests and ten informants. His tapes first revealed that many of the members and particularly ranking members of the family did not like hatchet man Anthony Capo. Soldiers and captains could be heard discussing how the family leadership did not know what to do with Capo. He was a soldier who had done dirty work for the family on numerous occasions, and thus he was feared for both his knowledge and his hair-trigger personality. Within a short time after his arrest, the FBI brought him in and played certain tapes. These were not tapes in which he discussed his golf handicap. On the tapes other wiseguys discussed murdering Anthony Capo with permission from higher-ups. He listened to the tape, thought about life for a few days, then decided to cooperate with the United States government.

Now it was time for Anthony Capo to mention something he'd been holding in for years. Anthony Capo told the FBI what he knew about Vincent Palermo and that morning in Staten Island more than ten years before. This would be the same Vincent Palermo who wasn't even on the government's radar screen during the first twenty-five years he was in the Mafia. The Vincent Palermo who was an up-and-coming crime boss. The Vincent Palermo who was talking about doing multimillion-dollar deals with Bob Guccione and selling cell phones to the Germans. The Vincent Palermo who had something going with the Gambino family, the Colombo family, the Genovese family, and the Bonanno family.

The FBI took down all that Anthony Capo had to say about the murder of Fred Weiss. Capo, the newly minted informant, put Vincent at the scene with a gun in his hands, pulling a trigger, shooting Fred Weiss in the face. Capo also implicated Vinny Ocean in the murder of John D'Amato, although in that case he—Capo—had pulled the trigger. He told them all about the abandoned plot to kill Big Ears Charlie Majuri and another unsuccessful effort to kill Frank D'Amato. In each case, Vinny Ocean was implicated. The FBI and the lead prosecutor in the case, Assistant United States Attorney John Hillebrecht, had enough information to charge Vinny Ocean with even more crimes. They took this information to Vinny Ocean.

From the start, Vinny was leaving his options open. The lawyer who represented him at bail was John Serpico, who had represented him on many other occasions. Within a month Vinny had fired Serpico and hired a new lawyer, Gregory O'Connell. To anyone who knew O'Connell, the implication was obvious. O'Connell was a veteran federal prosecutor from the Eastern Disrict of New York in Brooklyn. He had specialized in prosecuting gangsters—not defending them. He could not be called a "mob lawyer." He was, instead, a negotiator. This is an attorney who is known to accept clients who are willing to cooperate with the federal government. When a gangster hires a negotiator, it's clear right away he's at least thinking about going over to the other side.

In Vinny Ocean's case, the process of becoming an informant could certainly not be called, as it often is, "flipping." Flipping implies fast action.

For months Vinny Ocean sat down with O'Connell and prosecutors Hillebrecht and Korologos and the FBI, working to come up with a deal in which he would plead guilty to some of the crimes he committed, but not all, so that he would not have to go to jail forever. His major concern was to get a prison term that would allow him to spend as much time as possible with his three younger children, even if they did have a new last name.

That was the implication. If he decided to become an informant, his family would have to go into the Witness Security Program—Witsec. This would mean that his two youngest children would suddenly disappear from their Catholic high schools and never see their friends again. The daughter at Fordham would have to quit and enroll elsewhere. The United States marshals would arrange to have new transcripts made up to reflect lives lived elsewhere in the country so nobody could trace them back to New York. They would be given new social-security numbers, new birth certificates, new names. They would be told it was not wise to contact relatives. Vinny's son from his first marriage, Michael, had just had his first child—Vinny's first grandchild. Vinny would not be able to see his new grandchild, at least for a long, long time. The entire family would relocate to another neighborhood in another part of the country where they knew no one and where they could blend in. They would drive down unfamiliar streets and receive mail addressed to unfamiliar people. The Palermos would cease to exist.

The alternative was simple. Vinny Ocean could go to trial and watch the faces of jurors as the FBI played tape after tape after tape. Although he was not on many of the tapes, some of his trusted soldiers had had quite a lot to say. Between Joey O Masella's ghostly voice and the non-stop color commentary of Tin Ear Sclafani, Vinny would certainly face a tough audience.

He knew what he had to do. In the late summer of 2000, he agreed in principle to plead guilty to shooting Fred Weiss, as well as to his participation in the John D'Amato murder. And there was more.

Vinny Ocean told the FBI about the murder of Fat Lou LaRasso, a holdover from the days of Sam the Plumber, whom John Riggi had decided was a "subversive threat" to his leadership. In late 1991, Palermo and Capo participated in the decision to have LaRasso killed. His enormous body was found stuffed in the trunk of a car parked at Kennedy International Airport in Queens a short while later.

Vinny Ocean talked about attempts. There was the Big Ears Charlie Majuri matter, and the Frank D'Amato matter, and the aborted attempts to kill Thomas Salvata, his manager at Wiggles. Tommy had a bad heart and it was felt he would become an informant, so a decision was made to kill him. The same was true for Frankie the Beast Scarabino, for whom a hole was dug but never filled somewhere in New Jersey.

There was only one small concession. Vinny Ocean had been charged in the murder of Joey O Masella, his long-time driver and the guy who once made him laugh. The

FBI was no longer convinced that Vinny had anything to do with Joey O's death. If anything, it was an act of omission. It was thought that when Vinny told Joey O he would have to kill him and Joey O told everyone else, the end of Joey O came to be. The FBI came to agree that the allegations that Vinny Ocean deliberately and willfully ordered Joey O's death—the worst charge in the indictment, the death-penalty charge—were based on purely circumstantial evidence. The Joey O murder charge was dropped.

Vinny began to tell them everything he knew, starting back in 1965 when he first became a made man in the De-Cavalcante crime family. He told them about other crimes involving other people. He implicated just about everybody else in the crime family of his mentor, Sam the Plumber, three years in the grave. He started with the boss, John Riggi, and worked his way down and back in time.

One after another, the members and associates of Sam the Plumber's legacy fell. On the day in December 1999 when the FBI found Vinny Ocean at Long Beach with his bags packed, they had arrested him, an acting boss, along with two captains, three soldiers, and a busload of so-called associates—guys who hang around but are not made guys. Guys with names like Joey Cars and The Kid. Despite the press conference and the parade of officials, the first arrest was in a larger sense a minor event. It made the TV that night but barely registered in the next morning's papers. It hardly marked the end of the DeCavalcante family. There were, the FBI estimated, seventy members of the group, including the boss of the family, two other acting bosses, a consigliere, a half-dozen more captains, and a score of soldiers, all still on the street. They were now well aware that their organization was under siege, which meant that they would likely stop talking about their criminal activities except in the most cryptic manner possible.

They were on notice, so they would now be far more difficult to arrest. Probable cause would all but disappear.
Ralphie the informant—a lifelong resident of New York
City—was now out of town for the first time in his life and
unavailable for future government work. The game was
over.

With Vinny Ocean cooperating, all of that changed.

The wave wrought by Vinny Ocean and Anthony Capo
hit on October 19, 2000. That morning the FBI and NYPD
moved across New Jersey and New York and arrested most
of the rest of the DeCavalcante family hierarchy, starting
with boss John Riggi, who was sitting in jail expecting to
be out in two years. They worked their way down the list,
picking up Big Ears Charlie Majuri and Jimmy Palermo,
the two other acting bosses; Stefano Vitabile, the alleged
consigliere; and Frank Polizzi, a capo and sometime boss
of the family. They went further, adding on Phil Abramo,
another capo who was known for his involvement in Wall
Street schemes long before any gangster in New York and
was, perhaps, the family's biggest earner. For good mea-
sure they threw in a handful of soldiers and associates. All
were dragged before federal magistrates in Manhattan and
labeled dangers to the community.

Within days of the October arrests, paranoia once again
gripped Sam the Plumber's legacy. The indictment unsealed by prosecutors Hillebrecht and Korologos included
the names of eleven members and associates of the De-
Cavalcante family. One name was conspicuous in its ab-
sence—Giuseppe Schifilliti, known to all as Pino. The FBI
considered him one of the nastier members of Cosa Nostra
who'd been involved in at least one murder and conspired
with others to kill the Frankie the Beast they suspected was
an informant. Now it was Pino's turn. Pino had been in-

dicted separately and the court paperwork kept sealed. This occurred because Pino had fled to Italy shortly before the arrests. When the indictment was handed down, the FBI was still in the process of finding him. It made sense to the FBI to keep the indictment separate and sealed, but it had an unintended effect: other gangsters started believing that Pino had become an informant.

Within a month, the FBI discovered that other members of the family were conspiring to kill Pino, regardless of his locale or circumstances. The FBI alleged that an associate known as Charlie the Hat was hired for the job. As best they could tell, Charlie the Hat—who was sometimes called the Mad Hatter, though never to his face—devoted four months to the cause of finding Pino before realizing the FBI had done the job and was bringing him back as a defendant, not an informant.

Killing Pino because the family thought he was an informant fell within the alleged rules of organized crime. Informants were to be killed, no questions asked. But in the DeCavalcante family, rules often viewed as incidental. Another "rule" said no member of a member or associate's family was to be killed. Occasionally, although extremely rarely, this rule was broken. The Luchese crime family tried to kill the sister of an informant known as Fat Pete Chiodo (and did not succeed). In October of 2000, the De-Cavalcante crime family took this rejection of the rules one step further.

Francesco Polizzi was charged along with the rest of the family on the same October day. But he was not sent to jail, primarily because he'd told the court he was dying of spinal disintegration and several other ailments. He was, he said, confined to his bed on Long Island. This laundry list of physical problems allowed Frank Polizzi to show up in court by Speakerphone alone. During proceedings, his raspy voice would sometimes interrupt lawyers and say, "What? What did you say?" This arrangement, the FBI came to believe, afforded him an opportunity.

Polizzi, who had been released from prison seven years previous after claiming he was about to die but was, seven years later, still alive, was in a position to know better. He had been around since the days of Sam the Plumber, and had even been appointed acting boss for a period in the 1970s before Riggi. In the days after his arrest in October 2000, the FBI says he forgot all about any alleged rules and decided that Anthony Capo was an informant. He planned and plotted, and decided to seek retribution—not on Capo, but on his wife and three young children. This was a total rejection of mob protocol. Capo's family was moved from New York City shortly after Capo began cooperating, and by February 2001, nothing had come of Polizzi's alleged plot.

A month later, in March 2001, the disintegration of Sam the Plumber's family continued. Mary Jo White, the United States attorney for the Southern District of New York, had unsealed yet another indictment against Sam the Plumber's family, this time including just about everybody left on the street. Now a new group of made guys and wannabes was dragged through Manhattan Federal Court, and Prosecutor Hillebrecht was able to stand before a judge and announce the final blitz on the DeCavalcante crime family.

Hillebrecht sometimes had trouble keeping track of the numbers. There were now sixty individuals arrested, including ten defendants who had decided to cooperate with the FBI. Besides Ralphie and Vinnie Ocean and Anthony Capo, the list of informants now included several low-level associates, many of whom had been suspected by the family hierarchy at one point or another of helping

322   Greg B. Smith

the government. An astonishing one in six of those arrested was now working for the FBI, and nearly an entire Mafia family had been arrested and charged.

The decimation of Sam the Plumber's family illustrated just how far things had come since the days when the FBI dropped two thousand three hundred pages of transcripts recorded in Sam's Kenilworth, New Jersey, plumbing office into the public domain. The Staten Island developer Fred Weiss was killed. One of the conspirators in the Weiss killing, Joey Garofano, was himself killed. An old gangster who was once John Riggi's closest friend, Fat Lou LaRasso, had been ordered killed. John D'Amato, the acting underboss, had been killed. Joe Pitts, the old gangster in the wheelchair, had been killed. Joey O Masella was gunned down in a parking lot. And there were other killings no one had ever linked to the DeCavalcante crime family—a low-level associate named John Suarato. A street hustler named William Mann.

Conspiracy after conspiracy emerged from the testimony of Vinny Ocean and Anthony Capo and all the rest. The scope of the paranoia and bloodletting was astonishing, and the results of the investigation profound. The family that thought it was a TV show was now, more or less, cancelled.

John Riggi—the boss of Sam the Plumber's family—now sat in a prison cell in the Metropolitan Correctional Center in lower Manhattan, indicted once again. He was seventy-four years old and faced the likely prospect of remaining in jail for the rest of his life. This was how it was to be. Once he was a powerful man who sat in a hotel restaurant and received the praise of much of northern New Jersey's union leadership. In 1990, he was one of only three members of the DeCavalcante crime family invited to *the* Mafia event of the late twentieth century—the wedding of John Gotti's son, Junior, at the Helmsley Palace in Manhattan. He'd made a fortune, lived in a big house in Linden, and two days before Christmas 2000 an event occurred that made all of that seem like nothing.

His wife of forty years, Sarah, had been fighting cancer for months. She died early on the morning of December 23, 2000, at their home. Because Riggi was incarcerated and newly indicted, it was not a simple matter for him to attend his own wife's funeral. His lawyers had to ask the federal judge overseeing his new case permission in an emergency petition.

They filed papers, and on the day before Christmas Judge Michael Mukasey granted the request of Inmate No. 12317-016—to a point. He did not allow Riggi to attend the funeral service at St. Elizabeth's Church in Linden or the burial at nearby Rosewood Cemetery. He did allow Riggi a private "viewing," supervised by United States marshals. "The viewing," Judge Mukasey instructed, "is to last no longer than fifteen minutes."

Around noon on the day after Christmas, a marshals' van escorted by two sedans pulled up curbside at Second Avenue and John Street in Elizabeth. The temperature had warmed up from the teens but was still below freezing. The sky was nearly cloudless. Here was Corsentino's Home for Funerals, where three years earlier the funeral of Riggi's mentor and the man who started it all, Sam the Plumber DeCavalcante, took place. The marshals led Riggi through a frigid wind and upstairs to a second-floor viewing room.

No other family members were allowed to be present in the funeral home when Riggi was there, and no one—not even funeral-home staff—was allowed in the room. Riggi was led in and greeted by the owner of Corsentino's, who then left the room. The aging boss was then allowed to spend his last moments with his wife of many years in the company of two United States marshals, who were instructed to time the event.

He got exactly fifteen minutes, as dictated by the criminal justice system that would soon consider his fate. When the time was up, he was led back out of the funeral home and into the government van with tinted windows. He was headed out of the State of New Jersey and back to New York to a jail cell that would always be waiting for him. He was, perhaps, the last boss of a crime family started by a man who once said, "Honest people have no ethics."